# Port... W9-CBC-821
# English
# Handbook

3 2109 00095 4470

The
Portable
English
Handbook

# "The Portable English Handbook"

*An Index to Grammar, Usage, and the Research Paper*

**Second Edition**

## William Herman

The City College of
The City University of New York

WITHDRAWAL

**Holt, Rinehart and Winston**

New York   Chicago   San Francisco
Philadelphia   Montreal   Toronto
London   Sydney   Tokyo   Mexico City
Rio de Janeiro   Madrid

*For my darling daughter Lisa Jane Herman:*
*Some day you too will be a grammar!*

Library of Congress Cataloging in Publication Data

Herman, William, 1926-
  The portable English handbook.

  Includes index.
  1. English language—Grammar—1950-          I. Title.
PE1112.H38  1982              808'.042          81-6695
**ISBN 0-03-591212-X**                          AACR2

CBS COLLEGE PUBLISHING
Holt, Rinehart and Winston
The Dryden Press
Saunders College Publishing

# Preface

The second edition of *The Portable English Handbook* has been much revised in response to the experience of users of the first. Thus there are new entries in Part 2 on Diagramming, Logic and Examination, and Study Skills. A new model research paper ends Part 3, and many exercises have been sharpened; additional exercises have been provided for such continuing problems as Verbs, Comma Splice, Semicolons, Subject-Verb Agreement, and others. Nevertheless, the book is not at all longer than the first edition.

Like the first edition, the overriding purpose guiding the organization of the second edition has been to make it not only a book that is useful in the classroom but also one that students will be able to use on their own. To achieve this end, the book has five key features: (1) Its index organization makes it *easy* to use. (2) It is complete. (3) It contains many exercises. (4) Its coverage of the research paper is thorough, including an entire model paper. (5) It opens with a thorough and yet concise review of basic grammar.

1. Students will find this book easy to use. For one thing, there is no complicated letter-and-number coding system. Instead, the principal reference section, Part 2 on usage and effective writing, is arranged alphabetically. The Glossary of Usage is also, of course, alphabetical. In addition, Parts 1 and 3 on grammar and the research paper consist of units that progress in a logical teaching and learning order. Also, there are many cross-references throughout the book, and the index and the organizational chart on the inside front and back covers offer further aids to easy access by students.

2. The book is complete. The alphabetical Part 2, "An Index to Usage and the Principles of Effective Writing," contains entries ranging from Abbreviations to Verbs; it concentrates on errors in usage and such important rhetorical matters as Unity, Diction, Coherence, Paragraph Development, and Thesis Statement.

3. The book offers many exercises—"Test Yourself" sections by means of which students can consolidate the gains they make through understanding the text. Virtually every entry in Part 2 contains exercises, and they also appear at critical points in Parts 1 and 3.

4. The book is comprehensive in its treatment of the research paper in Part 3. This section takes the student through a step-by-step approach to writing a research paper. Sample note cards and reference materials are reproduced at the appropriate stages, and the section ends with a *complete* sample research paper.

5. Part I, "A Basic Grammar," gives students a basic grounding in the fundamentals they need to know before they start writing. This opening section is intended to be useful both for teaching in the classroom and for independent student study and review. The section clearly explains words, sentences, clusters, clauses, and phrases, in that order, with many examples and exercises along the way.

The book is, as its title denotes, portable—it is no burden to carry around and have handy; this feature is especially important. Finally, I should add that the basic approach to grammar here lays before students only what is essential for their grasp of the writing problems in their own work; I have avoided a top-heavy burden of fine exegesis which could only confuse students and take their attention away from their own writing. I hope, too, that I have written with plain diction and a lively style, so that students will not be led astray by *my* writing.

An *Instructor's Manual* to the text is available. Primarily an answer key to virtually all the exercises, it also includes a list of possible research paper topics. The *Manual* may be obtained through a local Holt representative or by writing to English Editor, College

Department, Holt, Rinehart and Winston, 383 Madison Avenue, New York, N.Y. 10017.

For the instructor who wants more exercise material in any particular area of student need, I have prepared and Holt has published *The Portable English Workbook*. Its Table of Contents is conveniently keyed to *The Portable English Handbook*.

I wish to thank my colleagues in the Department of English of The City College, CUNY, for their generous responses to my sometimes anxious queries. Special thanks are due Professor Arthur Zeiger for reading the manuscript and saving me from a number of potential errors. I must also thank Professor Edward Quinn for performing the same task and for his fine philological distinctions. In addition, the following, who reviewed the manuscript of the second edition and made constructive comments: Richard S. Beal, Boston University, Carol A. Baxter, Cypress College; Paul O. Clark, Manchester Community College; Charles W. Davis, DeKalb Community College; Leona M. Fisher, Georgetown University; James A. Fuller, Mesa Community College; Glenn R. Groenke, Scottsdale Community College; Tom Hemmens, Pittsburgh State University; Morris E. Husted, Ventura College; and Jean Torson Walker, Manchester Community College. My editor at Holt, Susan Katz, was a model of efficiency and unfailing kindness and encouragement. My wife Joanna knows a great deal about making books— and a lot of other things as well—and she generously shared that knowledge with me in the making of this one.

W. H.

# Contents

**Part**

**1**

# A Basic
# Grammar

# Why Study Grammar?

Grammar need not frighten you.

Grammar is simply a set of rules that describes how we all speak and write. The frightening word here is *rules*, because it makes us think of penalties for doing something wrong. But it need not. There are all kinds of rules, some of which we don't know are operating, and most of which we fall easily into obeying. For example, you understand what these words you are now reading are saying. The reason for this is that you are obeying the grammatical rules *you* already know.

For all of us, this understanding of some grammatical rules is unconscious, long ago learned and incorporated into our mental processes. The purpose of studying grammar here is to make more of these rules conscious and to do so for a number of very good reasons.

For one thing, grammar is interesting. Language is fascinating when you come to understand that its grammar is a remarkably coherent piece of human knowledge and that most human activities would be impossible without the subtle riches of linguistic communication. More important, however, the study of basic grammar can help you to improve your writing by reminding you of how it works. For example, if you know that a verb must agree with its subject, you are less likely to write "The humor and personal concern of Mr. Jones, my sociology professor, *is* what I like best about the course." Moreover, knowing grammatical terms can help you discuss your writing with instructors trying to make it more effective. If an instructor suggests that you *use subordinate clauses for subordinate ideas,* the suggestion will not get through to you if you do not know a clause from a hammock.

In Part 2 of this book, "An Index to Usage and the Principles of Effective Writing," you will find many suggestions for improving your writing. In order to use that index intelligently, you will need to understand the basic grammar we are about to discuss. We begin here with words and sentences, then go on to clauses and phrases.

# Words

Words traditionally have been placed into classes called *parts of speech* according to their forms and the ways in which they communicate meaning in sentences.

Before we begin to study the characteristic features of these classes, it is important to point out that some words can fall into more than one class, depending on how they are used in the sentence. For example, consider this group of sentences:

The *light* is hurting my eyes.
Let's *light* the Christmas tree.
Kathy has a *light* complexion.
She wore a *light* brown dress.

If your native language is English, you can make out the different meanings of these sentences quite easily. The fact that you *can* make out the different meanings is partly due to your ability to understand the word *light* in a different way in each sentence. In other words, in each sentence you are identifying *light* as a member of a different class, because in each sentence *light* has a different function.

You should be aware that hundreds of words can behave the way *light* does in those four sentences. Good dictionaries always define such words according to each of the various ways in which they can be used, and as we go along you will be able to see the logical processes governing the classification of these words. But you need to know the characteristic features of the various classes.

## Nouns

A noun is a word used to name something: a person, a place, an object, an idea. Examples of nouns are such words as *apple, table,* and *car.* The important features of nouns that will help you identify them are the following:

**1.** Nouns can usually be made into plurals by adding *-s* or *-es:*

| | | |
|---|---|---|
| apple—apples | peach—peaches | hope—hopes |
| table—tables | pass—passes | tragedy—tragedies |
| car—cars | tax—taxes | democracy—democracies |
| boy—boys | dash—dashes | |

**2.** Nouns can usually be made into possessives to indicate that something belongs to them. This is done by adding -'s.

*Danny's* shoes
*democracy's* advantages
*car's* engine

**3.** Nouns can be preceded by words like *a, an, the, my, each, this, that,* or even another possessive noun (*Judy's,* for example). These words *signal* that a noun is coming.

| | |
|---|---|
| a *horse* | that *stadium* |
| Linda's *boyfriend* | this *chicken* |
| his *shirt* | an *egg* |
| my *heart* | Aunt Vicky's *cake* |

In a phrase such as "an intelligent young man," the word *an* does its signaling several words away from the noun *man. An* is not signaling that *intelligent* or *young* is a noun.

**4.** Nouns are in the noun position in the sentence. Notice the position of the italicized nouns in the following sentences, and write in appropriate nouns in the blank spaces.

I bought the *apple*.        This *apple* is beautiful.
I bought the _____.        This _____ is beautiful.
I was unhappy with the _____.  _____ are available in Peoria.

**5.** Some nouns are formed by adding certain characteristic word endings (or *suffixes*) either to nouns or to other parts of speech such as adjectives or verbs.

mile + **age** = mileage
deny + **al** = denial
consider + **ation** = consideration
deliver + **ance** = deliverance
provide + **ence** = providence

tenant + **ancy** = tenancy
urge + **ency** = urgency
farm + **er** = farmer
govern + **or** = governor
social + **ism** = socialism
active + **ity** = activity
happy + **ness** = happiness
achieve + **ment** = achievement
hard + **ship** = hardship
dissent + **sion** = dissension
young + **ster** = youngster
introduce + **tion** = introduction

---

## *Test Yourself on*
## Identifying Nouns

Circle the nouns in each of the following word groups.

1. An American elephant.
2. The blue notebook.
3. I saw the light.
4. Cheese is available in Wisconsin.
5. The Trail Blazers are a championship team.
6. Alligators are fond of dating crocodiles.
7. I have a boat on the lake.
8. A message from my nose to my brain tells me it's spring.
9. I am going to invite Republicans to my party.
10. The fire is blazing in the fireplace.

---

## Verbs

A verb is used to describe an action or a state of being. A verb says something about what a noun *does* (action) or what it *is* (being).

Karl *plays* basketball. (describes the action of the proper noun *Karl*)

Karl *is* tall. (describes the state of being of the proper noun *Karl*)

The important features of verbs that will help you to identify them are the following:

**1.** Verbs can change form to indicate a change of time. Not only do verbs describe an action or a state of being, but they also tell us *when* the action is taking place or *when* the state of being was in force. When a verb changes form in this manner, we say that it has changed its *tense*.

Fred *walked* to the movies. (Action in the past; *walked* is the past tense—the past time form—of the verb *walk*.)

He *is* happy. (State of being now; *is* is the *present tense*—the present time form—of the verb *be*.)

One of the surest ways to identify a verb is to look for that word in the sentence that can be changed to a different tense to indicate a change of time.

**2.** Nearly all verbs have an *-ing* form. All verbs in the third person singular of the present tense, indicative mood, end in the letter *-s*. In addition, many verbs change to their past forms by adding *-d* or *-ed*. (See page 10 for what is meant by indicative mood.)

**-ing Forms**  jump*ing*, smok*ing*, act*ing*, play*ing*, try*ing*, do*ing*

**Third Person Singular Forms**  i*s*, ha*s*, goe*s*, doe*s*, help*s*, play*s*, move*s*

**Past Forms**  wait*ed*, need*ed*, want*ed*, leap*ed*, pray*ed*, wish*ed*, move*d*, love*d*

**3.** Verbs can be single words (*sings, worked, touched*) or they can consist of several words (*has gone, can play, was changing, will have studied*). *Has, can, was, will,* and *have* are called *auxiliary* or *helping* verbs. (For more detailed information about them, see below, pp. 11–14.)

## *Test Yourself on*
### Identifying Verbs

Circle the verbs in the following sentences. Keep in mind the features of verbs you have just read about.

1. Betsy plays the piano.
2. A civil engineer earns a good salary.
3. My sister is jumping rope.
4. Sally waited in the rain for an hour.
5. She trusted Jean to show up.
6. I tried calling her apartment, but she had left.
7. The mail will be late today.
8. I have given you perfect instructions for getting to the lake.
9. The Dean told her that she would graduate with the rest of her class.
10. I am curious about the history of slavery in this country.

## *Test Yourself on*
### Identifying Verbs by Changing Tenses

Identify the verbs in the following sentences by changing their tenses.

*Example:* Tom *played* basketball for his college team.
Tom *plays* basketball for his college team.
*Verb: played.*

1. Tom played basketball for his college team.
2. George passes his examination easily.
3. The apples were delicious.

4. Your help makes a lot of difference to me.

5. He seemed unhappy.

6. In fact, Arthur works for his father.

7. He will be happy with his birthday present.

8. Frank understood the lesson.

9. The piano piece will end the program.

10. He has taken his father's car to school.

11. We will sit at different tables.

12. He has taken a vacation.

---

**4.** Verbs occupy certain typical positions in sentences. In ordinary use, the verb follows the subject (the noun). Notice the positions of the italicized verbs in the sentences below:

People *listen.*
They will *play* soon.
They will *come* soon.
People _____.

They will *listen* soon.
They will _____ soon.

He *plays* from time to time.
He _____ from time to time.

**5.** Verbs have a property called *voice,* which indicates whether the subject of the verb performs the action or undergoes it. Where the verb is in the *active voice,* the subject does the performing.

John *ate* a rabbit. (*John,* the subject, did the eating.)
José *saw* the President. (*José,* the subject, did the seeing.)

Where the verb is in the *passive voice,* the subject is being acted on: the subject is *receiving* the action.

John *was eaten* by a rabbit. (*John,* the subject, is acted on.)
José *was seen* by the President. (*José,* the subject, is acted on.)

*Note:* Only an *action verb* can have a passive voice. See 7 below for the definition of an action verb. (For more detailed information on voice, see **Voice** in Part 2.)

**6.** Verbs also have a feature called *mood,* to indicate the manner (or mode) in which they are used: the *indicative mood* is used for statements of fact or other kinds of assertions or questions; the *imperative mood* is used for issuing commands or giving directions; the *subjunctive mood* is used for statements contrary to fact or those that are in the area of possibility or potential.

I *gave* him five dollars. (*Indicative:* a statement of fact.)
Can you *give* me a lift? (*Indicative:* an ordinary question.)
*Give* me five dollars. (*Imperative:* a command.)
*Turn* left at the hardware store. (*Imperative:* a direction.)
If I *were* President, I *would declare* a holiday. (*Subjunctive:* the speaker, "I," is *not* President.)

**7.** Verbs fall into two classes: *linking verbs* and *action verbs.* Linking verbs consist of all forms of the verb *be: is, am, was, were,* and so forth, as well as such other verbs as *seem, become, appear, feel.* They are called *linking verbs* because they link the subject of a sentence (a noun) with either another noun, a pronoun, or an adjective—describing the state of being of the subject.

Frank *felt* anxious.
You *are* gorgeous.
Uncle Al *seemed* quiet.
Fred *is* a dancer.

Action verbs, on the other hand, describe action rather than a state of being. They are divided into *transitive* verbs and *intransitive* verbs.

A transitive verb describes action that is received by something. This something is called the *direct object* of the verb.

Joe Namath *throws* the long *ball.* (*Ball* receives the action.)
Gravity *moves* the *planets.* (*Planets* receives the action.)
Women *date men.* (*Men* receives the action.)

Intransitive verbs describe action, too, but they do not act *upon* an object; they have no direct object but simply describe an action performed *by* the subject that also applies *to* the subject.

Christmas trees *burn* easily.
/This typewriter really *works*.

Some verbs can be used transitively or intransitively, in different sentences. Notice how the verbs used in the preceding examples can function as transitive verbs:

My stove *burns* coal. (*Coal* receives the action.)
Charley *works* the tractor. (*Tractor* receives the action.)

---

### *Test Yourself on*
### Identifying Types of Verbs

Circle all the verbs you can find in the following sentences. Above each circle, write T if the verb is transitive, I if the verb is intransitive, and L if the verb is a linking verb.

1. I feel wealthy.
2. Charley smokes too much.
3. He is riding his motorcycle.
4. My father plays golf every Sunday.
5. The bomb exploded.
6. Willie loves hats.
7. My brother needs a job.
8. Lawyers are officers of the court.
9. Judges make rulings.
10. My wife is very slender.
11. Jane played the piano.
12. Students read all day long.

---

### Auxiliaries

An auxiliary is often called an *auxiliary verb* or *helping verb*. Very frequently, auxiliaries signal a reader that a verb is coming. Words like those italicized in the following examples are all auxiliaries:

| | | | |
|---|---|---|---|
| *is* looking | *did* go | *have* played | *was* laughing |
| *can* offer | *may* believe | *would* find | *had* known |

The following aspects of auxiliaries will help you to understand their forms and functions:

**1.** Auxiliaries have different meanings and change the meanings of the verbs they couple with in different ways. For example, they indicate time and therefore change tense.

He *is* playing. He *was* playing.

A subgroup of auxiliaries called *modals* (*should, would, could, can, may, might, must, ought to, have to, shall, will*) add meanings that suggest possibility, ability, obligation, and so forth.

He *can* play.     He *should* play.     He *must* play.

Notice that these modals are always used with the present tense stem of the verb.

**2.** Auxiliaries are widely used in asking questions.

| | |
|---|---|
| *Did* you go? | How *did* you go? |
| *Can* you go? | When *can* you go? |
| *Must* you go? | Why *must* you go? |

**3.** One auxiliary appears with verbs ending in *-ing:* the forms of the verb *be.*

I *am* playing.
You *are* playing.
He *is* playing.

I *was* playing.
They *were* playing.

He *has been* playing.
They *have been* playing.
They *had been* playing.
They *will be* playing.
They *will have been* playing.

**4.** Only two auxiliaries are used with past verb forms like *known, played, gone, remembered;* they are the auxiliaries *be* and *have.*

| | | |
|---|---|---|
| I *am* known. | She *was* known. | He *has* played. |
| They *are* known. | You *were* known. | He *had* played. |
| She *is* known. | | They *have* played. |

**5.** The auxiliaries *be (am, is, are, was, were), have (has, had), do (did, does),* and *can* may also occur as verbs; this happens when they appear before a member of some other class of words.

**Do as Auxiliary**   He *does* believe. (*Believe* is a verb.)

**Do as Verb**   He *does* laundry. (*Laundry* is a noun.)

---

## *Test Yourself on*
## Identifying Auxiliaries

Place the proper auxiliary into each of the blank spaces in the following sentences.

1. You _____ visit your sick friend.

2. We _____ need some milk for our coffee.

3. He _____ planning to take a course in physics.

4. He says they _____ trying to climb the rocks.

5. When _____ you take the exam?

6. She _____ gone to the hairdresser's.

7. _____ you continue playing the piano?

8. _____ he see what we

   _____ doing with the fish?

9. He _____ decided to find out if

   they _____ taken.

10. He _____ laughing and we

    _____ crying but nobody

    _____ paying attention.

For the following group of sentences, supply verbs in each of the blank spaces. Be sure to use the correct verb form.

11. We could _____ the entrance on Grove Street.

12. Can you _____ with us this afternoon?

13. We are _____ to arrive by three o'clock.

14. Did you _____ the dinner was cooked?

15. We should _____ all the windows.

16. We will _____ your apartment on Saturday.

17. I am _____ you to school today.

18. They were _____ him about his mother.

19. May I _____ your word on that?

20. Has he ever _____ you play the guitar?

## Adjectives

Let us begin our discussion of adjectives by trying to identify a few nouns. One of the words in each of the following pairs is a noun; underline each.

| tasty hamburger | good answer | new moon |
| beautiful lake | honest man | young turkey |
| happy parent | hopeless case | typical day |

What about the other word in each pair?

What does each *do* to the noun it is paired with?

Each of these words describes further the noun it is paired with; not just *a hamburger* but a *tasty* one; not just *an answer* but a *good* one. Each of these words, a part of speech we call an *adjective,* modifies the noun it is paired with by describing it more specifically. The important features of adjectives that will help you identify them are the following:

**1.** Adjectives can be changed in form to compare two or more objects. This can be done by adding the ending *-er* to the basic adjective (called the *positive* form) to make the *comparative* form, and the ending *-est* to the positive form to make the *superlative* form.

| **Positive** | **Comparative** | **Superlative** |
| happy | happier | happiest |
| young | younger | youngest |

However, some adjectives form the comparative and superlative by adding the words *more* and *most.*

| **Positive** | **Comparative** | **Superlative** |
| beautiful | more beautiful | most beautiful |
| honest | more honest | most honest |
| recent | more recent | most recent |

Also, some adjectives form the comparative and superlative irregularly.

| **Positive** | **Comparative** | **Superlative** |
| good | better | best |
| bad | worse | worst |
| many | more | most |

The comparative form is used to compare two objects.

He is *happier* than I am.
Her cat is *more beautiful* than mine.
My cold is *worse* today. (i.e., "than it was yesterday")

The superlative form is used to compare more than two objects.

I am the *happiest* man in the whole world.
Here is the *most beautiful* hat I've seen.
He is the *best* player on the team.

**2.** Adjectives occupy certain typical positions in sentences. Notice the position of the italicized adjectives in the following sentences:

He was *happy.*
He was _____.

A very *happy* girl arrived.
A very _____ girl arrived.

**3.** Many adjectives have characteristic endings (suffixes) that can help you identify them. Here are just a few:

-al (international)
-ant, -ent (resistant, excellent)
-able, -ible (affable, irresistible)
-ar, -ary (solar, ordinary)
-ful (wonderful, soulful)
-ish (sluggish)
-ive (attentive)
-ous (generous)
-y (funny, sloppy)

Recognition of these suffixes can help you to identify adjectives.

For more information on adjectives, see **Modifiers** and **Dangling Modifiers** in Part 2.

---

### *Test Yourself on*
### Identifying Adjectives

The following sentences all contain adjectives; some contain more than one. Identify them by analyzing their positions in the sentence, whether they are in the comparative or superlative degree, the way they end (their suffixes), or some combination of these.

1. She seems courageous.
2. He looked funny in that costume.
3. My father was very kind to my mother.
4. He made her happier than she had ever been.
5. It is childish to be greedy.
6. He was riding a lively horse but his saddle was very old.
7. The greatest batter I ever saw was Ted Williams.
8. He is more confident now that he is in a good school.
9. She was athletic, girlish, and sensitive.
10. Of all the lovely cities of Europe, the one having the largest treasure trove of art is beautiful Florence.

---

## Adverbs

So far we have studied three of the parts of speech: nouns, verbs, and adjectives. Write N above the nouns in the following sentences, V above the verbs, and ADJ above the adjectives.

1. Young dogs eat noisily.

2. Old people often sit.

3. Happy farmers live there.

The words you have *not* marked are all adverbs. Each answers a question about the verb in the sentence.

1. Young dogs eat *noisily.* (*How* do they eat? *Noisily,* a way or manner of eating or doing other things.)
2. Old people *often* sit. (*When* do they sit? *Often,* which signifies the frequency with which they sit.)
3. Happy farmers live *there.* (*Where* do they live? *There,* which signifies a place.)

The adverbs that can replace *noisily* in sentence 1 are called *adverbs of manner;* those that can replace *often* in sentence 2 are called *adverbs of time* or *frequency;* those that can replace *there* in sentence 3 are called *adverbs of place* or *position.* Here is a list of some of them:

| *Manner* | *Time* | *Place* |
|----------|--------|---------|
| thus | then | there |
| badly | seldom | here |
| carefully | never | upstairs |
| rapidly | again | away |
| surely | soon | downstairs |
| sweetly | always | up |
| even | still | down |
| just | already | |
| only | | |

Adverbs can modify not only verbs but also adjectives, other adverbs, and even whole sentences.

**Modifying a Verb**   Old people *often* sit. (Modifies *sit*.)

**Modifying an Adjective**   She was *rarely* unhappy. (Modifies *unhappy*.)

**Modifying Another Adverb**   I spoke *too* harshly to my uncle. (Modifies *harshly*.)

**Modifying a Whole Sentence**   *Unfortunately*, we cannot have a vacation this year. (Modifies the whole sentence beginning with *we*.)

The important features of adverbs that will help you identify them are the following:

**1.** A few adverbs, like adjectives, can change form to compare degrees or qualities by adding the endings -*er* and -*est*.

| **Positive** | **Comparative** | **Superlative** |
|--------------|-----------------|-----------------|
| soon | sooner | soonest |
| quick | quicker | quickest |

However, most adverbs form the comparative and superlative by adding the words *more* and *most*.

| **Positive** | **Comparative** | **Superlative** |
|--------------|-----------------|-----------------|
| often | more often | most often |
| rapidly | more rapidly | most rapidly |

A few adverbs form the comparative and superlative irregularly.

| Positive | Comparative | Superlative |
|----------|-------------|-------------|
| badly | worse | worst |
| well | better | best |

**2.** Adverbs occupy certain typical positions in sentences. Notice the position of the italicized adverbs in the following sentences.

| | |
|---|---|
| He drove *in.* | She was lucky *rarely.* |
| He drove *seldom.* | She was lucky *there.* |
| He drove _____. | She was lucky _____. |

**3.** Adverbs can often be moved from one position in the sentence to another without changing the meaning of the sentence. This is in contrast to adjectives, which must remain relatively fixed if the sentence is to make sense.

*Often* she was lucky.
She *often* was lucky.
She was *often* lucky.
She was lucky *often.*

In this group of sentences, *often* is the adverb and *lucky* the adjective. You can see that whether *often* is made the first, second, third, or fourth word of the sentence, the meaning of the sentence remains essentially the same. By contrast, notice what happens when we try the same movement pattern for the adjective.

*Lucky* she was often.
She *lucky* was often.
She was *lucky* often.
She was often *lucky.*

Only the last two of these examples make sense. The first two are, of course, nonsense. Sometimes, however, adverbs are not as movable as *often* is in the above examples. (For more details on how to control the placement of adverbs, see **Misplaced Modifiers** and **Dangling Modifiers** in Part 2.)

**4.** Adverbs frequently end in the suffix *-ly,* and many adverbs can be formed by adding this suffix to an adjective.

| Adjectives | Adverbs |
|------------|---------|
| rapid | rapidly |
| sweet | sweetly |
| tense | tensely |
| brave | bravely |
| beautiful | beautifully |
| happy | happily |

The difficulty is that not all words ending in *-ly* are adverbs. Some nouns add *-ly* to form *adjectives*.* There are not many of these; here are a few:

| Noun | Adjective |
|------|-----------|
| beast | beastly |
| brother | brotherly |
| earth | earthly |
| father | fatherly |
| friend | friendly |
| heaven | heavenly |
| love | lovely |
| man | manly |
| neighbor | neighborly |
| saint | saintly |

Recognizing the noun base in these adjectives can help you avoid the mistake of thinking they are adverbs.

---

## *Test Yourself on*
### Identifying Adverbs

Take this test by changing the conditions indicated in each of the sentences below. That is, change the manner (*rapidly* to *slowly*), the time (*now* to *then*), or the place or direction (*here* to *there, up* to *down*). The word you change is the adverb.

*Example:* Gilda walked *slowly* into the lion's cage.
Gilda walked *quickly* into the lion's cage.

1. Gilda walked slowly into the lion's cage.

2. She drove in.

---

*Some adjectives ending in *-ly* are *not* formed from nouns, e.g., *unsightly* and *unlikely*.

3. He went up.

4. He put the apple here.

5. He answered the question sweetly.

6. She is often absent.

7. He did his homework sloppily.

8. She lived upstairs.

9. He is never happy.

10. She walked over.

---

*Prepositions* and *conjunctions,* the next two groups we will study, both act to tie together or connect nouns, verbs, adjectives, and adverbs.

## Prepositions

A preposition connects a noun or a pronoun with other parts of the sentence.

The man *in* the truck drove away. (Connects *man* to *truck.*)
Give me that book *on* the table. (Connects *book* to *table.*)
He went *to* the movies. (Connects *went* to *movies.*)

Each of the italicized words in these examples is a *preposition.* Each preposition, together with the two words that follow it (a determiner, *the,* and a noun), forms what is called a *prepositional phrase:*

*in the truck*
*on the table*
*to the movies*

In these phrases, we would call the word *truck* or *table* or *movies* the *object of the preposition,* the word that the preposition connects to the rest of the sentence. (More on the prepositional phrase will be found later under **Phrases.**)

Prepositions usually denote direction or position, as you can see from this list:

| | | | | |
|---|---|---|---|---|
| aboard | around | by | like | till |
| about | at | concerning | near | to |
| above | before | despite | of | toward |
| across | behind | down | off | under |
| after | below | during | on | until |
| against | beneath | for | onto | up |
| along | beside | from | over | upon |
| alongside | besides | in | since | with |
| amid | between | inside | through | within |
| among | beyond | into | throughout | without |

In addition to these, there are a number of prepositions in English that consist of more than one word. Here are some:

| | | |
|---|---|---|
| according to | by way of | in spite of |
| ahead of | contrary to | in view of |
| apart from | due to | instead of |
| as for | in addition to | on account of |
| as well as | in back of | out of |
| away from | in case of | up to |
| because of | in front of | |
| by means of | in place of | |

All the words in the first list *may* be used as prepositions. Some words on the list—*during, among, with,* and others—are regularly prepositions, but most of the words are also used as other parts of speech. For example, you may recall that the words *in, over,* and *by* were adverbs when used in the following ways:

He drove *in*. He drove *over*. He drove *by*.

But these three are prepositions when used in these ways:

He drove *in* the truck. He drove *over* the bridge. He drove *by* the house.

Prepositions occupy certain typical positions in sentences. Notice the positions occupied by those italicized in the following sentences:

The house *across* the road is mine.
The name *on* the door is my father's.

He wrote an essay *on* Shakespeare.
He was carrying a bag *of* potatoes.
He went *to* his class.
He lived *in* my building.

Notice that there is nearly always a small word (*the, his, my*) between the preposition and the following noun to form what we call a prepositional phrase (see p. 46 for more on this structure).

---

### *Test Yourself on* Using Prepositions

Using the following list of nouns, select twenty of the prepositions listed above and make prepositional phrases by using a small word (*the, a, my, his, her, your,* and the like) where appropriate.

*Example:* beyond our lake

*Nouns:* farm, apple, newspaper, automobile, ferry, chair, horse, tomato, pizza, chopsticks, burglary, television set, stadium, football field, day, camp, lake, room, cage, planet

---

## Conjunctions

The word *conjunction* means "the state of being joined." In grammar, conjunctions act to join together words, groups of words, or even whole sentences. Different kinds of conjunctions perform different jobs, and there are three different groups to consider.

### 1. Coordinating conjunctions

This group consists of the seven words *and, or, but, yet, for, nor,* and *so.* Consider the way *and* does its work:

Apples *and* peaches are delicious.
I bought a red Ford *and* a green Mustang.

My aunt gave my sister *and* my brother some money.
Melons smell *and* taste sweet.
She was young *and* pretty.
I plan to spend the summer working on my uncle's farm *and* studying for my exams.
He will play with us if he has the time *and* if he is not tired.
He is a student, *and* he is my friend.

In nearly all these sentences we can substitute the word *or* for *and*. But can replace *and* only in the last sentence. *But* is commonly used to join pairs of adjectives or adverbs that are somewhat opposed to each other in meaning:

He was poor *but* happy.
He looked quickly *but* carefully.

All seven of the coordinating conjunctions are commonly used to join together two sentences (independent clauses), as in the last sentence above, depending on the relationship between the two sentences.

He was poor, *but* he was happy.
He was dressed, *so* he went out.
He was angry, *yet* he was calm.
He was happy, *for* he had passed his exams.

*Note:* The punctuation of such sentences is important and you will find more about the subject in Part 2, under **Comma Rules.**

In addition to these coordinating conjunctions, there are four pairs of what are sometimes called *correlatives:*

both . . . and
not only . . . but also
either . . . or
neither . . . nor

These pairs are used very much as *and* and *or* are used.

*Both* apples *and* peaches are delicious.
*Not only* apples *but also* peaches are delicious.
He was *either* young *or* inexperienced.
He was *neither* young *nor* inexperienced.

## 2. Conjunctive adverbs

This is a group of words used to connect sentences; they act in a sentence like the word *therefore*.

The school year was over; *therefore,* he decided to take a long vacation.
The children were playing in the yard; *therefore,* he took a nap.

The following words are commonly used as conjunctive adverbs:

| | | | |
|---|---|---|---|
| besides | hence | indeed | subsequently |
| consequently | however | moreover | therefore |
| furthermore | in fact | nevertheless | thus |

He ate the whole pie himself; *furthermore,* he was not sorry.
He ate the whole pie himself; *moreover,* he was not sorry.
He ate the whole pie himself; *nevertheless,* he was not sorry.

Note that conjunctive adverbs can change position in the sentence and still act as connectors.

The clock struck twelve; *therefore,* Eddie got ready to leave.
The clock struck twelve; Eddie, *therefore,* got ready to leave.
The clock struck twelve; Eddie got ready to leave, *therefore.*

Note too that when words like *and* join two sentences together, they are preceded by a comma; when words like *therefore* join two sentences together, they are preceded by a semicolon or a period. (For more detailed information on punctuating with conjunctive adverbs, see **Comma Rules, Fragments,** and **Semicolons** in Part 2.)

## 3. Subordinating conjunctions

Subordinating conjunctions are words used to join a word or a word group to a sentence by subordinating, or making less important, that word or word group. Consider these sentences:

1. John sings well.
2. John is a member of the church choir.

Of the two sentences, which is more important? Obviously, either *could* be more important than the other.

But suppose, for example, that we thought sentence 2 were more important. We could then join the sentences together this way:

*Because John sings well,* he is a member of the church choir.

The italicized portion of the new sentence now corresponds to our old sentence 1. The only difference is that we have added the word *because,* a subordinating conjunction. Of course, we could join our two original sentences together in another way:

*Because he is a member of the church choir,* John sings well.

Now the italicized portion corresponds to sentence 2 and the new sentence makes old sentence 1 the more important one. Of course, each version of the joined sentences has a different meaning.

Subordinating conjunctions generally act like the word *because.* Depending on the kinds of word groups you want to subordinate, you can use any of the following words as subordinating conjunctions.

| | | |
|---|---|---|
| after | provided | whatever |
| although | since | when |
| as | that | whenever |
| because | though | where |
| before | unless | wherever |
| if | until | whether |
| lest | what | while |

Here are some further examples of how these subordinating conjunctions work:

*After* we had dinner, we went to the movies.
We went to the movies *after* we had dinner.

*Although* I am only a student, I have a good knowledge of chemistry.
I have a good knowledge of chemistry, *although* I am only a student.

*Whenever* I work hard, I get good grades.
I get good grades *whenever* I work hard.

Notice that the subordinated part can occur either at the beginning of the sentence or at the end.

## *Test Yourself on*
### Using Conjunctions

1. Write ten sentences in which a coordinating conjunction joins two sentences. Try to use each of the seven coordinating conjunctions at least once. See page 23 for examples to use as models.
2. Write eight sentences in which you use each pair of correlatives at least once.
3. Write a dozen sentences using each of the conjunctive adverbs at least once.
4. Take those sentences and change the position of the conjunctive adverb.
5. In how many of the sentences you have written can you substitute a coordinating conjunction for a conjunctive adverb? Try the substitution and find out.

## Pronouns

Pronouns are words that can replace nouns. Such words as *he, she, him, them, somebody, mine,* and *this* are all pronouns. An important word associated with pronouns is *antecedent.* Consider these examples:

I just saw *Alice. She* seems fine.
*Richard* put *his* money into real estate.

In the first example we say that the word *Alice* is the antecedent of the pronoun *she.* In the second example we say that the word *Richard* is the antecedent of the pronoun *his.*

Not all pronouns have antecedents in all cases, but you will want to keep the term in mind and be sure that pronouns agree with their antecedents in your writing. For more details on this subject, see **Pronoun References** in Part 2.

Here are the chief kinds of pronouns and the names they are known by:

**Personal**

| | | |
|---|---|---|
| I | me | my, mine |
| you | you | your, yours |

| he | him | his |
| she | her | her, hers |
| it | it | its |
| we | us | our, ours |
| they | them | their, theirs |

### Reflexive

myself, himself, herself, yourself, ourselves, themselves, yourselves, itself

### Relative

who, whose, whom, which, that

Relative pronouns are used to connect a subordinate word group to another part of the sentence.

John, *who* sings well, is a member of the church choir.
The foreign country *that* I like best is Italy.

The antecedent of *who* in the first example is *John,* and the antecedent of *that* in the second example is *country.*

Sometimes a relative pronoun is omitted but understood in a sentence.

The car [that] I liked was a Toyota.

### Interrogative

who, whom, which, what

These are used to ask questions.

*Who* is your friend? *Which* would you like? *What* did you say?

### Demonstrative

this, that, these, those

These act to *point* to a noun, but they may also be used by themselves.

*This* hat is mine. (Pointing to a noun.)
*This* is mine. (As a pronoun.)

### Indefinite

Common indefinite pronouns are the following:

one, no one, anyone, everyone, someone
anybody, everybody, nobody, somebody, other
another, anything, everything, something, nothing
all, few, either, neither, none, most, more

**Reciprocal**
each other
one another

All of the pronouns listed can occupy some of the typical noun positions in sentences, although not all can occupy every noun position.

**Sentence with a Noun**
The *man* is over there.

**Pronouns Substituted for the Noun**
*He* is over there.
*Mine* is over there.
*Somebody* is over there.
*Neither* is over there.

**Sentence with a Noun**
I know the *man*.

**Pronouns Substituted for the Noun**
I know *him*.
I know *hers*.
I know *somebody*.
I know *neither*.

---

## *Test Yourself on* Using Pronouns

A. Use each of the following words in two sentences.

| | | | |
|---|---|---|---|
| 1. many | 3. that | 5. either | 7. all |
| 2. his | 4. few | 6. several | 8. three |

B. Replace each of the italicized words in the sentences below with a pronoun. In order to do this, you will—in some cases—have to drop a few words from the sentence.

*Example:* My old *grandmother* needs false teeth.
　　　*She* needs false teeth.

1. My old *grandmother* needs false teeth.
2. My old grandmother needs false *teeth*.

3. My *boss* complained to me.

4. *People* are funny.

5. *Congressmen* are politicians.

6. No *lakes* can ever be emptied.

C. Underline all the pronouns you can find in the following sentences. Some sentences have more than one.

1. His shoes are brown.

2. Mine are black.

3. Everybody knows something.

4. You should be honest with yourself.

5. My brother wanted him to be nice to everyone.

6. Anyone can tell that you have a sunburn.

7. Students are friendly to one another.

8. Nothing bothers me when I myself am driving.

9. She put herself in his position.

10. Much will be gained and nothing lost if you go swimming with us this afternoon.

11. Neither will be enough.

12. Several will be fine.

## Sentences

Now that we have discussed words, we must begin to speak of sentences. Almost everything we say or write is made up of certain arrangements of words that we call *sentences*. When we speak a sentence, we signal its beginning and end by controlling the sounds of what we say; that is, our voices tell the listener when we have begun and when we have finished. When we write a sentence, we signal these things by beginning with a capital letter and ending with a period, question mark, or exclamation point.

There are three types of sentences, classified according to what effect they are generally intended to have on a listener:

Sentences can be commands or directions on how to do something or go somewhere (imperative sentences):

Turn on the lights.
Make a left turn.

or they can be questions (interrogative sentences):

Are you coming?

or they can be statements (declarative sentences):

I saw Uncle Fred this morning.

In this section, we will be concerned mainly with sentences that are statements. We will begin by studying certain basic facts about all sentences.

**1.** Every English sentence can be divided into two parts, because every sentence accomplishes two things: (1) It names something (an object, an idea, a person, a place), and (2) it says something about what it has just named.

| **Part 1**<br>**(what is named)** | **Part 2**<br>**(what is said about it)** |
|---|---|
| 1. Dogs | *bark.* |
| 2. Birds | *are* beautiful. |
| 3. Cats | *are* animals. |
| 4. Babies | *drink* milk. |
| **(Subject)** | **(Predicate)** |

What is named in each of the sentences we call the *subject* of the sentence; the subject is the doer or performer of the action, as in 1 and 4, or it is the thing whose state of being is described by the rest of the sentence, as in 2 and 3. What is said about the subject we call the *predicate* of the sentence.

Even when we make the sentence a bit more complicated, we can still show the basic two-part division.

| **Subject** | **Predicate** |
|---|---|
| Babies | can *drink* milk very often. |

What is said about babies in the predicate is now a bit more complicated, but the predicate still contains the words that do the saying about *babies*—still the subject, still the doers (the drinkers of the milk).

**2.** Every predicate contains at least one verb, though it may have an auxiliary and a verb. It can never have *only* an *-ing* verb and still be a sentence. Look at the italicized words in the examples above.

**3.** To find the subject of a sentence, first find the verb. You do this by understanding that the verb in the sentence is the word that denotes action or a state of being; you may also recall from studying verbs that verbs are words that can change tense.

Joanna *is* beautiful. (The verb: *is;* it denotes a state of being; it can be changed to *was,* the past tense.)

Now if you ask the question *who* (or in some sentences *what*) *is,* you get the answer *Joanna.* And *Joanna* is the simple subject of the sentence.

Many sentences have more than one subject; these subjects are called *compound* rather than *simple.*

1. *Dogs* and *seals* bark.
2. *Birds* and *tigers* are beautiful.
3. *Cats* and *squirrels* are animals.
4. *Babies* and *kittens* drink milk.

If you wanted to know the subjects of these four sentences and asked the questions *who* bark (in 1), *what* are (in 2 and 3), and *who* drink (in 4), the answers would be the pairs of words italicized in each sentence; each would then be said to have a *compound subject.*

---

### *Test Yourself on*
### Locating Subjects

In each sentence below, underline the subject. To find the subject, first locate the verb—the word that indicates action or a state of being and that can change tense; then ask the question *who* or *what* (of the verb); the answer will be the subject.

1. Whiskey burns my tongue.
2. She is beautiful.
3. My father is a policeman.
4. The meat tastes good sometimes.
5. Parents scold their children sometimes.
6. The truckdriver and his helper quit early.
7. Misery loves company.
8. You and he look happy.
9. The pipe blows bubbles.
10. Everybody seemed sad.
11. His pants are blue jeans.
12. My uncle pitches horseshoes.

---

It may strike you that these basic facts fit well the simple sentences we have used as examples but may not be so useful in analyzing more complicated sentences. The point is a good one, and we should begin to address ourselves to it by learning something about basic sentence patterns.

If you read a page or two of a good piece of writing in English, you will probably notice that there is a good deal of variety in the sentences. Maybe no two of them will look alike to you. But the fact is that these various sentences are built on just a few basic patterns.* These patterns can be modified or combined in a variety of ways to produce quite complicated statements, and it is this fact that accounts for the variety you generally find in English sentences. Let us therefore begin to examine

---

*Just how many of these basic patterns there are is a matter of some argument, but it won't affect what we shall have to say about the main point: that just a few basic patterns underlie all sentences.

these sentence patterns to see how the basic facts—and certain others—apply to them as well as how they can be expanded to make more complicated sentences.

## Pattern 1

This pattern consists of a subject (noun or pronoun) and a predicate that is or includes an intransitive verb (one that does not have to act *on* something):

Dogs bark. (*Who* bark? *Dogs*, the subject.)
Birds sing. (*Who* sing? *Birds*, the subject.)
He arrived. (*Who* arrived? *He*, the subject.)

The following are just some of the ways in which this pattern can be modified and expanded:

*My* dogs *can* bark *loudly*.
*All* birds *are* singing *sweetly*.
He *has* arrived *suddenly*.

So we can say that this pattern consists of a *subject + predicate*.

## Pattern 2

This pattern consists of a noun or a pronoun (*subject*) with a linking verb followed by an adjective (*predicate*). The most common linking verb is *be* (*am, is, are, was, were*), but others like *seem, become, feel, appear, taste,* and *grow* also are used.

Birds are beautiful. (*Who* are? *Birds*, the subject; predicate is *are beautiful*.)
She feels happy. (*Who* feels? *She*, the subject; predicate is *feels happy*.)
John looks young. (*Who* looks? *John*, the subject; predicate is *looks young*.)

## Expanded Pattern 2

*Tropical* birds are *sometimes* beautiful.

The adjectives that appear in the predicate in this pattern are called *predicate adjectives*. *A predicate ad-*

*jective* describes the state of being of the subject, thus completing the pattern.

## Pattern 3

This pattern consists of a subject (noun or pronoun) with a linking verb followed by a noun (or pronoun). The verbs *be* (*am, is, are, was, were*) and *become* usually occur in this pattern. These verbs tell the reader that the nouns are closely related, if not identical.

Cats are animals.
He is Harry.
She became my wife.

## Expanded Pattern 3

*These* cats *may* be *my* animals *soon.*

The nouns that follow the linking verb we call *predicate nouns*. A predicate noun also describes the state of being of the subject, thus completing the pattern.

## Pattern 4

This pattern consists of a subject (noun or pronoun) with a transitive verb (one that acts *on* something) followed by another noun or pronoun. Many verbs can appear in this pattern; a few are verbs like *see, throw, create, deliver.*

Babies drink milk.
He flies airplanes.
Everybody needs a job.

## Expanded Pattern 4

*Those* babies drink *their* milk.
*These* cats *can* drink *my* milk *often.*

We call the noun *milk* in the first example or the noun *airplanes* in the second or the noun *job* in the third the *direct object.* We say that the subject *does* the action; the direct object *undergoes* or *receives* the action of the verb.

You locate the direct object by asking still another question. Let us go through all the questions needed to identify all the parts of this basic pattern.

Cows chew grass.

What word can change its tense? (*Chew*, which can be changed to *chewed. Chew* is therefore the verb.)
*Who* chew? (*Cows*, the subject.)
Cows chew *what*? (*Grass*, the direct object.)

## Review of Sentence Patterns 1–4

Below are examples of patterns 1–4. Each part is identified for you. (d stands for determiner.)

                  predicate

             subj.  verb  (intransitive)
**Pattern 1**  Fish swim.

                    predicate

             subj.     verb (linking)  pred. adjective
**Pattern 2**  Clowns are          funny.

                    predicate

             d  subj.    verb (linking)  d pred. noun
**Pattern 3**  A cowboy is        a hero.

                    predicate

             subj.       verb (transitive)  direct object.
**Pattern 4**  Mechanics repair       automobiles.

---

## *Test Yourself on*
## Identifying Parts of Patterns 1, 2, 3, 4:
## Subjects, Predicates, Verbs, Direct Objects

A. To each of the sentences listed under "Review of Sentence Patterns 1–4" add a determiner or adjective or both to the subject and an auxiliary and an adverb to the predicate. In addition, you might add an adjective to the nouns in the predicates of patterns 3 and 4 (e.g., *happy hero; old automobiles*).

B. Underline the subjects of the following sentences:

1. My mother is a good cook.

2. Summers are too long.

3. He had an idea.

4. Everybody likes ice cream.

5. Some do not.

6. Musicians need formal training.

7. All politicians are the same.

8. She hated her dress.

9. They ordered steak infrequently.

10. A prince is a ruler.

C. Underline all the words that belong to the predicates of the following sentences:

1. My father seldom ate bananas.

2. His friend can play golf now.

3. Al was really a terrible villain.

4. A shopkeeper is really a small businessman.

5. Sharks are always dangerous.

6. Clouds are drifting slowly.

7. His clothes would often be messy.

8. They can travel soon.

D. Describe each word of the predicates you underlined in C by writing above each D (for determiner), VL (for linking verb), VI (for intransitive verb), VT (for transitive verb), ADJ (for adjective), ADV (for adverb), AUX (for auxiliary), PRED ADJ (for predicate adjective), PRED NOUN (for predicate noun), or DIR OBJ (for direct object).

## Pattern 5

This pattern consists of a noun (or pronoun) followed by a verb, another noun (or pronoun), and then a third noun (or pronoun). The verb in this pattern is a transitive verb, one of a small group that indicates giving or sending or teaching. Some of the verbs are words like *give, send, mail, teach, lend,* and *offer.* Here are some examples of pattern 5:

My brother *gave* his friend a camera. (Who *gave?* My *brother,* the subject; my brother gave what? A *camera,* the direct object.)

The professor *taught* his students biology. (Who *taught?* The *professor,* the subject; the professor taught what? *Biology,* the direct object.)

Your father *lent* you his car. (Who *lent?* Your *father,* the subject; your father lent what? His *car,* the direct object.)

In these examples, you can see that we have identified all the parts except the noun following the verb in each. In each example, the second noun is called the *indirect object.* The indirect object is the person or thing *to* or *for whom* the direct object is given, taught, lent.

My brother gave a camera—to whom? To his *friend.* (indirect object)

The professor taught biology—to whom? To his *students.* (indirect object)

Your father lent his car—to whom? To *you.* (indirect object)

This pattern, then, consists of *subject + verb + indirect object + direct object.* You can see that the second noun (the subject is the first noun) is the indirect object and the third noun the direct object; you can also see that the second and third nouns refer to different things. When they refer to the *same* thing, we have a slightly different pattern: pattern 6.

## Pattern 6

This pattern consists of *subject + verb + direct object + noun* (or pronoun). The verbs in this pattern are transitive verbs like those in pattern 4.

| d | subject | verb | d | direct object | d | noun |
|---|---------|------|---|---------------|---|------|
|   | We | considered | the | cowboy | a | hero. |
|   | They | called | the | policeman | an | officer. |
| My | committee | elected |   | Jim |   | chairman. |

Notice that in this pattern the second noun is the direct object and the third noun, which really refers to the same thing as the direct object, is called the *object complement*. A complement is something that *completes* something else. Thus the object complement completes the meaning of the direct object by identifying it further: *cowboy:hero; policeman:officer; Jim:chairman.*

## Pattern 7

This is only slightly different from pattern 6. It is the same except that the object complement is an adjective instead of a noun.

| d | subject | verb | d | direct object | adjective |
|---|---------|------|---|---------------|-----------|
|   | We | considered | the | cowboy | foolish. |
| That movie | | made | | my friends | angry. |

Like the first four patterns studied, these can also be expanded.

*My* very generous and loyal *brother gave his friend* Charlie who lives in California *a camera* as a birthday present.

You can see by reading the italicized words one after the other that this sentence is a complicated expansion of a basic sentence pattern: pattern 5.

---

### *Test Yourself on*
### Identifying Parts of Patterns 5, 6, 7: Indirect Objects, Object Complements (Nouns and Adjectives)

Circle the words in the following sentences that are either indirect objects or object complements. Mark the circles IO (for indirect objects), OCN (for object complements that are nouns), or OCA (for object complements that are adjectives). Probably you will need to find the direct object before you can locate the other parts.

1. My wife bought me a wedding present.
2. Frank thought the cop a hero.
3. During the meeting, we elected Jim our spokesman.
4. The boys considered the girls beautiful.
5. Sally taught her sons arithmetic.
6. Afterward, Uncle Joe sent Aunt Mina a letter.
7. His tailor made my friend a suit.
8. The people thought the mayor foolish.
9. I found the teacher interesting.
10. We made the beach a paradise.
11. After the party, we found the host happy.
12. He lent his brother the bike.

---

## Clauses and Phrases

We have studied basic sentence patterns and seen how they could be expanded by the addition of single words. Another possibility for expansion is the following:

Clowns *in the circus* are funny *when they work with animals.*

This is basic sentence pattern 2, but we have expanded it through the addition of the two italicized word groups. With this, we introduce *clauses* and *phrases. In the circus* is a *prepositional phrase.* Like other types of phrases (participial and infinitive), it has no subject and no verb. It acts in the sentence like an adjective, modifying *clowns.* The second of the italicized word groups is a *subordinate* (or *dependent*) *clause.* It has a subject (*they*) and a verb (*work*), but unlike a sentence, also called an *independent clause*, it cannot stand alone. It hangs on the word *when*, which introduces the clause.

By employing word groups like these, we can expand and vary the basic sentence patterns into very complicated statements. To understand just how these expansions and modifications take place, we must look in more detail at clauses and phrases.

## Clauses

Here we shall discuss clauses that can act as adjectives, adverbs, and nouns. We shall also discuss an important difference between these dependent clauses and sentences that are independent clauses.

### *1. Adjective clauses*

Cats are animals *that can scratch.*

The italicized group of words is an adjective clause. It modifies the noun *animals* by making it more specific; not just *animals,* but *animals that can scratch.* The word *that* is part of the clause. You can substitute *animals* for it and get a sentence:

Animals can scratch.

An adjective clause can modify a noun regardless of where the noun is positioned in the sentence.

Chairs *that are covered in velvet* look elegant. (modifies *chairs*)
I don't like professors *who lecture all the time.* (modifies *professors*)
Bob was the attorney *whom the court had appointed.* (modifies *attorney*)

Three points about adjective clauses are worth noting here:

**A.** We usually make this distinction in using *who* and *which:* When the noun being modified refers to a person, we use *who;* when it does not refer to a person, we use *which.* But we often use *that* in place of either:

The *doctor who* treats me is a graduate of Mount Sinai.
The *law which* was passed in 1964 prohibits discrimination in
   housing.

or

The *doctor that* treats me is a graduate of Mount Sinai.
The *law that* was passed in 1964 prohibits discrimination in
   housing.

**B.** Frequently, in both speech and writing, we use
adjective clauses and omit the subordinating conjunction.

The girl *I met* lives in Mill Valley. (*Whom* or *that* is omitted
   between *girl* and *I.*)

This happens only when we can turn the modified noun
into a direct object if we make a sentence out of it and
the words of the clause.

The *girl I met* lives in Mill Valley.
I met the girl. (*Girl,* noun originally modified, is now the direct
   object of *met.*)
The *party he gave* was a lot of fun. (*That* or *which* is omitted
   between *party* and *he.*)
He gave the party. (*Party,* noun originally modified, is now the
   direct object of *gave.*)

**C.** Sometimes a *which* clause can modify a whole
sentence—not just one noun in it.

He scored 87 points in one game, *which is a record for our
   team.*

## 2. Adverb clauses

Babies drink milk *when they are hungry.*

The italicized group of words is an adverb clause. It
modifies the word *drink* by answering the question:
*When* do babies drink milk? They don't drink it all the
time, only *when they are hungry.* The adverb clause
differs from the adjective clause in two ways: (1) Its
connecting word (*when,* in this case) is not part of the

clause but stands at the beginning of it; (2) it can be moved around in the sentence and still do its job.

Babies drink milk *when they are hungry.*
*When they are hungry,* babies drink milk.

Adverb clauses begin with one of the subordinating conjunctions listed on page 26 (words like *whenever, although, if, until, unless,* and so forth).

### 3. Noun clauses

*What I am eating* tastes good.

The italicized group of words is a noun clause. Occupying the place of a noun, it is the subject of the sentence. You can test to see if this is true by asking the question: *What* tastes good? The only satisfactory answer is *what I am eating.* Therefore, the clause is the subject. But the noun clause can also occur in most of the other positions typically occupied by nouns (that is, as predicate noun, direct object, or in the position of a noun in a prepositional phrase).

That is *what I am eating.* (predicate noun)
I love *what I am eating.* (direct object)
I am satisfied *with what I am eating.* (object of a preposition)

Noun clauses are very commonly signaled by words like *whoever, whatever,* and *what.*

I can supply *whatever you need.*
*Whoever runs* will be short of breath.
*What needs fixing* can go to the repair shop.

## Clauses and Sentences: Dependent and Independent

The clauses we have been discussing are to be distinguished from sentences by the way we punctuate them. That is, sentences are really *independent clauses;* they can stand on their own and are punctuated with periods or question marks or exclamation marks. Adverb, adjective, and noun clauses, on the other hand, are *dependent clauses* and cannot stand alone; therefore, they are never punctuated as if they were sentences.

**Independent Clause**   We are tired.

**Dependent Adverb Clause**   Whenever we are tired

**Dependent Adjective Clause**   The farm, *which we bought in 1970,* is worth a lot of money.

**Dependent Noun Clause**   I can give you *whatever you need.*

---

## *Test Yourself on*
### Clauses

A. Using the words *who, whom, which,* and *that,* construct clauses that modify the following words:

*Example:* 1. money: clauses constructed using *that* and *which:* money *that I spent yesterday,* money *which was given to me*

1. money

2. people

3. little boys

4. apples

5. laws

6. women

B. Using words such as *although, unless, because* (or any of those listed on p. 26), construct clauses to go with the following simple sentences:

*Example:* 1. The Scholarship Fund gave me what I asked for.
clause constructed to go with this sentence: *Although my grades weren't as good this year as they were in 1977,* the Scholarship Fund gave me what I asked for.

1. The Scholarship Fund gave me what I asked for.
2. It has hair on it.
3. Onions give me indigestion.
4. I can see my brother.
5. Parades make me nervous.
6. The office was empty.

C. Underline the clause in each of the following sentences and above each write ADV if the clause is acting as an adverb, N if it is acting as a noun, or ADJ if it is acting as an adjective.

1. What I want for supper is fish.
2. Until you come home, I have to babysit for our little brother.
3. The car that pleases me most gives good gas mileage.
4. Whatever you do is all right.
5. The man whom I pointed out is my uncle.
6. I don't know what will happen next.
7. Although I came early, the show was sold out.
8. I am disappointed because my grades were not higher this term.
9. The basketball court that is in the gym is occupied day and night.
10. The thing that hurts most is indifference.

D. Below are printed ten sentences. Part of each sentence is in *italics*. Place an I over the part that is independent, a D over the part that is dependent. After that, decide whether the clauses marked with a D are adjective, adverb, or noun clauses.

1. *The man* that was here yesterday *was Judy's father.*
2. *Although I never went past the tenth grade,* I can write pretty well.

3. Whenever you cross the yellow line at the center of the road, *you're in danger.*

4. *Whoever asks* should be directed to the Administration Building.

5. I can guess *what you're thinking.*

6. The doctor *whom I saw* said I'd recover in a week.

7. *The tractor,* which I bought last year, *is in terrible shape.*

8. You'd better look *before you leap.*

9. I'll wait for you *until nine o'clock.*

10. Because he was late getting up, *he missed the bus.*

## Phrases

When we discussed a more complicated expansion of basic sentence patterns (pp. 40–41), we identified the prepositional phrase. You saw that this type of phrase could be used as an adjective and that phrases differed from clauses in having no subject or verb. Several types of phrases can be used as adjectives, and some can be used as adverbs and nouns, too.

### 1. Phrases used as adjectives

1. The man *in the blue suit* spoke quietly. (Pattern 1)
2. The birds *flying toward the barn* are beautiful. (Pattern 2)
3. My father is a man *known for his kindness.* (Pattern 3)
4. I need shoes *to wear to the wedding.* (Pattern 4)

The italicized part of each sentence is a phrase used as an adjective. The phrase in example 1 should be familiar: It's a prepositional phrase used as an adjective. The phrases in examples 2 and 3 are somewhat different. Each begins with a verb. *Flying,* an *-ing* word, we call a *present participle; known* in example 3 we call a *past participle*—it is normally used with an auxiliary, as in *He* *had known.* Since both phrases begin with a participle, we call them *participial phrases*—but both are here *acting* as adjective phrases.

Notice that these two phrases, *flying toward the barn* and *known for his kindness,* consist of their headwords (*flying* and *known*) plus a prepositional phrase. But this type of phrase need not be structured this way. For example, we could say "The birds *flying there* are beautiful" and "My father is a man *known to be kind.*" However, they would still both be participial phrases acting as adjectives.

In example 4 above, the italicized phrase modifies the word *shoes* by making it more specific; not just *shoes,* but *shoes to wear to the wedding.* This type of phrase has two headwords: *to* and *wear.* *To wear* is the infinitive form of the verb *wear.* So we call this type an *infinitive phrase* according to its form, but it is functioning as an adjective and is an adjective phrase.

## 2. *Phrases used as adverbs*

He spoke *in the afternoon.* (Pattern 1)

The italicized group of words is a phrase used as an adverb. You may recognize it by its construction, *preposition + determiner + noun,* as a prepositional phrase. This phrase tells *when* he spoke, modifying the verb *spoke.*

There is one other kind of phrase that can be used as an adverb:

*To avoid fatigue,* he rested.

The italicized group of words in an infinitive phrase used as an adverb; it modifies the verb *rested.*

## 3. *Phrases used as nouns*

*Riding a motorcycle* can be dangerous. (Pattern 2)

The italicized group of words is a phrase used as a noun. It occurs in the noun position and acts as the subject of the sentence. You can test to see if this is true by asking *what* can be dangerous. The only satisfactory answer is *riding a motorcycle,* because the sentence does not say that *riding* can be dangerous or that a *motorcycle* can be dangerous.

You will notice in this phrase that the word *riding* resembles a verb in having the *-ing* ending. Here this word is not used as a verb. Instead we call it a *gerund,* that is, a verb form that acts as a noun—as in the sentence "*Swimming* is fun." Therefore, for purposes of recognizing the form of the phrase, we would call *riding a motorcycle* a *gerund phrase* because it begins with a gerund; but it acts like a noun and is called a *noun phrase* by function.

This type of phrase can occupy other noun positions:

I like *riding a motorcycle.* (direct object)

An infinitive phrase can also be used as a noun and occupy some typical noun positions:

*To ride a motorcycle* can be dangerous. (Pattern 2, subject)
I like *to ride a motorcycle.* (Pattern 4, direct object)
He asked me *to ride a motorcycle.* (Pattern 6, object complement)

Occasionally, a prepositional phrase is used as a noun in the subject position:

*Over the fence* is out.
*After supper* is all right.

But these uses are not common.

---

## *Test Yourself on*
## Phrases

A. Underline each phrase you find in the sentences below and above each write ADJ if the phrase is being used as an adjective, ADV if it is being used as an adverb, or N if it is being used as a noun. Some sentences have more than one phrase.

1. He traveled in the afternoons.
2. The cameras carried in stock were all cheap.
3. After a few minutes, he saw the sun set over the trees.
4. Known for his pure tenor voice, he often gave concerts in the park.
5. To love deeply is my goal in life.
6. I saw him riding a bicycle.
7. Come up to my house for an hour.
8. He wants to study chemistry.
9. I saw the shoplifter running down the street.
10. She stood next to my brother.

B. For each of the sentences or parts of sentences given below, construct the type of phrase that is called for to serve the given function.

*Example:* The man (participial phrase: adjective) looked sinister.
The man *walking alone* looked sinister. (The phrase acts as an adjective modifying *man.*)

1. The man (participial phrase: adjective) looked sinister.
2. Charley traveled (prepositional phrase: adverb).
3. (Participial phrase: noun) should be a pleasure.
4. She looked like a lady (participial phrase: adjective).
5. He talked (prepositional phrase: adverb).
6. (Infinitive phrase: adverb), he broke up with his girl.
7. He typed (prepositional phrase: adverb).
8. He loved (participial phrase: noun).
9. She begged me (infinitive phrase: noun).
10. She was a woman (participial phrase: adjective).

If you have worked your way carefully through this part of the book, you should now be ready to tackle any of the entries in Part 2. These entries all focus on specific writing problems or principles of effective writing. Most of them cannot be understood without reference to some of the ideas discussed in Part 1. Thus you should continue to use this part as a reference, or if you prefer, to use the "Glossary of Grammatical Terms"—or both. The improvement it can make in your writing is worth the effort.

# An Index
to Usage
and the
Principles
of Effective
Writing

**Part**

*Note:* Cross-references in **boldface** type are to other entries in Part 2. Cross-references in regular type are to sections in Part 1.

# Abbreviations

Abbreviations can be useful in saving the writer time and space, but not all abbreviations are acceptable in essay writing. Over the years there has developed a set of conventions (agreements) that tell us when we may and when we may not use abbreviations. Here they are divided into two classes, the appropriate and the inappropriate.

## Appropriate

### *Forms of address and titles*

It is permissible to use such abbreviations as *Mr., Mrs., Ms., Messrs.* (plural of *Mr.*), *Mmes.* (plural of *Mrs.*), *St., Jr., Sr., M.D.* (Doctor of Medicine), *D.D. S.* (Doctor of Dental Surgery), *A.B.* (or *B. A.*, Bachelor of Arts), *M. A.* (Master of Arts), *Ph.D.* (Doctor of Philosophy), and *Esq.* (Esquire; a title appropriately used only by attorneys).

### *Conventional foreign words and phrases*

The following abbreviations of certain useful foreign words and phrases may be used:

c *or* ca. (about)          i.e. (that is)
cf. (compare)               v. (see)
e.g. (for example)          viz. (namely)

### *Technical terms*

The following technical terms may be abbreviated:

BTU (British Thermal Unit)      kmh (kilometers per hour)
cc (cubic centimeter)*          mpg (miles per gallon)
cm (centimeter)                 mph (miles per hour)
gm (gram)                       rpm (revolutions per minute)
km (kilometer)

*$cm^3$ is preferable in technical writing.

### Organizations, institutions, government agencies, trade unions

It is common practice to abbreviate the names of institutions. Occasionally, an abbreviation forms an *acronym,* that is, a pronounceable word, such as WHO for World Health Organization. In an essay, first write out the whole name of the organization; subsequent references to it may be abbreviated.

The Committee on Dental Education (CODE) issued a stern warning about the use of kangaroo flakes in toothpaste. CODE officials noted that very few kangaroos have had good checkups this year. CODE stated that fluorides are the most effective additives for toothpaste.

Here is a brief list of some common abbreviations for well-known groups; some of them are acronyms, as you can see:

CARE (Cooperative for American Relief to Everywhere)
CBS (Columbia Broadcasting System)
FBI (Federal Bureau of Investigation)
GSA (General Services Administration)
UN (United Nations)
UNESCO (United Nations Educational, Scientific, and Cultural Organization)

### Expressions of time

These may be abbreviated:

1434 B.C. (before Christ)
A.D. 953 (anno domini; in the year of Our Lord)
8 A.M. *or* 8 a.m.
7:29 P.M. *or* 7:29 p.m.
EST (Eastern Standard Time)
DST (Daylight Saving Time)
MST (Mountain Standard Time)
CST (Central Standard Time)
PST (Pacific Standard Time)

## Inappropriate

It is inappropriate to abbreviate in the following ways in a written text. (Many of these abbreviations are acceptable in addresses and certain short references.)

## Titles

**Wrong**  *Prof.* Smith and *Sen.* Smith are brothers.
**Right**  *Professor* Smith and *Senator* Smith are brothers.

## Given names

**Wrong**  Geo., Wm., Thos., Ed., Jas., Theo.
**Right**  George, William, Thomas, Edward, James, Theodore

## Places

**Wrong**  I plan to spend my vacation in *N.M.*
**Right**  I plan to spend my vacation in *New Mexico.*

**Wrong**  Of all the underdeveloped areas, *S.A.* has the highest economic growth rate.
**Right**  Of all the underdeveloped areas, *South America* has the highest economic growth rate.

**Wrong**  To get to Sarah's, take County *Rd.* to Closter.
**Right**  To get to Sarah's, take County *Road* to Closter.

**Wrong**  Jerry lives at Elm *St.* and Carson *Ave.*
**Right**  Jerry lives at Elm *Street* and Carson *Avenue.*

## Days of the week, names of the months, and holidays

**Wrong**  The King died on *Tues.*
**Right**  The King died on *Tuesday.*

**Wrong**  The academic calendar runs from *Oct.* to May.
**Right**  The academic calendar runs from *October* to May.

**Wrong**  For *Xmas*, I'd like a new bathrobe.
**Right**  For *Christmas*, I'd like a new bathrobe.

## Units of measurement

**Wrong**  ins., ft., yds., mi., lbs., oz.
**Right**  inches, feet, yards, mile, pounds, ounces

### Academic courses

**Wrong**  Richard is failing *eco.* and *psych.* this term.
**Right**  Richard is failing *economics* and *psychology* this term.

### Miscellaneous items

Do not use an ampersand (&) unless it is part of an official company name, for example, *Earl H. Rovit & Son, Inc.* In ordinary circumstances, use *and* in place of &.

Do not abbreviate ordinary words through laziness or because you are uncertain about their spellings. Do not, for example, substitute *thru* for *through*, *tho* for *though*, *yrs* for *yours*, or *mtns* for *mountains*.

---

## *Test Yourself on*
## Abbreviations

By using abbreviations where appropriate, correct the errors in the following sentences. Place the letter C next to the sentences that you think are correct.

1. \_\_\_\_ Mister Tuten took the stand and stated that at 8 ay em, when the accident took place, he was traveling at 55 miles per hour.

2. \_\_\_\_ The physician on duty administered 100 cubic centimeters of insulin.

3. \_\_\_\_ He said he was able to get through the winter by taking a short vacation in Florida at Christmastime.

4. \_\_\_\_ By using the Panama Canal, ships can avoid going around the tip of S. A.

5. \_\_\_\_ The Council to Rehabilitate Urban Military Back Yards announced a fund-raising drive today. Officials of the Council to Rehabilitate Urban Military Back Yards set their goal at

$3,000,000 and said they hoped to reach it by
St. Pat's day.

6. _____ Many species of fish inhabit this lake, e.g.,
pike, perch, and catfish; some specimens have
measured as much as twenty inches and
weighed as much as fourteen pounds.

7. _____ On Mon., Wed., and Fri. I go from eco to philo
and then on to gym.

8. _____ Driving west toward California, you can pass
through Ill. and Kan.

9. _____ Before I started my diet on Thurs., I weighed
242 lbs.

10. _____ The mtns look toward Penn on one side and
W. Va. on the other.

11. _____ Gail & Grace have both broken up with their
boyfriends.

12. _____ His parents hope that Joseph Young, Junior,
will grow up to be like Joseph Young, Senior.

## Active Voice

See **Voice.**

## Adjectivals

An adjectival is any word, phrase, or clause that can act
as an adjective in a sentence. See **Modifiers.**

## Adverbials

An adverbial is any word, phrase, or clause that can act
as an adverb in a sentence. See **Modifiers.**

# Ambiguity

When something can be read in two or more ways then we say it is ambiguous, that is, it has ambiguity. *Mail leaves tomorrow* could mean that *the mail will leave tomorrow* or that the writer of the message wants *his leaves* mailed tomorrow. See **Modifiers, Pronoun References, Shifts.**

# Antecedents

An antecedent is what a pronoun may sometimes refer to and must always agree with. See **Pronoun References, Shifts;** Pronouns.

# Apostrophe

The apostrophe is a mark used by convention (agreement) to signal contractions, possessives, and certain special plurals.

## Contractions

The rule for contracting two words into one is to use the apostrophe in place of the missing letter or letters.

```
are not = aren't
Bud is = Bud's (see also Possessives, below)
cannot = can't
it is = it's (but its, without the apostrophe, is possessive)
let us = let's
we have = we've
would not = wouldn't
you will = you'll
```

## Possessives

In English, there are two ways to express possession, ownership, and similar relationships when using nouns.

The *office of the manager* is located at the top of the stairs.
The *manager's office* is located at the top of the stairs.

Both ways are correct. In general, we would use the first

method (using the word *of*) for nouns that stand for something inanimate and the second (using an apostrophe and -s) for nouns representing something animate.

**Animate**   Judy's room; Mark's office; Franny's eyes; Colin's book

**Inanimate**   the light of the moon; the color of the paint; the score of the game

Nevertheless, it is valuable to know that both forms mean the same thing: possession. For if you are having trouble with the apostrophe -s (*'s*) form, you can determine whether or not the *'s* is needed by using the fact we've just noted. For example, suppose that one of your essays contained the following phrases, and that you were unsure whether an apostrophe were needed in any of them.

1. Charlies horse
2. Clarences cross
3. Janeys boss
4. Marks loss
5. the Smiths went

Using the fact previously noted—that the *of* form and the *'s* form both mean the same thing—we can try to see whether any of the five phrases can be turned into the alternative *of* form.

1. Charlies horse = the horse of Charlie
2. Clarences cross = the cross of Clarence
3. Janeys boss = the boss of Janey
4. Marks loss = the loss of Mark
5. the Smiths went ≠ the went of Smith

We can see clearly that the first four examples *can* be changed into the alternative form and therefore need an apostrophe in the original form—as follows:

1. Charlie's horse
2. Clarence's cross
3. Janey's boss
4. Mark's loss

Example 5 needs no apostrophe because it contains no possessive.

### *Test Yourself on*
## Changing from One Form of Possession to the Other

Using the rule you learned, change the following into the alternative possessive form:

1. the outcome of the game
2. the tirade of Lenny
3. the argument of the Mayor
4. the future of the boy
5. the impatience of my father
6. the wit of Eddie
7. the engine of Phil
8. the winged chariot of time
9. the ale of Gail
10. the acting of Colin

---

### *Forming the possessive of singular nouns and indefinite pronouns*

In order to form the possessive of singular nouns and indefinite pronouns* that do not end in -s simply add *'s*.

| | |
|---|---|
| my father's cigarette | a doctor's appointment |
| my mother's comb | anybody's game |
| *TV Guide*'s features | teacher's pet |
| everybody's future | nobody's fault |

### *Forming the possessive of plural nouns*

To form the possessive of plural nouns, add *'s* to nouns with an irregular plural (e.g., *children, men, women*); but add *only* an apostrophe to plurals ending in -s.

*Note: Never use an apostrophe for any of the possessive personal pronouns. That is, *his, hers, its, yours, ours, theirs, mine* already indicate possession and need no additional marks to indicate that fact.

**Irregular Plurals**
*men's* clothing
*women's* liberation
*children's* growth

**Regular Plurals**
the *boys'* hats (the hats belong
  to more than one boy)
his *parents'* devotion (the
  devotion of two people:
  mother and father)
*students'* grades (the grades of
  more than one student)

## Forming the possessive of nouns ending in -s, -x, and -z

The rule here is the same as the previous one for plurals ending in -s.

Marx' philosophy
Lefty Gomez' career
the boss' daughter

the Joneses' garage
Ulysses' voyage
Venus' orbit

*However ...*

In the case of plural nouns ending in any of these letters (-s, -x, -z), you have a spelling option based on how you pronounce these possessives. For example, if you actually say *boss-es* in pronouncing *boss'* then you may spell it to conform with the pronounciation. Thus the following alternative spellings would also be correct:

Marx's philosophy
Lefty Gomez's pitching
the boss's daughter

## Forming the possessive of two or more nouns

Place the *'s* after the last item in the series of nouns if you want to indicate joint ownership; place the *'s* after each item if you want to show individual possession but talk about both items in the same sentence.

I stayed at *Fred and Ed's* house. (They own the house together.)
I have sympathy for *Fred's and Ed's* troubles. (Each man's troubles are his own; the speaker declares sympathy for that which belongs to each man—and does so in the same sentence.)

## *Forming the possessive of compound nouns*

In a compound noun, the last word takes *'s*:

my mother-in-law's generosity
the Attorney General's order
my brother-in-law's book

## Special Plurals

The apostrophe is used to form the plurals of certain signs, numbers, letters, and words.*

Count up all the t*'s* and -*'s*.
On her quizzes, she had all *8's* and *9's*.
He had trouble pronouncing his *s's* and his *th's*.
Don't use too many *which's* in your writing.

---

## *Test Yourself on*
## The Correct Use of the Apostrophe

Each of the sentences below has either a misplaced or an omitted apostrophe. Supply the apostrophes where needed and strike out those that are superfluous.

1. The womens' liberation movement grows stronger every day because of it's militant posture.

2. During the 50s, the outspoken would'nt speak; their's was the silent age.

3. Charleys horse had a Charley horse before Tuesday's race's.

4. The Attorney Generals office is flooded with work; federal crime's seem to be taking place at a record rate.

*The apostrophe is sometimes also used for plural dates: "The 1800's were a time of change." However, it is preferable to write *1800s* for this kind of date.

5. If you get 90s and 100s on your exams, your grade index this term will be higher than Max'.

6. If she wont give you her book's, thats all right; Grandmas grammars are hers to give.

7. Its in your pant's pocket.

8. My mother-in-laws kindness to others has made her famous in Waterbury.

9. Harry's and Frank's book is likely to be published this year.

10. Mrs. Gonzalez's fathers sister was the first member of his family to arrive in the United States.

11. My father-in-laws' storytelling is always fascinating.

12. I'm tired of Linda Ronstadts; play someone elses records.

13. Anybody's troubles are my trouble's.

14. Ham and egg's is my favorite dish.

15. Peoples interests are determined by the complicated fact's of their lives.

---

## Appositives

An appositive is a noun, or some structure that can take the place of a noun, that is set right next to a noun to further explain or define it. It is set in *apposition*—in the next position in the sentence—to the noun which it will expand on. An appositive can be a single word or a group of words. In the following examples, the first noun is in italics and the appositive is in boldface.

The *teacher,* **Davis,** spoke slowly. (word)
*Magic Johnson's skill,* **stuffing a basketball through a hoop,** earns him a large salary. (phrase)
The *teacher,* **a physics professor,** spoke slowly. (noun phrase)

An appositive can occur in a sentence in various positions where nouns occur.

That was *Eddie*, **my friend.**
He liked my *car*, **a '57 Chevy.**

A useful fact to understand about the appositive is that this structure is really an abbreviated clause.

The *teacher*, **Davis,** spoke slowly. (The appositive *Davis* is really a part of the clause *whose name is Davis.*)
*Magic Johnson's skill*, **stuffing a basketball through a hoop,** earns him a large salary. (The appositive, *stuffing a basketball through a hoop*, is really a part of the clause *which is stuffing a basketball through a hoop.*)

There is another important fact about appositives that you should understand. Some are not essential to complete the meaning of the sentence; these are therefore called *nonrestrictive*. They are set off by commas. The appositives are italicized in the examples:

The doctor, *Allan Peters*, treated me for the flu. (The essential meaning is "The doctor treated me for the flu.")
For Christmas, I got a camera, *a Kodak Instamatic*. (The essential meaning is "For Christmas, I got a camera.")

However, some appositives *are* essential to the meaning of the sentence; these are called *restrictive*. They are *not* set off by commas because they *belong* to the noun they are set beside.

The gas station attendant *John* gave my car a lube job. (The essential meaning here is not that *the* gas station attendant gave my car a lube job, but that the gas station attendant named John did the job—there was more than one attendant and *John* identifies the correct one.)
I was helped through college by my Aunt *Martha*. (If the speaker had had only one aunt, then the word *Martha* would have been nonessential; as it is, *Martha* identifies one of the aunts and is an essential word.)

(See also **Comma Rules,** 5, for more on restrictives and nonrestrictives.)

## *Test Yourself on*
## Appositives

The following sentences all contain appositives, but they are all improperly punctuated. First, underline the appositive; then decide whether or not to set it off by a comma or commas. *Remember:* If the appositive is essential to the sentence (restrictive), do not use the comma or commas; if the appositive is nonessential (nonrestrictive), do use the comma or commas.

1. We slept that night in the tent an old piece of canvas with a dozen holes in it.

2. The Colonel Thomas Jones commanded the regiment as if he were a drill sergeant.

3. The police arrested two people a pickpocket and a burglar.

4. My aunt who lives in California Rebecca Rose is a movie producer.

5. We had to read *War and Peace* a book by someone named Tolstoy.

6. The cop we liked best O'Reilly treated us like human beings.

7. We were in the hands of the mediator the one who would decide.

8. Arthur Hopkins was a law professor a status he had achieved at a very young age.

9. The fighter we were eager to see Jackson was up against a tough opponent.

10. The author of the book Grace Paley will be autographing copies at Macy's today.

# Auxiliaries

Auxiliaries or helping verbs are the following: forms of the verb *be* (*am, is, are, was, were*); *has, have, had; do, did; can, could; be able to; may, might; would; should; must; ought to; shall* and *will*. For detailed information on how auxiliaries are used, see Auxiliaries.

# Business Letters

In a world as complex as this one, nearly everyone has to write a business letter at some time or other. But what is a business letter as opposed to, say, a letter to a friend?

It is, first and foremost, a formal piece of communication that says you mean business. The formality, expressed in both the writing style and the conventions of typography and layout we shall discuss, declares the writer a serious and reliable individual with serious business to transact. This impression is distinctly different from that conveyed by an ordinary informal letter to friends or relatives, where the primary purpose is to convey personal and intimate information.

You may have to write a business letter in applying for a job or a place in a professional school; you may have to write one making an inquiry or a complaint. Whatever the purpose of your business letter, it should follow these conventions:

**1.** Type business letters on plain white bond paper, 8 ½ × 11 inches in size.

**2.** Use standard business envelopes, 3 ⅝ × 6 ½ inches or 4 ⅛ × 9 ½ inches.

**3.** Be sure to pay careful attention to all six parts of the business letter: the heading, the inside address, the salutation, the body of the letter, the complimentary close, and the signature (handwritten and then typed).

# Sample Letter: Modified Block Style

1. Heading

```
105 Wedgwood Drive
Waterbury, Conn. 06705
April 11, 1982
```

Mr. Richard Appleman
Manager, Architect's Service Corporation    2. Inside
54 East 8th Street                              address
New York, N.Y. 10003

Dear Mr. Appleman:    3. Salutation    4. Body

This letter is in answer to your advertisement
for a summer architectural apprentice published in
the March issue of Architectural Digest. I wish
to apply for this position and believe I am
well qualified.

As an architecture student at the University of
Connecticut, Storrs, I have completed thirty
credits of courses in mechanical drafting, design,
and stress and materials. My sophomore project, a
design for a domed stadium, won second prize in
the Architecture Department's competition. Last
fall, I was employed part time in the Department
of Buildings here in Waterbury. The job required
me to read blueprints and I am thus familiar with
building specifications and details.

Should you wish to see my employment folder, you
may contact Ms. Katherine Roe. She is empowered
to send you my résumé and letters of recommendation.

```
Ms. Katherine Roe, Director
Office of Student Employment
University of Connecticut
Storrs, Connecticut 06268
```

I am available for an interview at your
convenience any time after 12 noon on Fridays, or
during the entire week of April 18. Should you
wish to telephone, I can be reached at (203)
755-5900.

5. Complimentary close          Yours sincerely,

6. Handwritten signature        *Peter S. Mudd*

6. Typed signature              Peter S. Mudd

The sample letter is typed in modified block style. If it were done in full block style, the heading and the closing would, like the rest of the letter, be flush with the left-hand margin. (The main styles are listed at the back of *Webster's New Collegiate Dictionary.*)

### 1. The heading

Notice that no part of this three-line heading is indented and that there is no end punctuation. The lines are singlespaced. When letterhead stationery is used, the date is sometimes centered two or three spaces below the printed material.

### 2. The inside address

Four to six spaces separate the heading from the inside address. Like the heading, the address is in block form. Notice that the address is spelled out without abbreviation, except the state; if an address is judged to be too long, certain abbreviations can be used—for example, *3512 Runnymede Pl., N.W.*

### 3. The salutation

The salutation (or greeting) is flush against the left-hand margin and placed two spaces below the last line of the inside address. Notice the colon following the name of the addressee.

Where it is known, always use the surname of the addressee. Where it is not known, you have a choice of the following:

```
Dear Sir or Madam:
Dear Sir:
Dear Madam:
Gentlemen:
```

The salutation "To Whom It May Concern" is generally

used when a letter is not addressed to a particular company or organization.

## 4. The body of the letter

This is normally single-spaced, with double-spacing used to separate paragraphs. Paragraphs should be flush with the left-hand margin if you are using the full block or modified block style (or they should begin with equal indentations, depending on your use of other styles).

The subject matter should be appropriately organized into paragraphs—that is, each paragraph should be devoted to one general idea. Use the plainest and most direct writing style, and avoid informal phrasing.

## 5. The complimentary close

Business letters have a variety of closes: *Yours truly, Very truly yours, Yours sincerely, Sincerely yours.* Occasionally, it is appropriate in a business letter to use *Cordially yours,* or *Cordially*—when you are on very friendly terms with the recipient. *Note:* The second word of the complimentary close begins with a small letter.

## 6. The signature

*The handwritten signature:* The handwritten signature goes between the complimentary close and the typed signature. Do not in handwriting indicate your official capacity or title.

*The typed signature:* The typed signature may be followed by your official title or capacity.

Yours sincerely,

*William J. Mudd*

William J. Mudd, M.D.

Sincerely yours,

*Douglas Hurban*

Douglas Hurban
Professor of Physiology

Women have generally been accorded the option of enclosing in parentheses either Ms., Miss, or Mrs. beside

their typed names. A married woman may choose to add
Mrs. together with her husband's name in parentheses.

Yours sincerely,                    Yours sincerely,

*Janet Miller*                      *Louise Johnson*

(Ms.) Janet Miller                  Louise Johnson
                                    (Mrs. John Johnson)

## Envelopes

The envelope should be addressed as follows:

---

Peter S. Mudd
105 Wedgwood Drive
Waterbury, Conn. 06705


                    Mr. Richard Appleman
                    Manager, Architect's Service Corp.
                    54 East 8th Street
                    New York, N.Y. 10003

---

## *Test Yourself on* Writing Business Letters

Write the following business letters:

1. to your local light and power company requesting a
   clarification of their new rate schedules for both electricity and natural gas fuel;
2. to the manager of a seashore hotel in Florida requesting a room reservation with a terrace facing the ocean;
3. to your congressman, urging him or her to vote for a
   bill that you are interested in seeing passed;
4. to a former employer, requesting that a letter of
   recommendation be sent to the placement office of
   your college, where your folder is on file;

5. to a former professor, requesting a letter recommending your admission to medical school; remind the professor of the course you took and the progress you have made since that time.

---

# Capitalization

The use of capital and lower case (small) letters follows a number of clear rules. We can number these for convenience as follows:

## 1. Beginning a sentence

Capitalize the first words of sentences.

Lasagna and pizza are Italian delicacies.
Travel agents are now offering charter flights to Mars.

## 2. The pronoun I and the interjection O (or Oh)

Capitalize these no matter where they occur in the sentence.

Doug says I am an astronaut.
He had O such an elegant jacket!

## 3. Days of the week, months, holidays

Capitalize all of these no matter where they occur in the sentence.

| | | |
|---|---|---|
| Tuesday | April | Memorial Day |
| Friday | August | Easter |
| Sunday | January | Christmas |

## 4. Titles of books, plays, movies, television shows, short stories, poems

Capitalize all of these no matter where they occur in the sentence. Articles and conjunctions are not capitalized unless they begin the title.

*The Sun Also Rises* (book)
*Caesar and Cleopatra* (play)
*Star Wars* (movie)
*The Fitzpatricks* (TV show)
"Asparagus Soup" (short story)
"Lycidas" (poem)

*Important note:* These titles should also be either italicized or enclosed in quotation marks, as they are above. See **Italics** and **Quotation Marks** for further information.

## 5. Proper names, proper adjectives, and titles

Capitalize the names of persons or geographical entities. Capitalize an official title when (a) it is used in place of a name to refer to the titleholder or (b) when it is used with the titleholder's name. *Do not* capitalize when the title refers to the office but not the person.

| | |
|---|---|
| Kathy Roe | Oneonta, New York |
| Middle East | Mars |
| Italian | New Englander |

*Justice Holmes* is presiding. The *Justice* is late today.
We are electing a *senator* today. (Refers to office, not person.)

## 6. Historical events, historical terms, historical artifacts

Use a capital letter for items such as the following:

| | |
|---|---|
| the Civil War | the Enlightenment |
| the Declaration of Independence | the Augustan Age |
| the Magna Carta | the Battle of the Marne |

## 7. Terms associated with colleges and universities

Use a capital letter for courses that are specifically designated by number. Use a lower case letter for those that are not so designated (except languages, which are always capitalized). Use a capital letter for academic titles or where the title alone is used to refer to the person holding it.

Biology 137
Math 11
French
anthropology (as in, "I am taking anthropology this term.")
Dean Theodore L. Gross
The Dean (referring to Dean Gross)
Professor Blanche Skurnick
Dr. Dennis Turner

## 8. Miscellaneous items

Use a capital letter for the names of public or private buildings.

the White House     the Gardner Mansion
the Flatiron Building     the Kennedy Center
the World Trade Center     the Renaissance Center

Use a capital letter for the names of both private and public organizations.

the Agriculture Department
the United Nations
the New York Yankees
Hadassah
the Modern Language Association
the Missouri Historical Society

Use a capital letter for virtually all references to things religious: deities, churches, adjectives based on these.

God     the United Methodist Church
the Lord     Christian
Anglican     the Bible
Christ     Genesis
Moses

Use a capital letter for products referred to by brand name.

Xerox     Rice Krispies     Chevrolet
Scotch tape     Kleenex     Sony

## *Test Yourself on*
## Capitalization

Read carefully each of the following sentences. Where there is an error in capitalization, indicate the error by writing CAP in the space provided. Then correct the error. If the sentence is correct, write C in the space.

1. _____ On friday we are taking the venus Special to Mars.

2. _____ Senator D'Amato made his maiden speech in congress today; the senator spoke on rock 'n' roll.

3. _____ To be mayor of New York is a little crazy.

4. _____ He didn't say i was a graduate of City college—he said I was a prisoner.

5. _____ An arabian knight is oil right.

6. _____ President Reagan favors a policy of lasting peace in the Middle East.

7. _____ The level of pollution in lake Erie is superseded only by the level of pollution in the Passaic river, according to measurements conducted by the Environmental protection administration, made last january.

8. _____ The work of a college president would be no challenge to the Dean.

9. _____ Next semester, I plan to take chemistry, Biology 101, mathematics, History 98, and Physics.

10. _____ The junior colleges in this state are suffering great decreases in student enrollment.

11. _____ This year we plan a big Memorial day parade followed by a dinner dance in the evening.

12. _____ At the University of Michigan, we are required to take classes in english.

13. _____ During World War II, spam was invented.

14. _____ Ronald Reagan is one of the oldest residents of the white house.

15. _____ The judge will now charge the jury.

16. _____ He was a christian gentleman.

# Case

Case refers to the function of a noun or pronoun in a sentence. In the sentence *He lent me his father's car,* the nominative case form *he* shows it is being used as the subject; the objective case form *me* indicates that the pronoun is an object; the possessive case form *father's* shows that the noun is possessive.

Case endings were once important in English but have now all but disappeared. Nouns have just two case forms: (1) the common form, for example, *doctor,* and (2) the possessive form, *doctor's.* It is the case of pronouns—where there are three cases: nominative, objective, and possessive—that requires the writer's attention.

| Nom. | I | we | you* | he | she | it* | they | who |
|------|---|-----|------|-----|------|-----|-------|-------|
| Poss. | my, mine | our, ours | your, yours | his | her, hers | its | their, theirs | whose |
| Obj. | me | us | you | him | her | it | them | whom |

Following are the rules for the proper use of each case.

---

*As you can see, *it* and *you* do not change in the objective case, only in the possessive.

## Nominative

**1.** Use the nominative case for the word in the subject position in the sentence. We need hardly say more about this rule, since few of us are likely to write sentences like "*Us* have a date tomorrow" or "*Me* want an apple."

**2.** Use the nominative case *who* in a clause where it is clearly the subject of the verb; do not be tempted into using *whom* by the words that intervene between *who* and its verb.

clause

There is a professor *who I know works hard to make contact with students.* (*Who* is here the subject of *works;* you should not make the error of thinking that *whom* should replace it because of the words *I know.*)

clause

He saw some men in uniform *who he thought were Marines.* (*Who* is the subject of *were;* do not think that *whom* should replace *who* because of the words *he thought.*)

**3.** In formal writing, use the nominative case after forms of the verb *be* (*is, are, was, were,* and so forth). Many good writers and speakers use the objective case, but formal writing requires the nominative.

**Formal**　It is *I.* It might be *they.*
**Informal**　It's *me.* It might be *them.*

**4.** Use the nominative case, in formal writing, after the conjunctions *as* and *than.* In these constructions, the pronoun is the subject of an omitted verb. In informal writing and in speech the objective case is frequently used.

**Formal**　He is hungrier *than I* [am]. (*Am* in this sentence is omitted but understood by the reader, and *I* is the subject of *am;* therefore, *I* must be in the nominative case.)
**Informal**　He is hungrier *than me.* (Here the conjunction *than* is made into a preposition, with *me* as its object.)

**Formal** We are as intelligent as *they* [are]. (*Are* is omitted but understood by the reader; *they* is the subject of *are* and is therefore in the nominative case.)

**Informal** We are as intelligent as *them*. (*As* is made into a preposition, with *them* as its object.)

**5.** Use the nominative case when the pronoun appears as part of a compound subject.

Jack and *he* played cards last night. (The compound subject of this sentence is the words *Jack* and *he;* the whole sentence really combines two sentences: "*Jack* played cards last night" and "*He* played cards last night.")

**6.** Use the nominative case of a pronoun in an appositive where that pronoun explains or further identifies a noun that is either the subject or the predicate noun.

appositive
It was the *coach, he alone*, who held the team together. (*Coach* is the predicate noun; therefore, *he*, the appositive pronoun, is in the nominative case.)

appositive
Those *two*—the policeman and *he*—prevented a robbery. (*Two* is the subject; therefore, *he*, the pronoun in the appositive, is in the nominative case.)

*Note:* Not all pronouns in appositives are in the nominative case. See Objective, below, for examples of appositive pronouns in the objective case.

## Possessive

**1.** Use pronouns in the possessive case to indicate possession, source, authorship, and similar relationships.

I liked *his* speech very much.
I know *whose* house that is.
The legislature has *its* power limited by the judiciary.

**2.** In formal writing, use the possessive case of a noun or a pronoun before a *gerund*. A gerund is the *-ing* form of a verb that is used as a noun; for example, *swimming* is a gerund when used in the sentence "Swimming is fun." In informal writing, you will sometimes see the objective case used instead of the possessive.

**Formal**   There was a good reason for *his* working hard.
**Informal**   There was a good reason for *him* working hard.

**Formal**   She was glad about *Charley's* organizing the concert.
**Informal**   She was glad about *Charley* organizing the concert.

Notice the subtle difference in meaning in the last pair of examples. In the first, the emphasis is on the organizing of the concert. In the second, the emphasis is on Charley.

## Objective

**1.** Use the objective case where the pronoun is the object of a verb.

The weird noise troubled *him*. (*Him* is the object of *troubled*.)
*Whom* did you invite? (*Whom* is the object of the verb.)

It is important to understand that where the object is a compound construction containing, say, a proper name and a pronoun, the pronoun must be in the objective case.

The club elected Paul and *me* co-chairmen. (*Paul* and *me* are the objects of the verb *elected;* therefore, *me* is in the objective case; do not say "Paul and *I*" in a construction like this. You would not say, "The club elected *I* chairman.")

**2.** Use the objective case when the pronoun is the object of a verbal. A verbal is either a verb ending in *-ing* or an infinitive, that is, a verb with the word *to* preceding it (*to work, to play,* and so forth).

Knowing *him* was a pleasure. (*Him* is the object of *knowing*.)
Whenever I see babies, I want to kiss *them*. (*Them* is the object of *to kiss*.)

*Note:* An exception to this rule occurs when the infinitive is the verb *to be* and the subject of the infinitive is unexpressed; then formal usage requires that the nominative case be used after the infinitive.

**Formal**    I wouldn't want *to be he.*
**Informal**    I wouldn't want *to be him.*

**3.** Use the objective case for a pronoun that is the object of a preposition.

Three of *us* went to the movies last night. (*Us* is the object of the preposition *of.*)
He is the professor for *whom* I worked hardest. (*Whom* is the object of the preposition *for.*)

It is important to note that on occasion two pronouns will be objects of the same preposition. Both must then be in the objective case.

Bob and I both wanted the job; the boss would have to choose between *him* and *me.* (Both *him* and *me* are objects of the preposition *between.*)

**4.** In formal writing, use the objective case *whom* in a clause where it is clearly the object of the verb. In informal writing, *who* is widely used instead of *whom.*

**Formal**    She is the visitor *whom* we expected. (*Whom* is the object of *expected.*)
**Informal**    She is the visitor *who* we expected.

**Formal**    *Whom* are you criticizing? (*Whom* is the object of *are criticizing.*)
**Informal**    *Who* are you criticizing?

The word *whom* is now used less and less, even among well-educated writers and speakers. Still, in certain cases, *whom* is the much-to-be-preferred formal choice.

*Whom* do you want to see?
*Whom* are you waiting for?

*Note: Whom* is *always* used when the pronoun directly follows a preposition.

*For whom* are you waiting?
I don't know *to whom* he spoke.

**5.** Use the objective case of a pronoun following the conjunctions *as* and *than* if that pronoun is the object of a verb that has been omitted from the sentence.

He likes her more *than* [he likes] *me*. (*Me* is the object of *likes*.)
I treated her as fairly *as* [I treated] *him*. (*Him* is the object of *treated*.)

**6.** Use the objective case of a pronoun that appears in an appositive when that pronoun explains or further identifies a noun that is an object.

appositive
The coach fired two players, *Colin and me*. (*Me* is in the objective case because it further identifies the noun *players*, the object of *fired*.)

*Note:* Do not use the reflexive pronoun *myself* in place of the objective pronoun *me*.

**Wrong** My aunt willed her estate to my brother and *myself*.
**Right** My aunt willed her estate to my brother and *me*.

---

## *Test Yourself on*
## Using the Correct Case of Pronouns

Select the proper case of the pronoun from the choices in parentheses in each of the following sentences. Make your choices in accordance with correct formal usage.

1. She talked to Ed and (I, me) for a long time.

2. I can't imagine (his, him) accepting the job.

3. He didn't look it, but Paul was as tired as (I, me).

4. The Mayor, (he, him) alone, was responsible for slum conditions in our city.

5. The blue jeans fitted Bob as well as (I, me).

6. Somehow, Richard thought he was better than (I, me).

7. When Betty ran to answer the phone, she knew it was (he, him).

8. They never found out the names of the vandals (who, whom) they believed were destroying the highway signs.

9. Chris and (he, him) got drunk together last night.

10. The two of them—Irv and (he, him)—drove to California in three days.

11. I can do the job without (his, him) instructing me every minute.

12. The girls considered Jim and (I, me) the most attractive bachelors they knew.

13. (Who, Whom) are you waiting for?

14. They gave medals to two swimmers, David and (me, I).

15. After the party, the host was as tired as (I, me).

---

# Coherence

The word *coherence* means "a sticking together." When we used it to refer to writing, we mean (1) that the parts of a sentence stick together to form a correct and logical utterance; (2) that the sentences in a paragraph are in logical and smoothly connected order; and (3) that each paragraph in a piece of writing is logically and smoothly connected to the ones that precede and follow it.

## Achieving Coherence in Sentences

Many different kinds of errors contribute to the lack of coherence in sentences. Some of these are discussed in separate entries (**Dangling Modifiers; Diction** (especially Idioms); **Misplaced Modifiers; Parallel Construction; Pronoun References; Shifts**). In order to achieve coherence in the sentence, it is necessary to avoid the following kinds of errors as well.

### 1. Avoid split constructions

**A.** Do not needlessly separate the subject of the sentence and the verb.

**Poor**   *Lisa,* after gathering together her clothes, books, and papers, *packed.*
**Better**   After gathering together her clothes, books, and papers, Lisa packed.

**B.** Do not needlessly separate the verb and its complement.

**Poor**   The truck driver delivered, after driving all night in a terrible rainstorm, the new boiler we had ordered.
**Better**   After driving all night in a terrible rainstorm, the truck driver delivered the new boiler we had ordered.

**C.** Do not needlessly split an infinitive. To do so may destroy the coherence of the sentence. A split infinitive, however, does not always lead to incoherence; sometimes it cannot be avoided and produces perfect clarity.

**Awkward**   He asked me *to as quickly as possible drop over* to his house. (Notice how this very nearly produces a "squinting modifier": Was he asked quickly or was he supposed to drop over quickly?)
**Correct**   He asked me *to drop over* to his house as quickly as possible.

**Awkward**   I promised *to immediately try out* for the football team.
**Correct**   I promised *to try out* for the football team immediately.

**Appropriate**   IBM expects *to more than double* its business this year.
**Appropriate**   *To just miss* the train is a bad start for anybody's day.

## 2. Avoid illogical subjects and complements

**A.** Do not carelessly use a modifying phrase or clause as the subject of a sentence.

**Wrong**   *Because he drove too slowly* made him miss the first inning of the game. (The adverb clause cannot be the subject of *made.*)
**Right**   Because he drove too slowly, he missed the first inning of the game.
**Right**   Driving too slowly made him miss the first inning of the game.

**Wrong**  *By using power tools* will save a lot of hard work. (The italicized phrase cannot be used as the subject of *will save.*)
**Right**  Using power tools will save a lot of hard work.
**Right**  The use of power tools will save a lot of hard work.

**B.** Do not use *when* or *where* as part of the complement of the verb *is.*

**Wrong**  The thing I like to do most at parties *is when* I'm dancing.
**Right**  The thing I like to do most at parties *is dance.*

**Wrong**  A vacation *is where* you relax.
**Right**  A vacation is *a period of relaxation.*

## 3. Avoid using mixed or incomplete comparisons

**A.** Do not use comparisons that mix two comparative constructions.

**Mixed**  My biology course is as interesting, *if not more interesting* than, my chemistry course. (The modifying, italicized, phrase is misplaced, making the main clause read: "My biology course is as interesting than my chemistry course.")
**Unmixed**  My biology course is as interesting as my chemistry course, if not more interesting.
**Correct (but stilted)**  My biology course is as interesting as, if not more interesting than, my chemistry course.

**Mixed**  Willie Mays was one of the greatest, if not the greatest, players in all of baseball history.
**Correct**  Willie Mays was one of the greatest players in all of baseball history. He may even have been *the* greatest.

**B.** Do not use inexact or incomplete comparisons.

**Inexact**  New York City is farther from Albany than Newark. (Confusion: which place is farther from which?)
**Exact**  New York City is farther from Albany than Newark *is.* (Both terms of the comparison are filled in here.)
**Exact**  New York City is farther from Albany than *it is from* Newark. (Again, the comparison is now exact.)

**Inexact**  I like to watch television because it has more varied entertainment. (More varied than what?)
**Exact**  I like to watch television because it has more varied entertainment *than other media.*

**Incomplete**   Her prospects for a job after graduation looked lower than a laborer. (Is a laborer *low?*)

**Complete**   Her prospects for a job after graduation looked lower than a *laborer's.*

**Complete**   Her prospects for a job after graduation looked lower than *those of a laborer.*

## 4. Avoid omitting necessary words

**A.** Do not omit words that are necessary to maintain parallel structure in the sentence. (See **Parallel Construction** for a complete explanation of the term.)

**Wrong**   He told her that she was intelligent but she lacked confidence. (The omission of *that* between *but* and *she* makes it uncertain whether she was told she lacked confidence or whether she thought so herself.)

**Right**   He told her *that* she was intelligent but *that* she lacked confidence.

**B.** Do not omit necessary parts of verbs. When the two parts of a compound construction are in different tenses or there is a change of number between them, be sure to include all the parts of *both* verbs.

**Wrong**   Freedom *has* and always *will be* the most cherished American ideal. (*Be* goes properly with *will* to form the future tense; but *has* needs *been* to form the present perfect.)

**Right**   Freedom *has been* and always *will be* the most cherished American ideal.

**Wrong**   Jack *was fishing* and the other men *sleeping.* (*Jack* is singular and properly takes the singular auxiliary *was; men* is plural and needs the plural *were.*)

**Right**   Jack *was fishing* and the other men *were sleeping.*

*Note:* It is permissible to omit parts of compound verbs when both parts of the construction are in the same tense.

She *had read* the assigned books and [*had*] *done* the required term paper. (The tenses are the same, so the bracketed *had* may be omitted.)

**C.** Do not omit words through sheer carelessness; careful proofreading can usually pick up these errors.

But notice how careless omissions give a special incoherence to sentences.

**Omission**   He took a five-mile walk the pool. (A reader might think that the letter *p* in *pool* should be an *f*—what was actually omitted was the word *to*.)
**Complete**   He took a five-mile walk to the pool.

**Omission**   The moon gave him the *feeling wonder* and *romance*. (Did the moon give him three separate things, the italicized words? No. The word *of* has been omitted.)
**Complete**   The moon gave him the feeling of wonder and romance.

---

## *Test Yourself on*
## Revising Incoherent Sentences

Each of the following sentences is plagued by one of the problems we have been discussing in this section. Analyze each problem, and then write out what you consider to be a good revision of the sentence; be prepared to explain why you think your version is superior.

1. In the basket is where I put the apples.
2. Because cheating the consumer is so widespread that we need a permanent Department of Consumer Affairs.
3. Jack, after the heat, the crowds, and the excitement, fainted.
4. The doctor wanted, because he suspected a kidney problem and needed to be sure, a urine sample.
5. The invitation said that I was to only reply if I couldn't make it.
6. A good disco is where they play music for dancing.
7. Professor Gould is one of the best, if not the best, teachers in the department.
8. A Toyota is built better and gets better gas mileage.
9. The actor's makeup looked like a clown.
10. Northerners are just as friendly as the South or West.

11. Loneliness is when you are starved for intimacy.
12. The bookcase I built myself cost far less than a carpenter.
13. The music instructor told her that she had talent but she needed to improve her technique.
14. In lower Manhattan are a pair of skyscrapers reaching toward the clouds and which provide great sight-seeing for millions of visitors.
15. He was working and still does at the packing plant.

---

## Achieving Coherence in Paragraphs

Most kinds of writing require that sentences be written one after another to form coherent paragraphs. A coherent paragraph is one in which (1) there is a logical order to the sentences; some principle governs why each sentence in the paragraph occupies its particular place there; and (2) there are clear connections—smooth bridges—between these sentences.

**1.** To assure that your paragraphs have coherence, choose the appropriate logical plan with which to govern the order of your sentences. Usually, the subject of your paragraph will suggest the right plan to follow. If you are telling a story, a common plan is the chronological one; you order your sentences according to time. If your paragraph is describing something, say a house, then a common plan of organization would have you describe the house from the inside out or vice versa: We call this a spatial plan. Here are examples showing the difference a plan can make in the coherence of your paragraphs.

### Incoherent (sentences without order)

Last night, my father discovered that our car had been stolen. The detectives didn't hold out much hope for its return, but they said they would be in touch if there were any news. They took down all the information about the car and were very polite. My father asked my mother if she thought I had taken it without permission, but she assured him I hadn't. He just couldn't believe it wasn't parked in the usual place, and ran down the hill to see if maybe the brakes had given out and it had rolled down. When he was finally convinced that the car had been stolen, he phoned the police. After they left, my father was depressed.

### Coherent (chronological order imposed)

Last night, my father discovered that our car had been stolen. He asked my mother if she thought I had taken it without permission, but she assured him I hadn't. He just couldn't believe it wasn't parked in the usual place and ran down the hill to see if maybe the brakes had given out and it had rolled down. When he was finally convinced that the car had been stolen, he phoned the police. The detectives took down all the information about the car and were very polite. They didn't hold out much hope for its return, but they said they would be in touch if there were any news. After they left, my father was depressed.

### Incoherent (sentences without order)

A spiral ramp hugging the wall goes whirling up as far as the eye can see, leaving a huge cone of space in the center. The entrance hall is also very dramatic. When you first approach the museum, you notice that it's very different from the buildings around it—ordinary high-rise apartment houses. It is low, first of all, almost squat in appearance. The squat impression made by the outside is lost on the inside. The building is made of massive geometric forms: cones, tubes, rectangles, and squares, all solidly connected to form a unitary, dramatic mass of concrete, with here and there a strange vertical slit in the façade. Everything inside is airy and light, turning and curving. From the top of the ramp, what you see is so slender and spacious you can hardly believe it's the same building you saw from the outside.

### Coherent (spatial order imposed)

When you first approach the museum, you notice that it's very different from the buildings around it—ordinary high-rise apartment houses. The museum is low, first of all, almost squat in appearance. It is made of massive geometric forms: cones, tubes, rectangles, and squares, all solidly connected to form a unitary, dramatic mass of concrete, with here and there a strange vertical slit in the façade. The entrance hall is also very dramatic. A spiral ramp hugging the wall goes whirling up as far as the eye can see, leaving a huge cone of space in the center. Everything inside is airy and light, turning and curving. From the top of the ramp, what you see is so slender and spacious you can hardly believe it's the same building you saw from the outside.

### *Test Yourself on*
### Making Coherent Paragraphs

A. Write a coherent paragraph that incorporates all the following information about Ralph Ellison. Begin your paragraph with sentence 1.

1. Ralph Ellison, the distinguished American novelist, was born in Oklahoma in 1914.
2. Afterwards, he became interested in sculpture, and finally, of course, in writing.
3. While attending school in Oklahoma City, he had a decisive experience when he heard Lester Young play the saxophone.
4. Probably the whole experience helped orient him toward art in general.
5. In 1965, *Invisible Man* was voted the most distinguished novel to have been published in the previous twenty years.
6. Hearing the great jazz player prompted him to go to Tuskegee Institute, in 1933, with the intention of studying music.
7. Since 1952, he has also published a collection of essays, *Shadow and Act;* from 1958 onward, he has taught literature at various colleges.
8. Ellison started publishing in 1937, but it wasn't until 1945, after service in the Merchant Marine in World War II, that he began his famous *Invisible Man.*

B. Both of the following paragraphs are incoherent because the sentences are poorly arranged. Impose some orderly plan on each and make coherent paragraphs of them.

1. Most Americans have become increasingly interested in leisure activities these days. There is so much intensity invested in these activities that we can fairly say Americans now have two jobs: One is real work, the other real play. Jobholders work fewer hours and thus have more leisure. Besides, Americans have always been sociable and sociability goes hand in hand

with leisure. The reasons have to do with changes that have taken place in American life in the last twenty-five years. Interest in health has grown, and this has led many to take an active role in sports. Moreover, the idea has gained prominence that self-fulfillment means gaining skills in pleasurable leisure activities like photography, sailing, woodwork, painting, and many others.

2. The outside of the building is typical of old farm-houses in this part of the country. So is the blackened tin funnel that was once used to lead cooking fumes to the outside. Inside, the house has been modernized—a new stove, a refrigerator, wall heaters—but the old wood stove is still there. A chimney squirts into the air from the top of each addition. Even a faded print on the living room wall, showing the original house without the additions, testifies that what used to be is not entirely gone. The furniture also reflects the original identity of the house. It is a white frame square, with two little additions—after-thoughts—sloping off either side of the square.

---

**2.** To assure that there are clear connections between your sentences, you must keep in mind the following four considerations.

**A.** Present your ideas from a consistent point of view. This means that you must speak, in each sentence, from the same position or vantage point. You must not needlessly shift tense, number, or person within a paragraph.

### Shift in Tense
In the story, Tom *went* to Canada to make a life as a hunter and trapper. Then he *goes* to Alaska to search for gold. His restlessness *was* emphasized repeatedly. Thus by the end of the story, he *is* a sad man.

### Shift in Number
Young *people* who look for security in their jobs rather than satisfaction are likely to be disappointed. A young *person* needs

to choose a career that will stimulate his imagination while it is young and responsive. *They* can always gain security later on, at the appropriate age. *He* must be wary of experiencing the worst possible regret: looking back on life and knowing *he* hasn't lived.

### Shift in Person

Now more than ever, *parents* need to pay close attention to children's gaining basic skills like reading, writing, and mathematics. *You* need to do more than help them with their homework. *You* cannot expect children to honor those skills if *you* don't. Therefore, a *parent* must set an example for *children*.

**B.** For the purpose of presenting parallel or coordinate ideas, use parallel construction in sentences that follow each other.

My mother has passed along to me certain rules for getting along with others. Don't argue with parents; they'll think you don't love them. Don't argue with children; they'll think themselves victimized. Don't argue with husbands and wives; they'll think you're a tiresome mate. Don't argue with strangers; they'll not want to be friends. My mother's rules can be summed up in two words: don't argue.

Most of us feel the troubles we encounter are not of our own making. We think that the system has failed us. We think that our loved ones have failed us. We think that circumstances have failed us. It rarely occurs to us that the failure has been our own and that it might be temporary and perhaps even reparable.

(See **Parallel Construction** for more information.)

**C.** Repeat key words and phrases to keep before the reader the flow of your thought. If you fail to do this, gaps in your thought are created. Pronouns referring precisely to their antecedents can also serve this bridging function.

A *magic show* works by carefully directing our *attention.* But the *show directs* our *attention* where the *magician wants* it to be. *He wants* us to look away from the *place* where his transformations go on. For that *place* has no *magic;* it's a *work place.* The *magical* quality of the *show* depends on our not seeing the *work.* When we do not look at that *work,* we see the *magic,* and our *attention*—focused on the right *place*—is well rewarded.

**D.** Use transitional devices where they are necessary to further this bridging function between sentences. A transitional device is a word or a phrase that can serve as a point of reference (*finally, at last*) or that can actually indicate the relationship between one sentence and the next (*consequently, as a result*).

Soon, he was able to walk. *Afterwards,* he was even able to swim a little and he managed a few minutes in the pool every day. *Consequently,* when spring came, his physical condition had improved considerably. He was stronger, could walk without tiring, and was able to swim as long as he wanted to. *However,* he was still depressed by the ordeal of the accident and the recuperation period during which he was unable to work. *On the whole, though,* he had much to be thankful for.

Here is a list of some of these transitional devices, classified according to meaning:

**Time**  after a while, afterward, at last, at the same time, in the meantime, immediately, later, soon

**Place**  here, there, nearby, close by

**Addition**  again, also, besides, further, furthermore, in addition, likewise, moreover, next

**Result**  as a result, accordingly, consequently, hence, therefore, thus

**Comparison**  likewise, similarly, in such a manner

**Contrast**  after all, and yet, however, in contrast, in spite of, nevertheless, on the contrary, on the other hand, otherwise

**Concession**  it may be true, I admit, naturally, of course

**Summary**  in brief, in short, on the whole, to conclude, to sum up, finally, to summarize

**Illustration and Example**  for example, for instance, to be specific, in particular, indeed, in fact, that is, to illustrate

See also **Transitions.**

## *Test Yourself on*
## Revising Incoherent Paragraphs

The following paragraphs contain confusing shifts in person, tense, or number, or lack smooth transitions. Eliminate the shifts wherever they appear and add transitions where necessary to make them all coherent.

1. My parents always argue with me about my wanting a moped. They said the machines were dangerous, but I believed they were not. Mopeds go only twenty miles an hour. It ran cheaply and had no license or insurance requirements. They have been sold cheaply too.

2. Cooking is both easy and fun if one observes certain basic rules. First, you should have the right utensils. As the saying goes, "a cook is only as good as his pots." A cook should buy only fresh ingredients. You ought to learn how much heat to apply to particular foods. Save good recipes.

3. A professor I know who is older than I am says that rock and roll is terrible music. I said it's just a form of what he used to think was popular music when he was young. He says rock and roll lyrics can't be heard because the music is too loud. He said the lyrics are foolish. I pointed out that though he may be right about the lyrics, they have not been more foolish than *his* kind of pop music. The degree of loudness is a matter of taste.

## Achieving Coherence Between Paragraphs

As you might have expected, the rules for achieving coherence between paragraphs are identical with those that apply to achieving coherence *within* paragraphs. For example:

[1] Strong faith, no matter where it is directed, can also erase anxiety, fear, and doubt from the human soul. These are often direct causes of many modern illnesses both real and imaginary. Faith seems to have a calming and soothing effect on a troubled

mind. Thus in a sense the patient often cures himself by his own strong *faith, faith* which is stimulated by the efforts of the *healer* and reinforced by the *group traditions* surrounding the *healing* ceremony.

[2] Nonmedical *healing,* whether it be on the *folk or mass culture* level, contains many more components than power and *faith.* There are always rudimentary elements of auto-suggestion, crowd hysteria, thought transference, and subtle forms of hypnotism lurking in these rituals, but the healing ceremony always centers on these two key ingredients. When the balance between the two is right, when the patient and audience exhibit deep, sometimes emotional, faith, then this strange power called healing begins to flow. What this force really is, modern science, psychology, and technology have not as yet determined. Perhaps it is a creation of man's imagination. Perhaps it is a substantial and measurable force. But whatever it is, it should be considered an intrinsic part of both popular and folk medical belief.

Greg Johnson, "A Classification of Faith Healing Practices,"
*New York Folklore Quarterly,* Summer 1975

Notice in the example that the words *faith, healer, healing* constitute a bridge from paragraph 1 to paragraph 2 and that the idea "group traditions" acts as a bridge to the idea "folk or mass culture level."

# Colloquial

See **Diction.**

# Colon

The colon is a mark of internal punctuation that can be used according to the following rules:

**1.** Use the colon to introduce a series of items explained in the main clause of the sentence.

In order to enjoy camping, you need the right supplies: a tent, a sleeping bag, good walking shoes, foul weather gear, waterproof matches, and the right kind of food.

He had a bad group of symptoms: headache, nausea, fever, and an itchy rash.

**2.** Use the colon to direct the reader's attention to a final fact or explanation.

You lack the one thing that rich people have: money.
One quality is essential for the good teacher: patience.

**3.** Use the colon to introduce a direct quotation of some length and formality.

The problem was clearly outlined by the Mayor, who put it this way: "The cities are in a state of decay. Our lives, our children's lives, and the future of cities everywhere depend upon how we choose to confront the renewal of the urban environment. Either we undertake rebuilding our cities with enthusiasm or we suffer the consequences with shame."

Longer direct quotations can of course be introduced by a comma, too, but a comma *should* be used when the material is more informal and shorter:

John smiled and answered softly, "You can do as you please."

**4.** Use a colon for the purposes of mechanical separation.

Matthew 8:10 (separating chapter and verse in Biblical citation)
Dear Mr. Kojak: (after the salutation in a formal letter, to separate it from the body)
2:32 a.m. (separating numbers in a time designation)

*Note:* Do not use a colon interchangeably with a semi-colon.

Do not use a colon after a verb or a preposition in a sentence to introduce a series.

**Wrong**    My priorities *are:* home, country, and God.
**Right**    My priorities are as follows: home, country, and God.
**Right**    My priorities are home, country, and God.

**Wrong**    This summer I am planning *to:* study French, get a part-time job, and swim a half-mile every day.
**Right**    This summer I am planning to do the following: study French, get a part-time job, and swim a half-mile every day.
**Right**    This summer I am planning to study French, get a part-time job, and swim a half-mile every day.

### *Test Yourself on*
### the Use of the Colon

In each of the sentences below, insert colons where they are needed or change their position after inserting another word.

1. It is now 245 p.m.

2. Whatever he wanted from Sarah, he got love, affection, kindness, money, or food.

3. The things that need repairing around the house are: the rain gutters, the front steps, the upstairs storm windows, and the leaks in the attic.

4. What do I spend my money on? I spend my money on: food, clothing, shelter, movies, medicine, skateboards, lobsters—a lot of things!

5. You need only one thing for a perfect golf swing, control.

## Comma Fault

Another term for **Comma Splice.** Both apply to independent clauses joined *only* by a comma.

**Wrong**   We were very tired, we went to bed early.
**Right**   We were very tired, *so* we went to bed early.

For more detailed information, see **Run-on Sentences.**

## Comma Rules

The comma is used to separate sentence elements. It is the most frequently used of all the punctuation marks. Its appearance signals the reader that something is interrupting the flow of the main statement (main clause), that something is being added or subtracted, usually something that is not so closely related to that main flow of thought. The specific rules given below are aimed at ensuring that a writer's flow of thought is presented with clarity; they should be applied with that aim in mind. When there is a conflict between applying these rules and your own sense of the fitness of a comma placement, consult your instructor.

**1.** Use a comma to separate independent clauses joined by the coordinating conjunctions *and, but or, nor, for, so, yet.*

Greene has washed and cleaned his old car, *and* he hopes that it will attract a buyer.

The plan was to leave on Sunday morning, *but* we found that we couldn't get ready on time.

We can stay home and have leg of lamb for dinner, *or* we can eat out and have pizza.

Jones could not name any of the original thirteen states, *nor* could he identify any of the original signers of the Declaration of Independence.

*Note:* A comma may be omitted between short independent clauses.

I laughed and he cried.
I asked but he didn't answer.

**2.** Use a comma to separate items in a series. These items may consist of words, phrases, or clauses.

**Series of Words:** I'd like a big bowl of fruit with *apples, pears, peaches,* and *plums.*
**Series of Phrases** He liked *going to the movies, eating at fancy restaurants,* and *visiting museums.*
**Series of Clauses** She liked him *when he was thoughtful, when he was kind,* and *when he was relaxed.*

Note that in each of these examples, there is a comma as well as the word *and* between the last two items in the series. In the case of items in a series, you have the option of following the practice in the above examples or of omitting the comma just before the *and* preceding the final item. Both procedures are correct; probably the retention of the comma is more formal than its omission. But whatever you choose to do, *be consistent.* Do not use one system with one series and another with a second series.

The series of words separated by commas in the first of the above examples is of nouns. A series of adjectives can present a slightly different problem in punctuation. For example, consider the following sentences:

They were *energetic, pretty, intelligent,* and *sensitive* girls.
They had an *interesting European summer* vacation.

In the first example, we could substitute the word *and* for each of the commas—energetic *and* pretty *and* intelligent. We could also alter the order of these adjectives; it would make little difference to the sense of the sentence if we wrote "sensitive, pretty, energetic, and intelligent." Therefore, the adjectives in this example are *coordinate adjectives* and are properly separated by commas.

By contrast, the adjectives in the second example are not coordinate. We could not logically join them by the word *and* (interesting *and* European *and* summer is illogical). And we could not alter the order of these adjectives: We could not say "summer European interesting vacation." In fact, the word *interesting* really modifies *European summer vacation;* the word *European* then modifies *summer vacation* and the word *summer* modifies *vacation*—there are layers of modification, so to speak. Where we have such a series of adjectives that are not coordinate we do not use commas to separate them.

**Coordinate** It was a *happy, productive,* and *prosperous* season in his life.
**Not Coordinate** He was wearing a *light green* belt.

**Coordinate** His remark was *foolish, rude,* and *embarrassing.*
**Not Coordinate** Last night we went to a *lively little* party.

**3.** Use a comma to separate introductory elements from the rest of the sentence. These elements can be words, phrases, adverb clauses, or transitional expressions.

**Introductory Word** *Usually,* he took a nap after lunch.

**Introductory Phrase**  *Coming through the alley,* the car swerved to avoid a garbage can.

**Introductory Clause**  *Although he had already eaten dinner,* he sat down to have a sandwich.

**Transitional Expressions**  *In other words,* I'm in love.
*On the other hand,* meat loaf is fattening.

*Note:* Certain introductory elements do not need to be followed by a comma, if they are short and omitting the comma does not cause a lack of clarity in the sentence.

*Probably* he won't win.
*Naturally* he found what he was looking for.

But note too how confusion can enter a sentence when a comma that *should* come after an introductory element is omitted:

After he ate the horse took a romp in the fields.
Because he needed to hit the catcher choked up on the bat handle.

As we have shown, introductory adverb clauses should be set off from the rest of the sentence by a comma. The need for a comma when the adverb clause comes at the end of a sentence depends on the relationship of the adverb clause to the main clause of the sentence. When the information contained in the adverb clause is essential to the meaning of the sentence, no comma is needed.

I will keep knocking *until they open the door.*

The speaker here tells us that *until they open the door,* the speaker will keep on knocking; therefore, that information is essential—it gives the motive for the information in the main clause—and no comma is needed.

I came to this school *because the engineering courses are so good.*

This states the essential reason that the speaker came, and so the clauses need not be separated by a comma.

However, when the adverb clause merely gives nonessential explanatory material, a comma should be used between it and the main clause.

Our seats were in the last row of the balcony, *although we had ordered a pair in the orchestra.*

Here the italicized clause has no *essential* relationship to the main clause: It gives no *reason* that the seats were in the balcony (far from it, in fact; it suggests a contrast) nor any motive for the seats being where they were. Therefore, it needs a comma, as if to emphasize the separateness of its information from that in the main clause.

**4.** Use a comma to set off a parenthetical element at the beginning of a sentence; use one comma before and one after a parenthetical or appositive element that occurs in the middle of a sentence. A parenthetical element is one which is not essential to complete the meaning of the sentence but which supplements a part or parts of the sentence.

**Parenthetical Element at Beginning of Sentence**
*To be frank,* I'm completely broke.
*Certainly,* he has a right to do what he wishes.

**Parenthetical Element in Midsentence**
The car, *you see,* is in the garage.

**Appositive**    Mr. Morris, *the patient in room 950,* has been wheeled down to occupational therapy.

**Appositive**    My uncle, *Harry Jackson,* was a stingy millionaire.

It should be clear from the above examples that appositives and parenthetical elements do not affect the meaning being delivered by the sentence; they can be omitted without loss of meaning.

Notice that if only one comma is used in each of the last two examples, some confusion in meaning results.

Mr. Morris, the patient in room 950 has been wheeled down to occupational therapy. (Meaning, possibly, that the speaker is addressing a Mr. Morris and advising him that the patient in room 950 has been wheeled down.)

My uncle, Harry Jackson was a stingy millionaire. (Again, it is not clear that *my uncle* and *Harry Jackson* are the same person.)

**5.** Use commas to set off nonrestrictive elements in a sentence. Another way of talking about a parenthetical or appositive element is to say that it is *nonrestrictive:* it does not *restrict* or essentially modify what it refers to; therefore, it *must* be set off by commas. On the other hand, if the element in question is *restrictive* or is essential to what it modifies, it must *not* be set off by commas.

**Restrictive Element**   The audience *that gave him the most applause* pleased him the most. (No commas necessary.)

**Nonrestrictive Element**   The audience, *which paid a fortune for its seats,* applauded for five minutes.

Sentence 1 is not about the *audience*—it is about *the audience that gave him the most applause.* Therefore, the clause must not be separated by commas from the subject word *audience;* the clause is part of the complete subject (italicized in this paragraph), and if it were separated the sentence would lose its essential meaning. On the other hand, the second sentence *is* about the *audience;* it is only incidental, not essential, information that this audience paid a fortune for its seats. Therefore, the clause in that sentence must be separated from *audience* by commas.

Try to figure out which of the following sentences contain restrictive elements and which nonrestrictive elements. Answers follow immediately below.

1. People *who live in glass houses* shouldn't throw stones.
2. Students *who take this film course* are guaranteed an exciting experience.
3. My doctor *who is on vacation this month* leads a busy professional life.
4. The foreman at the factory *who was a conscientious worker* was taking evening courses in business administration.
5. The man *leaning over the edge of the balcony* is being reckless.

*Answers:* 1, 2, and 5 all contain *restrictives.* In these, no commas should be used. But commas *are* needed in 3 and 4 because they contain *nonrestrictive* elements.

3. My doctor, who is on vacation this month, leads a busy professional life.
4. The foreman at the factory, who was a conscientious worker, was taking evening courses in business administration.

The reason that we need commas in these examples is that in each, the material between the commas is not essential to the writer's message. In 3, it is only incidental that the doctor is on vacation, not essential. Similarly, in 4, the material between the commas is also incidental; it has nothing to do with the main message of the sentence—that the foreman was taking evening courses in business administration.

On the other hand, the reason we do not use commas in 1, 2, and 5 is that, in each, the italicized material is essential to what is being said about the subject.

1. People *who live in glass houses* shouldn't throw stones.

This writer doesn't mean that "people shouldn't throw stones" and that incidentally those people live in glass houses—although "People shouldn't throw stones" is a grammatical sentence and may even be a pretty good rule to live by. The writer means that *only people who live in glass houses* shouldn't throw stones; therefore, we must have *people* and all the words that follow it as one single unit, unbroken by commas.

2. Students *who take this film course* are guaranteed an exciting experience.

The writer of this sentence doesn't mean that "students are guaranteed an exciting experience," and incidentally, that those students are taking this film course. "Students are guaranteed an exciting experience" is a grammatical sentence and may even be true, but the writer of 2 really means that *only students who take this film course* receive the guarantee. Therefore, we must take these words as a single unit, unbroken by commas.

Try analyzing 5 as we have just analyzed 1 and 2.

**6.** Use a comma to separate a contrasting element from the rest of the sentence; a comma emphasizes the contrast.

He came to the dance with me, *and not with you.*
She says she loves exercise, *but doesn't do it.*

**7.** Use a comma to achieve clarity, even in places where you ordinarily might omit it.

In brief, dresses will be longer this year.
People who like to see wild birds, walk through the woods.
Whatever he did, did no good.
The soldier dropped, a bullet in his leg.

**8.** Use a comma in dates, addresses, and letter forms.

**Dates**     August 4, 1982 (or 4 August 1982)
              Friday, November 30, 1983

**Address**   Waterbury, Connecticut

**Letter Forms**   Dear Mary Lea,
                   Yours sincerely,

---

## *Test Yourself on* the Use of the Comma

A. 1. Construct five compound sentences, each with two independent clauses; use the coordinating conjunctions *and, but, or, nor,* and *so* once each—and place commas in the correct position.
   2. Construct five sentences, each beginning with an adverb clause and followed by a simple main clause. Place the comma in the correct position.

B. Some of the following sentences use the comma correctly; next to these, place the letter C. In the others, either there is a comma missing or too many commas are used. Supply those that are needed; cross out those that are superfluous.

1. _____ The boys in the back of the room are noisy.

2. _____ Women, who are very poor drivers should have their licenses revoked.

3. _____ During the summer days are long.

4. _____ Above all the rooftops are filled with TV antennas.

5. _____ I saw you talking to a pretty slim girl.

6. _____ I'd like to be rich married secure and famous.

7. _____ The ship, which docked yesterday is the *Queen Elizabeth II.*

8. _____ People, who live beyond their incomes, shouldn't complain about money.

9. _____ I will keep taking the test, until I pass it.

10. _____ I need to buy a gray, summer suit and a pair of white seersucker pants.

11. _____ Wherever you're going to get there requires planning and purpose.

12. _____ On Friday, November 30, 1973, I met my wife, and my life, has not been the same, since.

13. _____ In fact I stole the books.

14. _____ George, who is very nearly my age, is much further along in his career than I am in mine.

15. _____ The revolution in education which so many educators talk about has yet to take place.

16. _____ A college really consists of a group of students who want to learn, a group of teachers who want to teach, and a good collection of books.

17. _____ I paused but he went on.

18. _____ Either he goes or I go.

19. _____ He eats drinks and talks too much.

20. _____ Usually living alone is a matter of personal choice.

# Comma Splice

When two independent clauses are joined only by a comma, and *not* by a comma and a coordinating conjunction, we call the error a comma splice or comma fault.

**Wrong**   We went to work very early, we came home very late.
**Right**   We went to work very early, but we came home very late.

For a detailed discussion of this problem, see **Run-on Sentences.**

# Contractions

When two words are joined together with one or more letters omitted and an apostrophe in its place, we have a contraction.

do not = don't      is not = isn't      we will = we'll

See **Apostrophe** for more detailed information.

# Dangling Modifiers

A dangling modifier is a phrase or a clause that either modifies no word in the sentence or refers to the wrong word.

**Dangling Participial Phrase**   *Walking home from school,* the fire engine came screeching around the corner.

The thing to notice about this example is that it *says* one thing but *intends* to say another. Because *walking home from school* modifies *fire engine,* it *says* that the fire engine, as it was walking home from school, came screeching around the corner. Clearly this is ridiculous.

It *intends* to say that as *someone* was walking home

from school, the fire engine came screeching around the corner, or that walking home from school, *someone saw* the fire engine come screeching around the corner.

Therefore, to correct the dangling phrase, we must get *someone* into the action, either by giving the phrase something to modify in the main clause (*the fire engine came screeching around the corner*):

Walking home from school, *I saw* the fire engine come screeching around the corner. (Now the phrase modifies the word *I* in the main clause.)

or by turning the phrase into a dependent clause and getting the *someone* into the action that way:

*As I was walking home from school,* the fire engine came screeching around the corner. (Now someone—*I*—has been gotten into the action by appearing in the italicized clause.)

How you decide to correct this dangling modifier depends on where you want to place the emphasis. Since emphasis naturally falls on the subject of the main clause, you would use the first revision if you wanted to emphasize the speaker *I,* and the second if you wanted to emphasize the *fire engine.*

Writers who produce dangling modifiers do so usually because they write hastily and do not proofread carefully. Learn to recognize and correct the various kinds of dangling modifiers likely to appear in your work.

## 1. Recognize and correct dangling participial phrases

These are similar to the example just discussed.

**Dangling** *Smoking a cigar,* the horse stood on its hind legs. (The phrase seems to modify *horse*—the wrong word.)

**Revised** *As I was smoking a cigar,* the horse stood on its hind legs. (Phrase turned into a clause—a person getting into the action.)

**Revised** Smoking a cigar, *I saw* the horse stand on its hind legs. (Now the phrase clearly modifies the new subject of the main clause: *I.*)

**Dangling**   Our summer passed happily, *swimming and play-ing baseball.* (Note that the dangler can come at the end, not just at the beginning of the sentence; the summer did not swim and play baseball—*we* did; therefore, the phrase modifies the wrong word.)

**Revised**   We passed our summer happily, swimming and play-ing baseball. (Note that the addition of the word *we* as the new subject does the correcting job nicely.)

**Revised**   *Because we were swimming and playing baseball,* our summer passed happily. (The phrase has been converted into a clause.)

**Dangling**   *Lying on my back on the raft,* the stars burned brightly in the sky. (It is not the *stars* that are lying on the speaker's back—but the speaker; the phrase is modifying *stars,* the wrong word.)

**Revised**   *As I was lying on my back on the raft,* the stars burned brightly in the sky. (The phrase is turned into a clause.)

**Revised**   Lying on my back on the raft, *I could see* the stars burning brightly in the sky. (Adding the words *I could see* to the main clause gives the phrase the correct word to modify: *I.*)

## 2. Recognize and correct dangling gerund phrases

A gerund is an -*ing* word that functions as a noun. A gerund implies the presence of a *someone.*

**Dangling**   *After drilling my tooth,* my cavity stopped aching. (The *cavity* did not do the *drilling.*)

**Revised**   *After the dentist drilled my tooth,* my cavity stopped aching. (The phrase is now a clause.)

**Revised**   *After drilling my tooth,* the dentist stopped my cavity from aching. (Now the phrase refers clearly to the new subject of the main clause: *dentist.*)

**Dangling**   *In planning a college education,* careful prepara-tions are needed. (*Careful preparations* cannot do the *planning;* a *someone* is needed.)

**Revised**   *In planning a college education,* a *student* needs careful preparations. (The someone, in the form of a *student,* has been added to the main clause; now the phrase correctly modifies *student.*)

### 3. Recognize and correct dangling infinitive phrases

An infinitive phrase has for its headwords the *to* form of a verb: *to play, to work, to love,* and so forth.

**Dangling** *To become a movie star,* talent and luck are needed. (*To become a movie star* does not logically refer to *talent* and *luck,* the subject of the main clause; people become movie stars.)
**Revised** *To become a movie star,* one [or *a person*] needs talent and luck. (Now the phrase refers logically to *one*—or *a person.*)
**Revised** *If you want to become a movie star,* you need talent and luck. (The phrase has been converted into a clause.)

**Dangling** *To make a delicious stew,* fresh ingredients must be used. (The *ingredients* do not cook the stew; people do.)
**Revised** *To make a delicious stew,* you must use fresh ingredients. (We have supplied the subject in the main clause, *you,* to which the phrase can logically refer.)
**Revised** *If you want to make a delicious stew,* you must use fresh ingredients. (The phrase has been converted into a clause.)

### 4. Recognize and correct dangling elliptical clauses

An *elliptical* expression has words missing. An *elliptical* clause is missing either a subject or a verb; these are understood instead of being stated. You can correct dangling elliptical clauses either by making the subject of the elliptical clause agree with the subject of the main clause or by supplying the missing subject and verb.

**Dangling** *When driving,* my seat belt is always fastened. (The *seat belt* is not *driving;* the italicized clause is missing the words *I am,* so the implied subject, *I,* does not agree with the *seat belt* of the main clause.)
**Revised** *When driving,* I always fasten my seat belt. (Now the implied subject, *I,* is the same as the new subject of the main clause.)
**Revised** *When I am driving,* my seat belt is alway is fastened. (With the missing words supplied, the clause is expanded and refers, properly, to *is fastened.*)

**Dangling**    *When at the age of six,* my Uncle Fred gave me my first haircut. (*Uncle Fred* was not *at the age of six* when the haircut was given—the speaker was: *I was* are the words missing.)

**Revised**    *When at the age of six,* I was given my first haircut by my Uncle Fred. (The implied subject of the clause now matches the new subject—*I*—of the main clause.)

**Revised**    When I was at the age of six, my Uncle Fred gave me my first haircut. (The missing words supplied expand the clause and make it modify, properly, the verb *gave.*)

*Note:* Some verbal phrases do not intend to modify any single portion of the main clause. Rather, they make statements about the whole sentence. These are called *absolute constructions;* using them puts the writer in no danger of creating a dangling modifier.

*Considering the time,* we're not doing badly.
*Parking regulations having been suspended,* we decided to leave the car on 12th Street.
*The air being nippy,* we brought along our parkas.
*Winning being impossible,* we figured we'd just have fun playing.

---

## *Test Yourself on*
## Recognizing and Correcting Dangling Modifiers

Some of the following sentences are correct; place a C next to them. For those that have dangling modifiers, underline the dangling modifier; then correct it according to the methods just discussed.

1. _____ Before leaving for California, hotel reservations must be made.

2. _____ Being an American, his knowledge of Italy was limited.

3. _____ Arriving in Chicago, his suitcase was in California.

4. _____ To understand one's spouse, good communications should exist.

5. _____ After putting my son to sleep, I settled down with a good book.

6. _____ After changing my shoes, my girlfriend took me for a walk.

7. _____ To understand true happiness, you need to know true love.

8. _____ Although planning to get married, my girl's parents didn't know it.

9. _____ His eyes caught the glint of a strange seashell walking barefoot on the beach.

10. _____ Listening to the concert, the Rolling Stones seemed like the funkiest group in the world.

11. _____ My examinations were passed, sweating and praying.

12. _____ To travel in grand style, money is essential.

13. _____ Driving through Ohio, I decided to stop in Akron.

14. _____ If sleepy, your car can be very dangerous.

15. _____ Before going up for a parachute jump, the airplane was thoroughly inspected.

16. _____ While visiting in France, the wine was excellent.

17. _____ On opening the garage door, the cat and dog came leaping out.

18. _____ While relaxed, I am able to jog two miles easily.

19. _____ In cooking the roast, the meat was impregnated with vegetable juices.

20. _____ When a baby, my Great Aunt Sarah died.

21. _____ To operate on a patient, a careful diagnosis must first be made.

22. _____ Stephen kept watching the traffic light till green.

23. _____ Knowing what he liked, I was able to buy him a satisfying birthday present.

24. _____ To sleep comfortably, a good mattress and peace of mind are required.

25. _____ To understand how automobiles work, the Chevy was taken apart.

---

# Dash

The dash is a mark of internal punctuation that has the separating effect of the comma or parentheses but that confers emphasis on what follows it. (See **Parentheses** for a brief discussion of the differences in the use of the three marks.)

If you use a typewriter, the dash is made by striking the hyphen key twice: --. If you write by hand, make the dash twice as long as the hyphen. In either case, do not leave a space before or after the dash—run it directly up against the letters of the preceding and following words. The dash may appropriately be used in the following circumstances.

**1.** Use the dash to set off a final appositive that is short and would benefit from emphasis.

What was in the package was what he feared and desired—
poison.
After he read the thesis, one word came to mind—nonsense.

**2.** Use the dash to set off nonrestrictive appositives that would benefit from emphasis or that need dashes for clarity.

My doctor—my friend for thirty years—always told me the truth.
Three girls—Jackie, Leslie, and Margo—came to my birthday
party.

Note that we could replace the dashes in the last example with commas, but see what confusion might result if we did:

Three girls, Jackie, Leslie, and Margo, came to my birthday
party.

In this sentence, we cannot be sure that the names given are those of the three girls; it is possible, in this case, that six people came and that Jackie and Leslie are men. The dashes, however, clear up any possible confusion.

**3.** Use a dash to set off a series of items, occurring either at the beginning or the end of a sentence, where the items are separated by commas.

**Beginning of Sentence** Love, friendship, caring for children, personal fulfillment, protecting nature's bounties, concern for others—these are the values that free men strive for.

**End of Sentence** We look for the same qualities in an athlete that we find in a soldier—agility, stamina, strength, courage, and competitiveness.

**4.** Use a dash to off parenthetical elements that abruptly interrupt the sense of the sentence.

In the blackness of the mine shaft, we started climbing slowly—
what else could we do?—until at last we saw a pinpoint of
light.
The character of the voting population—8,500 registered Democrats—makes it impossible to elect a Republican to office.

## *Test Yourself on*
## the Use of the Dash

In some of the following sentences, the dash is used correctly; place a C next to these sentences. In other sentences, it is possible to use the dash to improve the clarity, emphasis, and meaning of the sentence; in these, insert a dash where you think it would be helpful.

1. _____ You owe me one thing, loyalty.

2. _____ There is a possibility that we who have paid our rent will be evicted from our apartment.

3. _____ The pilgrims went devoutly to Rome—Catholicism's holy city.

4. _____ That's what I would call it—a crying shame!

5. _____ The crises in his life, divorce, separation from his children, the loss of his job, the attack of pneumonia, these were all too much for him.

6. _____ I notified the Dean of my decision, resignation.

7. _____ Job training programs, increased educational opportunities in the professions, federally sponsored housing, improved day-care facilities, all these are necessary to begin the attack on poverty.

8. _____ The defeat of communicable diseases and the increase in the food supply—these have been partly responsible for the rise in world population.

9. _____ One of the world's great religions Islam was begun by an Arab merchant, Mohammed.

10. _____ He drove in a cold fury not for one minute taking his eye off the prisoner beside him.

# Diagramming

Diagramming a sentence is a way to graphically represent how its parts go together—to enable the student to *see* what he or she is trying to grasp as an abstraction.

Here is how the standard method works:

### 1. The basic sentence

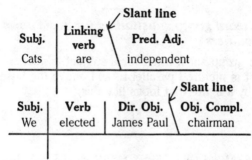

### 2. Modifiers

*Modifiers of all types are placed below the base line.*

*Words that modify modifiers* are attached with a right angle structure to the words they modify.

The pale blue flower wilted very suddenly.

An *indirect object is treated as a modifier*—equivalent to a phrase beginning with *to* or *for*—and placed in the diagram as follows:

### 3. *The word group substituting for basic parts and modifiers*

A word group substituted for a subject, object, or complement is pictured parallel to and above the base line joined by a figure that looks like this:

EXAMPLE OF A GERUND PHRASE AS SUBJECT

*Making a glass bottle is skilled work.*

### EXAMPLE OF A NOUN CLAUSE AS COMPLEMENT

Her idea was *that she needed some advice.*

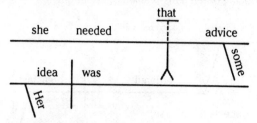

### EXAMPLE OF AN INFINITIVE PHRASE AS OBJECT

My Uncle Fred has decided *to live in France.*

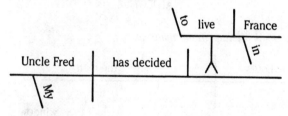

## 4. The word group substituting for single-word modifiers

A word group substituted for single-word modifiers follows the procedure for modifiers and is *placed below the base line.*

### EXAMPLE OF A CLAUSE USED AS AN ADJECTIVE

The student *who needs help* goes to his adviser.

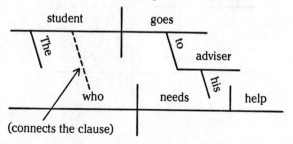

(connects the clause)

EXAMPLE OF A PARTICIPIAL PHRASE USED AS AN ADJECTIVE

*Having ordered his breakfast*, he sat quietly.

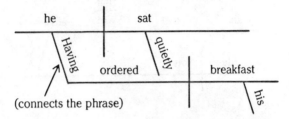

(connects the phrase)

EXAMPLE OF A PREPOSITIONAL PHRASE USED AS AN ADJECTIVE

Louis is the man *in the window*.

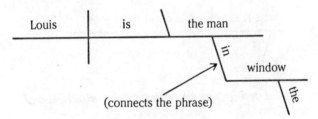

(connects the phrase)

EXAMPLE OF A CLAUSE USED AS AN ADVERB

*After the plane takes off*, we can relax.

EXAMPLE OF A PREPOSITIONAL PHRASE USED AS AN ADVERB

The police came *in a hurry*.

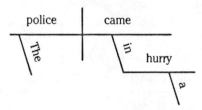

## 5. *Compound constructions*

Compound constructions are placed in parallel, as follows:

### COMPOUND SUBJECT

*Donuts and coffee* taste good.

### COMPOUND VERB

Cats *scratch and claw*.

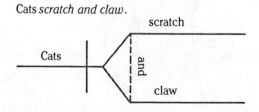

## COMPOUND SENTENCE

He wanted to go home for Christmas, but he couldn't afford the fare.

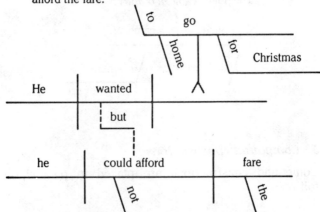

## Alternative Method of Diagramming

Some authorities prefer an alternative method of diagramming which proceeds as follows:

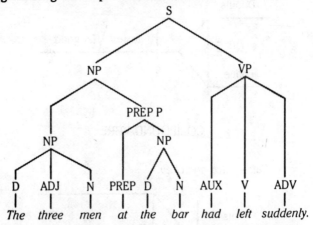

**Key to abbreviations:** ADJ (adjective); ADV (adverb); AUX (auxiliary); D (determiner); N (noun); NP (noun phrase); PREP (preposition); PREP P (Prepositional phrase); S (sentence); V (verb); VP (verb phrase).

## *Test Yourself on*
### Diagramming Sentences

A. Use the standard method to diagram these sentences.

 1. Eggs are oval.
 2. Fordham defeated Columbia.
 3. John loves Mary.
 4. The dark clouds covered the far horizon.
 5. In the morning, he shaved.
 6. He decided to give his mother a ring.
 7. When you eat spaghetti, you get indigestion.
 8. A man who lives on my block is the owner of a new car.
 9. Cats and mice love to play.
10. They swam, fished, and played tennis.

B. Try diagramming the following by using the alternative method.

1. The silver fish floating in the lake are feeding slowly.
2. The new secretary in our office is typing furiously.

C. Go back to the standard method for the following:

1. Although he considered himself a workhorse, he could not maintain the pace set by his sister.
2. Myra's basic principle was that language was the most important element in a short story.
3. He had a tractor for which he had paid a thousand dollars, and a car for which he had paid much more.
4. Television is not only entertaining, but it is also educational.
5. His great ambition, which he had told no one, was to make money soon and retire early.

# Diction

Diction means "the use of words." The use of words always involves choice, and in this entry we will discuss the considerations that govern a writer's choice of words. Before we do so, however, we must consider two preliminary matters: (1) the sources where writers can find words and (2) the standards commonly applied to the use of language.

## Sources

### 1. Dictionaries

The dictionary is an invaluable source of words. It is not just an alphabetical list of definitions; for each word, a good dictionary will also give such information as the part of speech the entry belongs to (i.e., noun, verb, preposition, etc.), its level of usage (archaic/obsolete, informal/colloquial, nonstandard, dialect, slang, etc.), plural spelling, pronunciation, synonyms and antonyms, and more. You should become familiar with the dictionary and take advantage of what it has to offer. The following are recommended in the event that your instructor does not suggest a particular dictionary:

*The American College Dictionary*
*The Random House Dictionary*
*Webster's New Collegiate Dictionary*
*Webster's New World Dictionary*
*The American Heritage Dictionary*

A specimen entry from *The American Heritage Dictionary of the English Language* (The American Heritage Publishing Company, Inc., and Houghton Mifflin Company, Boston, 1973 rpt.) is reproduced at the top of page 121.

Here we find a main boldface entry followed by a pronunciation guide in parentheses and in italics the designation *n.* for noun. Within this entry, following the seven numbered definitions of the sense of the noun *worm,* there follows a smaller boldface line, *wormed, worming, worms,* following the designation—*v.* for verb. These three smaller boldface words tell us that the verb form is regular, that is, has an *-ed* ending. Directly following the main entry for the noun, are parentheses

**worm** (wûrm) *n.* **1.** Any of various invertebrates, as those of the phyla Annelida, Nematoda, or Platyhelminthes, having a long, flexible rounded or flattened body, often without obvious appendages. **2.** Any of various insect larvae having a soft, elongated body. **3.** Any of various unrelated animals resembling a worm in habit or appearance, as the shipworm or the slowworm. **4.** An object or device that is like a worm in appearance or action, as a threaded screw or a zigzag road. **5.** An insidiously tormenting or devouring force: *"The worm of conscience still begnaw thy soul!"* (Shakespeare). **6.** A pitiable or contemptible creature; poor wretch. **7.** *Plural. Pathology.* Intestinal infestation with worms or wormlike parasites. In this sense, also called "helminthiasis." —*v.* **wormed, worming, worms.** —*tr.* **1.** To make (one's way) with or as if with the sinuous crawling motion of a worm. **2.** To elicit by artful or devious means. Used with *out of.* **3.** To cure of intestinal worms. **4.** *Nautical.* To wrap yarn or twine around (rope). —*intr.* **1.** To move in a sinuous manner suggestive of a worm. **2.** To make one's way by artful or devious means. Used with *into* or *out of.* [Middle English *worm,* Old English *wyrm,* worm, serpent. See **wer-³** in Appendix.*]

enclosing *würm,* which indicates pronunciation. Referring to the pronunciation key at the front of the dictionary, we find that the *ü* is pronounced like the *-ere* in the word *were.*

The definitions that follow that first entry are divided into the senses of the word by boldface numerals and proceed from the most common and exact senses (entries 1, 2, and 3) to later accretions (4, 5, 6) which show how the word has come into other than exact, scientific uses. The numeral 7 gives the sense—when used in the plural—of a special usage, a term in the field of pathology.

In a similiar way, definitions are given for the verb form, following first the designation —*tr.* which stands for *transitive,* that is, a verb taking an object. As in the series of definitions given for the noun, the last numeral here—4—carries the special sense, the technical sense of the verb in nautical use. After this portion of the entry come two further definitions following the designation —*intr.* meaning *intransitive,* that is, taking no object. At the end of the whole entry, within square brackets, is the etymology, or derivation of the word.

We see that the word derives from the Middle English word *worm,* from Old English *wyrm,* whose original sense was *worm* or *serpent.* The user is then referred to a useful Appendix entry, the third (see superscript 3) given under *-wer,* following the main vocabulary, where

Indo-European roots are discussed. There we would find that one of the original meanings of the root was "to turn or wind."

## 2. Dictionaries of synonyms and antonyms

Dictionaries of synonyms and antonyms are especially valuable in helping you to expand and enliven your vocabulary and to help you in choosing the exact and accurate word—a crucial aspect of good diction. Two kinds of synonym dictionaries are available. One simply lists under the word you are looking up a whole group of words having similar meanings. A second type discriminates between synonyms by way of a discussion of shades of meaning. The following are recommended:

Norman Lewis, *The New Roget's Thesaurus of the English Language in Dictionary Form* (hardcover; lists synonyms)

*Webster's New Dictionary of Synonyms* (hardcover; makes discriminations)

*Roget's II: The New Thesaurus* (hardcover; lists synonyms)

*The Merriam-Webster Thesaurus* (softcover; lists synonyms)

*The Merriam-Webster Dictionary of Synonyms* (softcover; makes discriminations)

## 3. Other people's writing

An important source for fresh and lively words is your reading. When you read, do so with a sharp eye for what is well said. It is not only permissible, it is desirable, to use—in your own way—words and expressions that other writers have used well. This does not mean that you should, in response to a writing assignment, *lift* (plagiarize) a whole essay or even a couple of sentences from someone else's writing and try to pass them off as your own; rather it means that you should feel free to incorporate into your own work the best words and expressions that other writers have used and that seem to you especially eloquent.

# Standards

Good English is a relative term. Linguists define it as the level useful to the particular situation in which it is spoken and written. Thus good English varies from one social or regional group to another and from one particular kind of writing and speaking to another. What is *good* for speakers and writers in southern Australia differs from what is good for users of the language in western Ireland—or middle America. Many kinds of variations have been described for speakers of our language; but the most important for our purposes are the distinctions made between *standard* and *nonstandard* English, and, within standard English, the distinction between *formal* and *informal.*

Standard English is the spoken and written language used by well-educated people when they wish to communicate as effectively as they can. People who use standard English enjoy a certain measure of social prestige; their language is used routinely in business, law, science, the humanities, and whenever an occupation or a profession requires written communication. Journalism, literature, and the great bulk of printed matter also use standard English. On the other hand, *nonstandard* English is the term given to the speaking and writing characteristics of the relatively uneducated. Writers and speakers of nonstandard English have usually had little opportunity to use written communication, and, more often than not, they have had little formal education.

## Standard

Most people today feel politically powerless. A relatively small group participates in nominating candidates for office, and not many more go to the polls to elect these candidates. More important, few citizens have access to government at any level. Thus politicians are not in touch with the real needs of their constituencies. The people know it, and this is the source of the feeling of powerlessness. Unfortunately, that feeling leads to apathy.

## Nonstandard

We was asking ourselfs the other day what we would be doing if we was rich. Charlie didn have no idea, he say it couldnt never happen anyway, so whats the difference. Herbie said he buy himself a car—a Cadillac—a house, a boat, and so many pair of shoes he couldn't never wear them out, cause he couldn't never wear em at all. Me, I say if I was rich, I just keeps on *buying.* I don't care *what.*

The advice given in this book is directed toward helping you to achieve competence in standard English. Since most students using this book will be seeking to enter the world where standard English is considered the appropriate level of spoken and written communication, we adhere to this standard. What we mean by good diction, then, will refer to standard English.

Within standard English, good diction depends on three basic considerations: the use of language that takes into account both your subject matter and your audience—in other words, the levels of usage called *formal* and *informal* and the appropriate uses of the *colloquial* and *slang;* the use of the *exact* word that will convey your *exact* meaning; and the use of words that are fresh, clear, and concrete.

# Levels of Usage: Subject Matter and Audience

## *1. Formal*

The formal level is appropriate whenever you want to establish an impersonal relation to your subject and your audience. It is a useful level for conveying serious information to an audience wanting exact information, because formal writing strives for clarity and precision. Serious books and articles in science, social science, technology, law, and the humanities employ the formal level. Characteristically, the formal is found mainly in writing, but it is also used in speeches, lectures, and discussions—such as those commonly held at formal meetings. Formal writing is characterized by seriousness of tone, complexity of sentence structure, and elaborate vocabulary—all in the interest of conveying exact, serious, and clear information.

Ginseng is the perennial herb *Panax* native to North America and Asia. Asiatic ginseng (*Panax schinseng*) has been known in Asia for centuries and particularly prized by the Chinese as an important item in their herbal formulary. They have used ginseng as a virtual panacea, prescribing it for conditions ranging from flatulence to pneumonia. The demand for ginseng in America is a recent development. For the purpose of export, China and Korea have developed the North American *Panax quinquefolius.* Here ginseng root is also virtually a panacea, but most users employ it to enhance natural vitality.

## 2. Informal

In recent years, it has become increasingly difficult to separate the formal from the informal. Still, there are distinct differences. The informal is the everyday language employed by well-educated people. It is the language used in private letter-writing, ordinary conversation, and even books and articles that aim to catch the attention of an audience that feels at home with a familiar tone.

Policemen make friends with other policemen. It isn't that they're not friendly; they're just busy. In fact, they spend so much time on the job, they don't have much time for socializing. So they just naturally tend to be friendly with the people they see most: other policemen. Most policemen enjoy each other's company, but most wish they had a wider range of acquaintances.

Note that this sample of the informal is conversational in tone; that it has a speaker's vocabulary, uses contractions, and has a less complicated sentence structure than the formal sample. All but the most sternly academic, scientific, or legal writing has some informal cadences in it.

An important thing to bear in mind—regardless of whether your writing is formal or informal—is to maintain consistency of tone, except when you are so well in control of your material that you are able to mix tones purposefully.

**Unintentionally Mixed Tones**
The beauty of the uninhabited desert regions *doesn't do a thing for me.*

**Revised to Maintain Formality**
The beauty of the uninhabited desert regions *does not impress me.*

**Intentionally Mixed Tones**
The President's tour of European capitals must be described as a *bust*—considering that he failed to negotiate any of the trade agreements he had hoped for.

Some discussions (and some dictionaries) regard the *colloquial* level as synonymous with informal or nonstandard or both. But the word *colloquial* really means *spoken* and can be used to describe a wide range of language that appears in standard, nonstandard, formal, or informal writing.

Here is a small list of words and expressions that are considered colloquial, along with their more formal counterparts:

| Colloquial | More Formal |
|------------|-------------|
| boss | superior, supervisor |
| bug | germ |
| brainy | intelligent |
| flunk | fail |
| hunch | premonition |
| job | position |
| kid | child |
| snooze | nap |
| splurge | spend lavishly |
| stump | puzzle |
| alibi | excuse |
| funny | strange |
| phone | telephone |
| guy | man |
| slob | unkempt person |

## 3. Slang

Slang is highly informal language, mostly spoken, rarely used in written standard English—but not absolutely forbidden there. Slang consists of both newly coined words and expressions and new and extended meanings attached to older words. It develops from attempts to find fresh and colorful language—funny, pungent, sur-prising. It also develops as a kind of shorthand, and that is frequently at the root of its downfall. As shorthand, slang comes to be so overused that it falls into disuse. For example, *heavy,* a "heavy" expression of the late sixties and early seventies, is no longer in frequent use by those who habitually use slang. *Groovy* has also been banished by many slang users, and *let's tip,* meaning *let's leave* (on the analogy of "let's tiptoe out"), is so short a piece of shorthand that it never really caught on.

Nevertheless, slang has its place in both formal and informal writing and it is unwise to suppose that slang is "bad" English. In fact, many words and expressions that began as slang have passed into general (formal) usage, and our language is richer for having them. The use of slang, like the use of other words, should be determined by audience and subject matter. Some purists would object to a slang expression like the following:

The new Woody Allen movie is *a real kick in the head.*

although, conceivably, it might prove a highly effective concluding sentence for a first paragraph reviewing that movie, especially if the review were addressed to a suit-able audience (the subject matter is certainly suitable for slang expression).

Woody Allen is a comic on his way up; Diane Keaton is a lovely, scatter-brained, painfully shy Midwestern singer-model; *Annie Hall* is a hilarious and touching film that depicts the bittersweet progress of an on-again, off-again romance be-tween a New York ethnic and a middle American. Conclusion: *the new Woody Allen movie is a real kick in the head.*

Examine carefully the following three examples. Are these effective uses of slang? Can you think of a way to improve the one or ones you think are ineffective? Can you think of contexts in which one or more of them might be effective?

I didn't want to get hung up on a 9–5 trip but I needed the money that this gig had to offer, so I rapped about it with my old lady and got a good handle on the whole shebang. Then I said okay.

To me his apartment was pure raunch. It looked like he had
    pigged out there over the weekend.
Man, don't get all bent out of shape!

---

## *Test Yourself on*
## Identifying Slang and Colloquial Language

Using your own sensitivity to language, put a C next to
those words or expressions below that strike you as
colloquial and an S next to the ones that seem to be
slang. After you have marked all of them, look each of
them up in a good dictionary and check the dictionary
labels against your answers. How many did you get?

1. bitch (verb)   5. bust (verb)   9. stuff (belongings)

2. freak (fan,     6. cool it     10. mad (angry)
   enthusiast)   7. awful      11. sloppy

3. flunky        8. cop (noun) 12. cute

4. jazz (noun)

---

## *Test Yourself on*
## Selecting the Proper Level of Usage for a
## Specific Piece of Writing

Think about each of the specific pieces of writing
given below and for each one choose the proper level of
usage. Prepare to defend your choice with a logical
argument.

1. A report to the Board of Directors of IBM Corporation on the sales prospects of a new product: a tiny,
   portable minicomputer.
2. A review of the movie *The Empire Strikes Back* written for an underground newspaper.
3. An introduction to the form of popular music called
   *punk rock,* written for *Time* magazine.

4. The same—written for the Sunday magazine section of your hometown newspaper.
5. An article for the campus newspaper on a recent budget crisis at your college.
6. An account of your football (or basketball or baseball) team's fortieth consecutive loss—written for your school newspaper.
7. An essay written for a course in sociology giving an account of how your family (including aunts, uncles, and cousins) celebrates weddings.
8. A speech at a fraternity or club dance announcing the dissolution of the club or fraternity.
9. A basic explanation of enzymes for a scientific journal.
10. A review of children's literature published in the past year—for a journal of psychology.

## Using Exact Words to Convey Exact Meaning

Writers who care about their work—which is another way of saying writers who care about their readers—will expend the time and energy necessary to write with precision, that is, they will go over what they have written to make sure that the words they have used convey their exact meaning.

### 1. Precise expression

Writers who want to increase the precision of their word choices must be prepared to acquire the habit of re-reading and then revising their written work. They must develop the habit of *seeing* and changing constructions like the following:

**Inexact**   Americans are *totally* interested in sex.

It's hard to say exactly *what* this sentence intends to express; it may mean something like "Americans are *completely* interested in sex" but more likely a word like *exclusively* or *solely* or *only* was intended, instead of either *totally* or *completely*. The writer may have meant to say that "Americans have an *absorbing* interest in sex"—but the failure to be exact asks the reader to consider many possibilities.

**Inexact**   Lisa was asked to testify as an *uninterested* observer of the burglary.

Here the writer simply confuses two words: *uninterested,* which means "without interest," and *disinterested,* which means "free of bias; impartial." Obviously, then, the exact expression would be "Lisa was asked to testify as a *disinterested* observer of the burglary."

**Inexact**   We swam until we were tired, played volleyball on the sand, ate too much seafood, and got bad sunburns. We had a *nice* time.

Here the offending word is *nice;* it's simply too vague and doesn't in the least describe what has gone before. Better would be "We had an *exhausting but exhilarating day.*"

---

## *Test Yourself on* Using Exact Expressions

In each of the following examples, the italicized word or phrase is not as exact as it should be. Supply a better expression in each case.

1. Corruption in the District Attorney's office was *first known* in the *Times.*
2. He *fulfilled* the court orders.
3. By the time the summer was over, he *knew* his desires.
4. Summer jobs for students were *not easy.*
5. Unemployment was an important *fact* in our economy.
6. Many of those who were flower children have *lost their appeal* for working on the land.
7. Her *immaturity* may improve as she gets older.
8. The rural atmosphere *subjects* a person to the beauties of nature.
9. He decided to *except* the job.
10. After the meal, he felt *nice.*

## 2. *Idioms*

An idiom is an expression whose meaning cannot be determined by the ordinary meanings of the words used in it. Native speakers of English have no trouble recognizing the idiom in the sentence "A gunman *held up* the supermarket." They would not think that the gunman *lifted high,* but rather that he *robbed,* the supermarket. Thus we could not literally translate *held up* into, say, French, and expect a Frenchman to understand it to mean *robbed.* Logic also offers no help in understanding idioms. Because it is *customary* in English to say "He was acquitted *of* the charges" rather than "He was acquitted *from* the charges," we say that the use of certain prepositions after certain words is idiomatic—that is, not logical but just peculiar to our language.

Although most native speakers of English automatically use idiomatic expressions, some writers have difficulty with verbs or adjectives that must be followed by particular prepositions in order to deliver their intended meaning. Here is a brief list of some troublesome combinations:

*absolved by, from*   I was *absolved by* the court. I was *absolved from* blame.

*accompany by, on*   I was *accompanied by* Tom. I was *accompanied on* my trip by Tom.

*acquitted of*   He was *acquitted of* all charges.

*adapted to, from, by*   The gasoline engine can be *adapted to* air-conditioners. The movie script was *adapted from* a novel; it was *adapted by* William Goldman.

*agree to, on, with*   We *agree to* the terms. We *agree on* a course of action. He *agreed with* me.

*angry with, at, about*   Terry was *angry with* me, *angry at* her mother, and *angry about* her situation.

*argue with, for, against, about*   I *argued with* Harry *about* air pollution; he *argued for* and I *argued against* government controls.

*capable of*   He was *capable of* being deceitful.

*compare to, with*   *Compared to* me, he's a saint. He *compared* a Volkswagen *with* a Toyota.

*communicate with, about*   I asked him to *communicate with* me soon. The two countries *communicated about* agriculture.

*confide in, to*  Can I *confide in* you? Then I want to *confide to* you that I broke the law once.

*conform to, with*  You must *conform to* (or *with*) this standard.

*conformity with*  You must act in *conformity with* prevailing customs.

*connect by, with*  The hose is *connected by* a coupling. I am *connected with* the English Department.

*correspond to, with*  I *correspond with* my colleagues regularly. A French province *corresponds* roughly *to* an American state.

*describe as, to*  It was *described as* a blessing. I *described to* him my latest project.

*despair of*  He *despaired of* ever understanding algebra.

*differ about, from, with*  We *differ about* the best wine to drink with fish. My ideas *differ from* his. I beg to *differ with* you.

*different from**  My plans are very *different from* yours.

*enter into, on, upon*  We *entered into* an agreement. The United States *entered on* (or *upon*) a new era in foreign relations.

*free from, of*  We were *free of* him at last. I need to be *freed from* my obligations.

*identical with*  Your hat is *identical with* mine.

*independent of*  He is *independent of* his family.

*interest in*  He *interested* himself *in* politics.

*live at, in, on*  He *lives at* 525 East 89th Street. He *lives in* an elegant mansion. He *lives on* his independent income.

*listen to, at*  He *listened to* nobody. She *listened at* the door.

*necessity for, of*  The *necessity for* vitamins has been proven. There is no *necessity of* your catching cold.

*object to*  I don't *object to* your statement.

*overcome by, with*  Sarah was *overcome by* sadness. Arthur was *overcome with* admiration.

*parallel between, with*  There is a *parallel between* his attitudes and his behavior. The course of his career ran *parallel with* mine.

*persuade of, to*  I was *persuaded of* the rightness of his argument. I was *persuaded to* accompany him on the trip.

*preferable to*  Hawaii is *preferable to* Alaska for a vacation.

*superior to*  His stereo set is *superior to* mine.

*vary from, in, with*  Ideas *vary from* one another just as shoe sizes *vary in* width. My mood *varies with* changes of weather.

*worthy of*  He is *worthy of* my sympathy.

---

*\*Different than* is the colloquial usage when a clause is the object of the prepositional phrase. *Formal:* The farm looks different *from what* I had expected. *Colloquial:* The farm looks *different than* I had expected.

Idiomatic expression also requires that some verbs be followed by a gerund and some by an infinitive.

| Infinitive | Gerund |
|------------|--------|
| able to go | capable of going |
| like to go | enjoy going |
| eager to go | cannot help going |
| hesitate to go | privilege of going |
| need to go | purpose of going |
| ask to go | consider going |
| consent to go | deny going |
| want to go | put off going |

## *Test Yourself on*
## Using Correct Idiomatic Expressions

In each of the blank spaces, write the correct idiomatic expression needed for the sentence. The expression required may be a preposition, an infinitive, or a gerund.

1. With fish dinners, white wine is preferable _____ red.

2. I hesitate _____ him what I think of him. (Use a form of *tell.*)

3. He lives comfortably _____ his pension.

4. They argued _____ who would do a better job as major.

5. He was described _____ me as a liberal, which was quite different _____ what I had been led to believe.

6. She was capable _____ making her feelings known.

7. Because she was angry _____

    me, I was overcome _____ guilt.

8. I was not eager _____ (use a
form of *leave*) school, but there was a necessity

    _____ doing so.

9. We entered _____ a contract;
therefore, we were legally connected

    _____ each other.

10. George confided _____ his
friends that he was breaking up with Kathy.

---

## Fresh, Specific, and Concrete Language

A writer's language should be fresh, specific, and concrete; it should avoid clichés and try to make a vivid impression on the reader. Plain language can do this if it strives for a proper balance between the abstract and the concrete, the general and the specific.

### 1. Clichés

The word *cliché* (pronounced *clee-shay*) comes from the French word for stereotype plate or printing block. Hence any word or expression whose freshness or clarity has been lost through constant usage is called a cliché, a stereotype. Such words or phrases are also called tired, stale, trite, or worn out. Writers who habitually use clichés not only use tired words but also present the reader with tired ideas.

Nevertheless, we all use clichés in ordinary conversation. In those circumstances, they are frequently forgiven—perhaps because we make up for the tired expression with a lively presence. In any case, whether your writing is formal or informal, you should develop an ear for clichés and avoid using such expressions as the following:

| | |
|---|---|
| the beginning of the end | the last straw |
| better late than never | mother nature |
| bigger and better | neat as a pin |
| cool as a cucumber | on balance |
| a crying shame | pretty as a picture |
| deep, dark secret | right on |
| do justice to | rotten to the core |
| free as a bird | sadder but wiser |
| hard as nails | tell it like it is |
| hot under the collar | variety is the spice of life |
| last but not least | viable options |

Writers who persistently use clichés are not in control of their material. Writers who are in control of their material can *use* clichés to make fresh points.

The fact that Harry was so often late for appointments made it obvious that he would never be known as *a regular guy.*

My response to what you've just proposed is *wrong on.*

*The bigger the better* simply does not apply to things like budget deficits and the headaches they invariably bring on.

---

## *Test Yourself on*
### Identifying Clichés

Circle any words or expressions you find in the following passages that you think are clichés; then supply better—fresher—words or expressions to replace them.

A. Although I was financially embarrassed, I decided to eat out anyway. I didn't care that I was getting to be fatter than a pig; I wanted to do justice to a great meal—and the bigger the better. I settled on McDonald's and started eating like there was no tomorrow. I had six Big Macs, four large orders of fries, and three large shakes. Last but not least, I topped the whole thing off with four apple turnovers. That, however, was the last straw. My stomach really started to growl, and later on that evening I realized that I had eaten myself sick. The next morning I was, believe it or not, sadder but wiser.

B. In this day and age, the American way of life demands that college students get on the ball and learn more than just the stuff taught in classes. Students should get out and mingle. This is the only way to develop a well-rounded personality and the ability to get along with others. There are all kinds of things students can do to become more interesting personalities. They can join a club, attend dances, or just start being friendly—straight from the shoulder—with their fellow students in class. Hitting the books isn't the only way to go in college. If you want to get what you pay for, you have to pass the acid test. Beyond a shadow of a doubt, if you want to get more out of life, you have to put more into it.

---

## 2. Concrete and abstract language

Writers should use the concrete wherever possible. A concrete word is one that appeals directly to the senses—it points to something that exists. Thus *engine* is a concrete word: We can see, hear, and feel one when we lift the hood of a car. But what the engine supplies, *power* (or *energy*), is an abstract word: *Power* cannot be directly perceived; but many concrete things deliver power: *an engine, a turbine, a locomotive, a football fullback,* and so forth. We would not say, giving the reason that we would not buy a specific car, "The Ford had no power" if we meant that it "had no engine," but we might say "The Ford had no power" if we meant that its engine wasn't efficient. So both abstract and concrete language have their uses. But the advice still holds: Writers should use the concrete word whenever they can, because the mind's ability to picture a concrete word makes the writing more vivid. This policy also applies to sentences. Sentences with abstract ideas can be made clearer by supporting them with concrete illustrations.

**Sentence Containing Needlessly Abstract Words**
The *grounds* were *sloppy* and the *planks* on the porch were *bad.*

**Revised to Supply Concrete Words**
The *front yard* was *littered with broken furniture and rusted tools* and the *steps* of the porch were *rotted and splintered.*

**Abstract First Sentence of a Paragraph**
When dealing with institutions, people are made to feel small.

**Concrete Follow-up Sentence**
They are made to fill out needlessly complicated forms, to spend long hours waiting on line, and frequently to visit an office several times in order to get what they came for.

## 3. Specific and general language

The terms *specific* and *general,* applied to words or expressions, mean much the same as is meant by the labels *concrete* and *abstract*—with this difference: *Specific* and *general* attest to the relative degrees of concreteness of a particular set of words.

meat—poultry—chicken
animals—primates—gorillas
military—soldier—Pvt. Mudd
foliage—trees—oak
clothing—trousers—blue jeans

Note that as you read from left to right, the words become more specific—the reader is better able to *picture* the concrete object; though we would not say that the words in the left-hand column are abstract, they are *more general* terms than those in the other two columns. Good writing requires that the writer use the more specific term whenever possible. Although it is true that good writers use general terms as well as specific ones, more often than not there is a loss of freshness and clarity in writing when writers abandon control of their work and use constructions like the following:

**General**   Shade was provided by a big *tree* on the *grass.*
**Specific**   Shade was provided by a *spreading maple* on the *lawn.*

**General**   College students are forced to waste a lot of time.
**Specific**   A college student's time is often wasted by waiting on registration lines, filling out forms, and making more than one trip to a professor's office to obtain a grade. (Notice how this idea gets expanded by having to be made more specific.)

## *Test Yourself on*
## Using Specific, Concrete Language

A. For each of the italicized words in the sentences below, find at least two other words that convey a more specific meaning.

1. He *slept* for half an hour.
2. He *ate* his food as if it were his last meal.
3. He decided not to *tell* that he'd had an accident.
4. She *called* for help.
5. Al didn't want to *show* his feelings.
6. He *ran* all the way home.
7. He *worked on* his essay for an hour; then he gave up.
8. Out of the corner of his eye, he *noticed* someone approaching.
9. He *walked* lazily down to the corner market.
10. They *wrote* their compositions in class.

B. Follow each of the general statements in the sentences below with two more sentences, giving concrete details to illustrate them.

*Example:* When I woke up this morning, I felt as if I'd been drugged.
*Follow-up with concrete details:* My head ached dully, and my vision was blurred. When I tried to move, it felt as if I were walking through water.

1. When I woke up this morning, I felt as if I'd been drugged.
2. My garden is growing beautifully.
3. I don't think my parents understand that I'm an adult.
4. Most college freshmen have special problems.
5. Registering for classes at this college takes its toll on a student.

# Double Negative

The use of an additional negative to reinforce an already negative statement is called a double negative and is not acceptable in standard English. Usually, the writer of a double (or even a triple) negative is intent on being emphatic in his no saying, and several hundred years ago this usage was acceptable, but not now.

**Double Negative**   Nobody loves me no more.
**Revised**   Nobody loves me *anymore.*

**Double Negative**   He can't hardly walk anymore.
**Revised**   He *can* hardly walk anymore. (*Hardly* is the negative.)

**Double Negative**   Scarcely none of my friends likes rock music.
**Revised**   Scarcely *any* of my friends likes rock music. (*Scarcely* is the negative.)

**Triple Negative**   He never had no faith in nobody.
**Revised**   He never had faith in *anybody.*

One form of the double negative *is* acceptable, however, and its use is a form of stylistic choice. For example, we could say, "He was frequently late to my classes," or to achieve a slightly different emphasis, "He was *not infrequently* late to my classes." Another example: "She said she was willing to go out on dates with Tom," or "She said she was *not unwilling* to go out on dates with Tom." The slightly different emphasis in the two sentences using the acceptable double negative is one of qualification.

---

## *Test Yourself on*
## Eliminating Unacceptable Double or Triple Negatives

Each of the sentences given below contains an unacceptable double or triple negative. Correct them in the spaces provided.

1. I don't want nothing to do with you.

---

2. There was never nobody like him.

---

3. He never had no reason to give nobody a present.

4. He didn't hardly have any friends.

5. There wasn't scarcely a soul in the library when I was there on Saturday night.

# Ellipsis

The omission of a portion of quoted text is called ellipsis. Spaced dots (ellipsis points) are used to indicate where text has been omitted.

**The Full Text Being Quoted**
Mr. Ross Alexander's play moves across the stage like a dream of yesterday, stinging us with its wit and wisdom, arguing our case before an ethical court, lifting our spirts as we contemplate our battered selves.

Edward Quinn

**A Portion Quoted from This Text with Some Words Omitted**
Quinn says "Alexander's play moves ... like a dream ... arguing our case ... lifting our spirits. ..."

The spaced dots in this quoted portion are ellipsis points. When the ellipsis comes at the end of a sentence, use a period followed by three spaced dots to indicate omitted material.

Ellipsis points are also used to indicate a pause or an unfinished statement, especially in dialogue.

"Be careful, John. If you're not ..."
"I don't know ... I just don't know."

# End Punctuation

The punctuation marks that end sentences—periods, exclamation points, and question marks—suggest how a reader is to understand the whole sentence. Internal punctuation (colons, commas, dashes, parentheses, and semicolons) indicates relations of the parts of the sentence. See **Colon, Comma, Dash, Exclamation Point, Parentheses, Period, Question Mark, Semicolon.**

## Examination Skills

See **Study and Examination-Taking Skills.**

## Exclamation Point

The exclamation point (!), which always signifies strong emphasis, should be used as follows.

**1.** Use the exclamation point to mark the end of an exclamatory sentence, phrase, or clause. An exclamatory expression is an abrupt, forceful outcry—very emphatic.

How he must be suffering! (sentence)
What a tragedy! (elliptical clause, i.e., one with words missing:
    full clause is "What a tragedy this is!")
No kidding! (phrase)

A single exclamation point does the job. Don't use more than one for extra emphasis.

**2.** Use the exclamation point to emphasize a form of direct address or an interjection when there is strong feeling being conveyed.

George! I need help!
Hurray! We won!

**3.** Use an exclamation point to add emphasis to an imperative sentence (a command) where strong feeling is being conveyed.

Shut your mouth!
Stay away from me!
Give me an answer now!

**4.** Do not use an exclamation point for (a) statements that are not exclamatory, (b) ordinary forms of address, (c) unemphatic interjections, or (d) mild commands.

| | |
|---|---|
| **Wrong** | That's too bad! |
| **Wrong** | George! I'd like to speak to you. |
| **Wrong** | Well! we've arrived. |
| **Wrong** | Turn left at the corner! |

*Note:* When the exclamation point is overused, it gives your writing an air of phony excitement—almost hysteria—and robs you of the opportunity to provide real emphasis where it is needed. So use the exclamation point sparingly.

---

## *Test Yourself on* Using the Exclamation Point Appropriately

Some of the sentences below use the exclamation point appropriately; next to these, place the letter C. In the rest, strike out the exclamation points that are unnecessary.

1. \_\_\_\_\_ War is hell!
2. \_\_\_\_\_ How the mighty have fallen!
3. \_\_\_\_\_ College courses ask too much of a student!
4. \_\_\_\_\_ Get your hands off me!
5. \_\_\_\_\_ How he must have suffered!
6. \_\_\_\_\_ This coffee is terrible!
7. \_\_\_\_\_ I need aspirin!
8. \_\_\_\_\_ What a crazy man!
9. \_\_\_\_\_ Turn the car around!
10. \_\_\_\_\_ What big teeth you have, Grandma!

---

## Fragments

The word *fragment* means a piece or a part; therefore, a sentence fragment is a piece of a sentence. Beginning writers frequently write pieces of sentences because they distrust the *length* of what they are writing, and they think that if they insert a period after they have written a certain number of words their writing will "look" better. This is an error. Length is not the main factor in determining when to end one sentence and begin another.

[A] Whenever I try to hold a long and serious conversation with my parents about my career. [B] They get me angry by raising irrelevant issues and arguments.

The writer of this material decided to place a period after the word *career* because the string of words looked long. In fact, however, the portion that is marked A is an incorrect *sentence fragment*. The reason it's a fragment is that it is a *dependent clause;* that is, it has a subject (*I*) and a finite verb (*try*)—which all sentences need—but it also has a subordinating conjunction, *whenever*. The whole structure hangs from this conjunction—which signals us that the structure must be connected to an independent clause—and therefore it cannot stand alone.

We can make A independent and therefore able to stand alone by eliminating *whenever;* this detaches the clause from what it depends on and makes it a whole sentence—an independent clause.

The second method of correcting the fragment error is to take the fragment, A, and hook it onto an independent clause. This we can do by substituting a comma for the period after *career* and making the capital letter in *they* into a lower-case letter, for the B portion of the example *is* an independent clause. (If you have forgotten the meaning of dependent and independent clauses, go back to Part 1, pp. 43–46, and study the subject.)

**Original Example**
Whenever I try to hold a long and serious conversation with my parents about my career. They get me angry by raising irrelevant issues and arguments.

**Example Corrected by the First Method**
I try to hold a long and serious conversation with my parents about my career. They get me angry by raising irrelevant issues and arguments.

**Example Corrected by the Second Method**
Whenever I try to hold a long and serious conversation with my parents about my career, they get me angry by raising irrelevant issues and arguments.

Which of the corrections do you think is better?

In this case, the second method is better because retaining the word *whenever* establishes a clear relation between the two parts.

**Fragment**
While I was listening to some punk rock on the stereo the other night. Someone came along and stole my car.

**Corrected by First Method**
I was listening to some punk rock on the stereo the other night. Someone came along and stole my car. (Grammatically correct, but gives no sense of how the two parts are related.)

**Corrected by Second Method**
While I was listening to some punk rock on the stereo the other night, someone came along and stole my car. (Also grammatically correct, but a better correction because the two parts are better related.)

---

## *Test Yourself on* Correcting Sentence Fragments

The following are all incorrect. Rewrite each as a complete sentence.

1. They wouldn't let Agnes on the basketball court. Because she wasn't wearing sneakers.
2. I'm worried about my final exams. Which come in about three weeks.
3. Professor Urban took me out for an expensive dinner. Although he had mentioned to me that he was short of money.
4. Unless I'm given the salary I want. I won't take the job.
5. Whenever he hears the Beatles sing "Yesterday." He's reminded of the sixties.

---

Another kind of sentence fragment is made when beginning writers mistake verbals for verbs and think that the structure containing a verbal can stand alone. (See Phrases.)

**Incorrect** Joey has an overwhelming desire. *To leave town.*
verbal

**Incorrect** Arthur believes he has one purpose in life. *To teach.*
verbal

**Incorrect** Uncle Bud is happy doing only one thing. *Running.*
verbal

Even if you haven't written much, you would not be likely to make the errors in these examples, because in each case the verbal is limited to just a few words. The problem remains the same, however, when these verbals are extended into long verbal phrases.

**Incorrect** Joey has an overwhelming desire. *To leave town in order to start a new career.*

**Incorrect** Arthur believes he has one purpose in life. *To teach youngsters the fundamentals of mathematics.*

**Incorrect** Uncle Bud is happy doing only one thing. *Running ten miles a day to prepare himself to compete in marathon races.*

The italicized phrase in each of these examples is dependent and cannot stand alone. Each must be connected, with or without a comma, to the sentence that precedes it. Besides having no subjects, these phrases have no finite verbs—only verbals—and a sentence must have a subject and a finite verb.

A third type of fragment appears when you punctuate prepositional phrases as if they were complete sentences (see Phrases). But only complete sentences should be punctuated as such.

1. Financial aid at this college is given. *To students.*
prepositional phrase

2. Financial aid at this college is given. *To students who show need.*
prepositional phrase

3. Financial aid at this college is given. *To students who show need and whose records are outstanding.*
prepositional phrase

Once again, it is unlikely that beginning writers will make the error shown in the first example, because the prepositional phrase there consists of only two words. But in the other two examples, the possibility is greater because the number of words is greater. In all three examples, of course, the period after the word *given* is incorrect and creates the fragment that follows it.

A fourth type of fragment is created when you fail to recognize that a portion of what you are writing is really a final appositive and not a sentence.

appositive
1. This summer, I'm spending my vaction with George. *A friend.*

appositive
2. This summer I'm spending my vacation with George. *A friend, a sportsman, a very funny guy.*

The first example contains an error that a beginning writer probably won't make, because the appositive consists of only two words. But the error in the second example is more likely to be made because the appositive has more words. In fact, appositives can be quite long and complicated, but no matter how long they are, they cannot stand as sentences. To correct the fragments above, change the period to either a comma or a colon.

---

## *Test Yourself on*
## Recognizing and Correcting Sentence Fragments

A. Turn the following sentence fragments into sentences by crossing out a word in the fragment.

1. Until I reached home.
2. Although he seemed like a nice enough man.
3. Whenever I have gone to the movies.
4. Unless the college gives me some financial support.
5. Because you have dry skin.
6. If I saw her at a party.
7. After the doctor changed my bandage.
8. Since he wasn't a practicing Christian.

9. While the cows were being milked.
10. As my uncle walked through the door.

B. Correct the following fragments by adding an independent clause to the beginning or the end of each.

*Example*

*Fragment:* Which cost me twelve dollars.
*Fragment connected: His birthday present was a shirt,* which cost me twelve dollars.

1. Which cost me twelve dollars.
2. Although I rarely eat at a restaurant.
3. If I never buy another automobile again.
4. Running along the side of the road.
5. To understand auto mechanics.
6. In the woods behind my house.
7. A friend, a teacher, an adviser.
8. To students who are able to undertake advanced studies.
9. Unless I hear from you tonight.
10. To people who are interested in art.
11. Traveling all over the world.
12. Enough time, enough equipment, enough spirit.

C. Read carefully each of the following examples. Underline a sentence fragment wherever you see one, and correct it. Some of the examples are complete sentences, containing no fragments; next to these, write C.

1. _____ Horses racing together through the surf.

2. _____ When Americans celebrate a holiday, they usually have a picnic and a parade.

3. _____ The Founding Fathers had a wish. To leave to us a good model for democratic living.

4. _____ She cooked a large and elaborate dinner. To impress her husband's parents.

5. _____ Last summer we visited Niagara Falls and then crossed over into Canada. Which is what I had always wanted to do.

6. _____ Although I am not at all sure what I will do after graduation. I am very sure that I want to spend four years studying ecology.

7. _____ They drove 3,000 miles across the country to see their son's graduation. An event that they had yearned to see for four long years.

8. _____ The black experience in America has been a frightful one. Which accounts for the revolutionary tone of recent black writing.

9. _____ Although television programming seems innocuous, its effects are not.

10. _____ I'm not leaving here. Until I get my money back.

---

## *Test Yourself on*
## Correcting Fragments by Proofreading

The following passage contains eight sentence fragments. By careful proofreading, find and correct each one.

My father was a farmer. Although he'd gone to college, where he studied engineering. Life on the farm was hard, but my father was ingenious, probably because of his training as an engineer, and he took delight in solving mechanical problems. Problems that would come up with the tractors or the milking machines or even the plumbing in our house. He never had time for long vacations. Which doesn't mean he ever in any way felt "burnt out." The way so many of us feel today when we work for long periods without appropriate rest. My father's secrets were two: He was a champion at resting whenever rest periods came, at night, for example. When he'd settle down with the weekly paper by the fire after a good supper. The other secret was the real sense of joy he took in his work. No aspect of the work on the land or with the livestock ever seemed to bore him. Although some of the tasks required constant repetition. In fact, whenever he needed to leave the farm to be present at ceremonious occasions, a wedding, a funeral, a party. He'd be nervous and irritable for all the time he was away. It would be fine if all of us could live a work life like my father's. Loving the labor we performed.

---

## Homophone

A homophone is a word identical in sound with another word, but different in spelling, origin, and meaning. Examples are *sun* and *son, bear* (to carry) and *bare* (naked), and so on. See **Spelling.**

## Hyphen

The hyphen is used between words or between prefixes and words to indicate that the hyphenated structure should be taken as a unit (*anti-war, twenty-two, low-level*); to separate prefixes from words when the combination is spelled like a word with another meaning (e.g., *re-creation,* "a creation again," and *recreation,* "leisure"); and to divide a word at the end of a line of text to show that it continues on to the next line. This last use is a matter of convention; we will begin with it.

**1.** Use a hyphen when you must divide a word at the end of a line of text and continue it on the next line. When you must do this, place the hyphen between syllables. A syllable is a unit of spoken language consisting usually of a vowel alone or a vowel with one or more consonants. Good dictionaries give the proper syllables of a word in each entry. Here is the proper syllabication of a few multisyllable words. Notice that each syllable is pronounceable.

| | | |
|---|---|---|
| a-bove | con-ver-sa-tion | pa-tience |
| ac-tor | dis-trib-ute | pic-ture |
| bap-tism | hy-dro-gen | rev-er-end |
| bi-cy-cle | op-po-nent | sep-a-ra-tion |
| bur-y | | |

Here are examples of proper word divisions at the end of a line.

It turned out on Friday that our *conversa-
tion* had been unnecessary. We were really agreed on everything.

After graduating from college, Henry became an *actor,* something I had not thought possible when I knew him.

If you are unsure of the proper syllabication of a word, consult a good dictionary. But never leave a single letter on one line even if it *is* the proper syllabication. And never divide a word of one syllable, such as *France* or *trout*.

**Wrong**   There was a line of low, threatening clouds *a-
bove* the mountains.
**Right**   There was a line of low, threatening clouds *above*
the mountains.

**Wrong**   We decided it would be in our best interest to *bur-
y* the hatchet and be friends again.
**Right**   We decided it would be in our best interest to *bury*
the hatchet and be friends again.

**Wrong**   In the fall, when we finally left for *France,* we were very excited.
**Right**   In the fall, when we finally left for *France,*
we were very excited.

**2.** Use a hyphen to join words or words and prefixes together. The hyphen used in this way is, in most cases, a transitional mark. For example, usually (but not always), when words are first linked to each other, they are written separately—as in *basket ball*. Later, this word became *basket-ball,* and it is now, of course, always written *basketball.* Thus, just how to use the hyphen for any compound word at any particular moment is difficult to determine, because usage is continually changing and even good, recently published dictionaries are likely to be behind the times. Still, the dictionary is the soundest authority and should be consulted when the writer is doubtful about some case of hyphenation.

The following rules were accurate when this book was written.

A. Words beginning with *all, self,* and *ex* (meaning *former* ) are always hyphenated.

He is a *self-made* man.
In Washington, the President's staff is *all-powerful.*
The *ex-President* has hardly any influence on national policy.

B. When the root word is a proper noun or proper adjective, use a hyphen to separate prefixes.

anti-Nixon        un-American        pro-Reagan

C. Prefixes ending in a vowel are frequently hyphenated, especially if the root word begins with the same vowel.

| | | |
|---|---|---|
| anti-intellectual | semi-invalid | pre-election |
| re-educate | de-escalate | re-evaluate |
| co-ordinate | | |

*Note:* Some constructions with a double vowel are acceptable without hyphenation.

cooperate, preeminent, preexisting.

D. Certain prefixes are hyphenated to avoid confusing a word with another whose spelling is identical.

A work of art is a *re-creation* of experience. (to avoid confusion with *recreation,* "leisure")
Since the math teacher couldn't follow his logic, the student had to *re-prove* the theorem. (to avoid confusion with *reprove,* "rebuke")
Now that my wife has emptied our closets, we have to *re-store* all our things. (to avoid confusion with *restore,* "return to a former condition")

**3.** A good many compound nouns are hyphenated; a good many others are not; and some are written as single words. (A compound noun is one that consists of more than a single word.)

| Hyphenated | Unhyphenated | Single Words |
|---|---|---|
| air-brake | busboy | blackbird |
| bee-sting | diving board | headache |
| bull's-eye | first cousin | highway |
| cave-in | high school | landslide |
| free-for-all | ice cream | madman |
| merry-go-round | oil spill | newsstand |

*Remember:* If you are unsure about a particular case, consult a good dictionary.

**4.** Compound adjectives—groups of words that when taken together act like a single-word adjective—are usually joined together by hyphens.

*able-bodied* seaman     *low-level* official
*devil-may-care* attitude     *middle-of-the-road* politician
*double-parked* car     *out-of-work* actor
*fence-busting* outfielder     *two-tiered* stadium

*Note:* When these adjectives are in the predicate adjective position, following a linking verb, the hyphen is omitted.

The actor is *out of work.*
His car was *double parked.*

**5.** Hyphens are used between parts of compound numbers—twenty-one to ninety-nine—and in specifying fractions. Hyphens are also frequently used to connect numbers in specifying dates.

This is my *twenty-second* birthday.
My professor is only *thirty-one* years old.
He is taxed *two-fifths* of his income.
The meetings will take place September *4-11.*
My vacation runs *July 31-August 14.*

*Note:* Do not use a hyphen in noncompound numbers.

one hundred twelve

## *Test Yourself on*
## the Appropriate Use of the Hyphen

Some of the sentences below contain uses of the hyphen that are correct; next to these, write C. Some sentences, however, contain word groups that need a hyphen. Insert a hyphen wherever you think one is missing.

1. _____ Sarah is a well trained teacher, but she would rather be a well paid researcher.

2. _____ Resort the laundry so that we can get all the white things together.

3. _____ Everything Jeffrey does is self-serving.

4. _____ Call in a carpenter; those bookshelves are not a doityourself job.

5. _____ Ed's colorblindness is due to a genetic defect.

6. _____ If you don't like spaghetti and meat balls, you're unItalian.

7. _____ Coal mine caveins are preventable.

8. _____ The actor used to be an able bodied seaman.

9. _____ Ex naval officers frequently become business executives.

10. _____ The all-powerful Internal Revenue Service takes two-fifths of my income in taxes.

11. _____ He was a semiinvalid and a proKennedy pseudoliberal.

12. _____ He scored a bullseye in target shooting, but she was uninterested.

## Idiom

See **Diction.**

# Internal Punctuation

See **End Punctuation**.


# Italics

*Italics is the name given to the typeface in which these words are printed.* On the other hand, the typeface in which these words are printed is called roman. In hand-written manuscripts or typescripts, underlining is the equivalent of italics. Italics are conventionally used in the following special cases.

**1.** Use italics for the names of books, plays, movies, television shows, newspapers, magazines, ships, aircraft, long musical compositions.

Shakespeare's *Hamlet*
Melville's *Moby Dick*
*The New Yorker* (magazine)
The Los Angeles *Times* (Note that the name of the city is not in italics here.)
S.S. *Rotterdam, Queen Elizabeth II*
*The City of Birmingham* (name of aircraft)
Beethoven's *Ninth Symphony*
*Star Wars* (movie)
*All in the Family* (TV show)

**2.** Use italics for foreign words and phrases that have not become part of the English language.

He lived in Peekskill but kept a small *pied-à-terre* in New York. (*pied-à-terre* = temporary or secondary lodging place)
Writing poems was his whole *raison d'être.* (*raison d'*être = reason for being)
Dave is known as a *bon vivant.* (a person who enjoys good food and other pleasant things)

*Note:* Some foreign words and phrases *have* become part of the English language and should not be italicized. Here is a small list of them:

| cliché | gamin | guru | genre | lacuna |
|---|---|---|---|---|
| café | bona fide | ensemble | elite | Gesundheit |

**3.** Use italics for words and phrases considered for themselves.

The word *elegant* is derived from Old French.
The term *end of the line* is a cliché.

**4.** Use italics for scientific terms in Latin.

The constellation Great Bear (*Ursa major*) is in the northern hemisphere.
For genetic research, the species of mosquito known as *anopheles* is most useful.

**5.** Use italics for giving special emphasis to ordinary words. You should achieve emphasis by placing the important word or words in an emphatic position in the sentence—not by carelessly using italics. Italics should be reserved for words that cannot be emphasized enough by ordinary work on structure.

**Weak**   I'm taking about *love,* as an emotion.
**Revised**   Love is what I'm talking about. (Here the position of *love* as the subject gives it enough emphasis without italics.)

**Weak**   He said he would *never* marry.
**Revised**   To the question of when he would marry, he replied with one word: never. (The final position of the word in the rewritten sentence is very emphatic; note, too, that the sentence has been designed to emphasize *never.*)

**Proper Use of Italics**
What's important is not what she *was,* but what she has *become.* (Italics point up the contrast between *was* and *become.*)
Charley is henpecked not because he has a wife but because *his wife has him.* (Italics call attention to the reversal.)

---

## *Test Yourself on*
## the Use of Italics

Some of the following sentences show the correct use of italics. Next to each of these, write C. Some sentences, however, need to have italics added or removed; in these, make the appropriate corrections.

1. _____ The current craze for *nostalgia* knows no limits.

2. _____ The expression freaked out is slang.

3. _____ The New York Daily News has only one competitor.

4. _____ Great books like Moby-Dick and Anna Karenina occupy the mind long after we've read them.

5. _____ My Uncle Ted is on the cover of *Time* this week.

6. _____ The program includes Beethoven's Sixth Symphony and his Fidelio Overture.

7. _____ I felt much better after I spoke to my *guru*.

8. _____ The porcupine anteater belongs to the family *echidna*.

9. _____ The Transatlantic Review published Myra's first story.

10. _____ We're sailing on the *S. S. Rotterdam*.

11. _____ She worked as a *fille de chambre* [lady's maid].

12. _____ It was his last performance as Hamlet.

---

# Logic

Clear and forceful writing always involves clear thinking and the presentation of honest evidence. Therefore, in this brief treatment of a complex subject, we shall deal with aspects of logic useful to writers who wish to impart to their work the rigor and strength of solid thought. The topics to be covered are these: (1) fairness in argument, (2) the careful use of evidence, (3) methods of clear reasoning, and (4) errors in thinking.

## Fairness in Argument

To be sure that your arguments or generalizations (or thesis statements) are fair and not prejudiced, you should avoid the errors discussed here.

**1.** Avoid basing your argument on belief rather than knowledge.

*Prejudice* is prejudgment, before the facts are known. We may *wish* to believe something is true and argue a case using that something as a generalization. But we would only be displaying prejudice.

Sally doesn't know how to drive a car. I always see her sitting in the back seat of her parents' automobile.
(How does the speaker know that Sally isn't just following family custom by sitting in back?)

She must have a sugar daddy somewhere. Every time I see her, she's wearing a new outfit.
(The speaker is merely *assuming.* Sally may have money that is *not* the gift of an "admirer" but that she has earned or been given as a gift by a relative.)

These leaps in logic are frequent in ordinary conversation or in careless discourse elsewhere. They are prejudicial and lead to serious distortions. Consider the way that racial prejudice follows the same model of slack thought; for example, all Italians are loud, blacks on welfare, Jews rich and stingy, and so forth.

**2.** Avoid arguing by discrediting an opponent or his idea.

This is known as *argumentum ad hominem,* or "arguing to the man." It is a form of nonevidence that fails to notice a person might be wrong about one thing and right about another.

Don't believe Quinn when he says our college isn't doing right by its students. He never went to school himself.
(Quinn may have been wrong in avoiding a formal education— although we can't tell from what the speaker says—and right in his analysis of the way the college functions.)

Tuten is wrong about the town's need for more roads. He's a
   contractor and naturally he wants the money.
(Tuten doesn't *know* he'll get the contract; besides, he could be
   right about the need for roads.)

The examples given show that the speaker in both
cases is arguing to the man rather than to the issues
involved.

**3.** Avoid making capital by associating your idea or
argument with a great name.
   This is called the *argumentum ad verecundiam,* where
it is hoped that the association of one's position or
thought with a great name will transfer the authority or
prestige of that name onto one's own thought. It also
works in reverse. By associating an opponent's ideas
with some person or movement of low prestige, one
discredits one's opponent.

If John Kennedy were alive today, he'd be fighting to put this bill
   through Congress.
Like all radicals, he believes in sharing the wealth.

---

## *Test Yourself on*
## Judging the Fairness of Generalizations

Read carefully each set of statements printed below.
Then prepare for each a discussion of its fairness or
unfairness according to the discussion you've just read.

1. The Bible says "honor thy father and thy mother," so I
   never disobey mine.
2. College students don't work as hard as they did in my
   day. Nowadays all they do is listen to rock music.
3. Business is nothing but thievery. How else could they
   make so much money?
4. Black people make terrific athletes.
5. I would never hire an ex-convict to work for me. Once
   a thief, always a thief. That's what I say.

## The Careful Use of Evidence

Instead of using prejudice and low blows, the logical writer employs evidence that appeals not to passion but to reason.

Good evidence is the proper use of facts, opinion, or statistics. Evidence honestly and carefully used supports a generalization (a thesis statement) in such a way as to persuade a reader that the case being presented is solid to the point of being unassailable.

Failure to be careful leads to errors in handling evidence, and these usually fall into the following categories:

### 1. Biased evidence

This is a form of evidence so unreliable that it is sure to do the arguer more harm than good. If you were to argue that the American people are in favor of the economy going on a war footing on the basis of a poll taken among aircraft workers in Seattle who favor stepped-up production, your evidence would be biased. Those workers would not necessarily favor making warplanes alone—though surely they are saying they want more work. Similarly, if you were to argue that Europe has a weak capacity to defend itself from aggression, citing its weak defensive capacity compared to the offensive might of the Russians, you would also be arguing from biased evidence. Europe's defense is not only in its own but in American hands as well.

Biased evidence is frequently the mainstay of advertising and other forms of commercial presentation. There the evidence is made biased by taking things out of context. Soft drinks advertised as sugar-free (good) do not, in the same ad, acknowledge that they contain saccharin (bad).

The testimony of character witnesses at trials can also be seen as a form of biased evidence, for such witnesses are always prepared to say only good things about a defendant.

Advertising blurbs and character witnesses are, among others, notoriously deliberate employers of biased evidence. But writers need to be careful that they do not inadvertently use such material. The way to make sure is to use only the most rigorously impartial and respectable sources.

## 2. Insufficient evidence

It is December in northern Minnesota. For three days, the temperature hovers around 55 degrees. A native exclaims, "We're having a mild winter." This is a clear case of insufficient evidence. What about the other days between December and March?

Another case: If after your first week at the college you attend you have failed to make a friend, are you justified in thinking, "This school is a drag; everybody's unfriendly"? Not really. You have insufficient evidence because it has only been a week and you haven't been exposed to *all* the possible friends you might make.

Thus insufficient evidence most frequently involves having too few cases on which to build a generalization. Writers must be sure to make their evidence plentiful enough to be convincing.

## 3. Poorly evaluated statistics

Faulty evidence in the form of poorly evaluated statistics is easy to present if the writer is not wary. For example, the U.S. Department of Labor, Bureau of Labor Statistics, issues a statistic on unemployment for a particular month: 8.7 percent. Before citing this figure in support of an argument that the U.S. economy is performing about as well as expected, you had better consider this question: as well as expected with regard to whom? For buried in that single 8.7 percent statistic there may be others, for example, that teenagers suffer an unemployment rate of 26.7 percent and black teenagers an even higher one. The economy does not perform for all the people all the time.

Another example, closer to home, will make this issue even clearer. Suppose you've been working during all of 1982 at your usual part-time job for the salary of $100 a week. Then in 1983, your boss recognizes your true value (at last) and starts paying you at the new rate of $200 a week. Can we assume that you now have twice as much money? Would that be a fair way to make inferences from the statistics? Not at all. It should be fairly obvious that you've jumped into a new tax bracket and more taxes are withheld from your paycheck and that more Social Security payments are being deducted as well.

The point is that all of us need help with statistics. For this reason, although statistics are very useful in an argument, we need to be wary about how we use them.

---

## *Test Yourself on*
### Recognizing Biased, Insufficient, and Statistically Unreliable Evidence

Each of the following groups of statements is a case of evidence poorly conceived. Give a name to each error in each case.

1. Twelve percent of the American people earn 50 thousand or more dollars a year. Let's look for the millionaire on this campus: there are 3,000 of us, so there must be 360 who earn that much.
2. Everybody I know is buying a motorcycle. They must be terrific.
3. If you live in Alaska, you must have warm blood.
4. I read that the lumberjacks in Oregon want to cut down more trees. That must mean nobody in the state is interested in ecology.
5. My sister's not doing well in math. Women can't handle math and sciences.
6. The price of cars has doubled in the past ten years. Detroit must really be raking in the money.
7. A cigarette ad showing two lean and leathery horsemen riding in a beautiful range of western American mountains.
8. I can't hire that ex-convict; he might steal something.
9. Now that I've bought a car, I need a bigger allowance.
10. Inflation last year was 8 percent; this year it's 16 percent; next year, it'll be 24 percent.

## Methods of Clear Reasoning

Logic refers to clear reasoning, and reasoning involves two basic processes called *induction* and *deduction*.

*Induction* is the name we give to a process involving rational movement from particular facts to general statements. Scientists and the scientific method rely on induction. For example, when a number of cases of influenza are diagnosed in the same part of the country (particular facts), we can say (make the generalization) that there is a flu epidemic there. Similarly, when a physicist determines, after a number of experiments, that metal *A* is a more ready conductor of electricity than metal *B,* the determination (the generalization) is made possible by the many experiments (particular facts). Induction can also be thought of as an ordinary mental process—the way we are influenced by experience: If after a number of attempts to make friends with Jack come to nought and we think to ourselves that Jack is unfriendly, we are only making use of the inductive process. Similarly, one important way in which the thesis statement comes into being is induction: We examine the facts and make a generalization from them.

However, a warning must be given here about induction. First, we can never be as sure about a conclusion based on a certain number of facts as we can about a conclusion based on all of them. When a scientist says that water freezes at 32 degrees Fahrenheit, he means that having observed it to do so on a number of occasions, he predicts that it will always do so. Similarly, if you should conclude, having met seven bright graduates of Stanford University, that *all* Stanford graduates are bright, your certainty will still be limited by the principle involved: It is never an absolute certainty when one leaps from *some* to *all.* Still, we can be more sure that physical nature is uniform than we can that human nature is.

Thus in inducing a generalization, the writer must bear this warning in mind; that is, he must at least be sure that he has a sufficient number of cases (facts) on which to base his conclusion (generalization), that these are typical cases (e.g., that the Stanford graduates were not all honors people who graduated *summa cum laude* but just ordinary graduates), and that exceptions can be explained (e.g., one of the Stanford graduates seems not so bright when you ask her a tough question; is it true that she is not bright or is it that when you asked, she had been without sleep for a few days and wasn't performing well on that one occasion).

*Deduction,* on the other hand, is a kind of thinking that proceeds from a generalization to a particular fact. From the generalization that people who are overweight tend to die earlier than those who are not, you can deduce that it is best to watch one's diet carefully. Or if you know that a particular restaurant serves wonderful food (generalization), you can deduce (particular fact) that it would be a good place to take a friend to dinner.

You may now understand that there is a relationship between induction and deduction, and so there is. For example, sound conclusions reached through scientific induction may be just the useful generalizations from which to make particular deductions—about health for instance. The National Institutes of Health has records showing causes of death in millions of cases; it has concluded (induced) that death by heart attack is hastened by the intake of cholesterol-rich foods. From that generalization, you can deduce that it is bad for your health to eat too many eggs or too much cheese or red meat.

In order for the inductive process to yield a true generalization, the facts must be true; similarly, in order for the particular fact deduced to be true, the premises from which it was made must be true.

In the case of deduction, there is a process for testing the validity of conclusions; for in its most familiar form, the deductive form is exemplified by the *syllogism.* A *syllogism* is nothing but a little argument in the form of two premises and a conclusion drawn from them.

**Major premise**   All citizens pay income taxes.
**Minor premise**   All Americans are citizens.
**Conclusion**   All Americans pay income taxes.

To understand why the conclusion in this syllogism is valid, we can think of those mentioned as belonging to classes and begin to represent these classes visually.

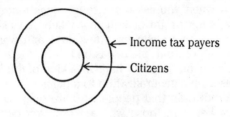

This is a visual representation of the major premise. Within the outer circle are all those who belong to the class of income tax payers. The inner circle encloses the class of citizens. Now let us represent the minor premise in the diagram.

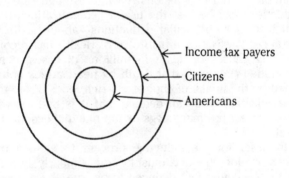

Now the innermost circle encloses the class of Americans. That circle is enclosed not only within the circle of citizens but also in the circle of those who pay income tax. Hence it is clear visually that all Americans pay income tax (are a class included within the class of income tax payers). But notice that if we had started with a major premise stating that "*some* citizens pay income tax," our conclusion could not be so straightforward.

Now we would need to conclude that *some Americans pay income taxes*.

Some Americans pay income taxes.

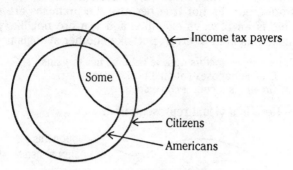

You will rarely if ever encounter a syllogism either in written work or in conversation. More likely in conversation is the appearance of part of a syllogism: Either one of the premises or the conclusion is missing.

*The Electric Horseman* is playing at the movies. I hate Westerns. (Conclusion missing: I won't go to the movies.)

It's Tuesday, so I'd better go to work. (Missing premise: Tuesday is payday.)

But a syllogism is not useful unless our premises are true, because a syllogism can validate an untruth. For example, here's a syllogism that provides a perfectly valid conclusion:

All cats are gray.
All gray things are stupid.
All cats are stupid.

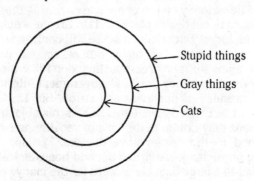

It certainly follows from the premises that all cats are stupid, but it's not true because the premises are not. This is an obvious example, and you are not likely to make this kind of error. But take another syllogism:

Conservative doctors oppose national health plans.
Dr. Greene opposes national health plans.
Dr. Greene is a conservative doctor.

Here is a visual representation:

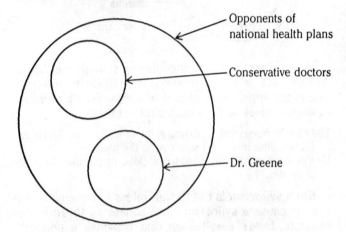

Opponents of national health plans

Conservative doctors

Dr. Greene

Notice that Dr. Greene is not included in the class of conservative doctors. He doesn't have to be. If the major premise had been that *only* conservative doctors oppose national health plans, the conservative doctors' circle would lie virtually on top of the one enclosing those who oppose national health plans, and Dr. Greene would have to be included. But common sense will confirm what the diagram indicates, for many others oppose national health plans for many reasons: they don't like the plans so far proposed; they don't like government interference in all avenues of our lives; and so on. But Dr. Greene need not be conservative either; that is, his objections to the plans may not lie in the area of venality presumably ascribed to the conservative doctors. Perhaps he's a young physician just starting out and honestly feels he's entitled to a large financial reward for the many years he spent preparing for an exacting profession. Perhaps he believes that a national health plan will deliver poorer health care than private plans. In any case, it is clear that although the premises here are true—conservative doctors *do* oppose national health plans as does Dr. Greene—the conclusion is clearly false.

Thus in addition to using the diagram method of checking syllogistic deduction, the writer needs to check carefully the truth of his premises. Another way of putting it is to say that the writer must check his evidence, the facts from which he draws his conclusions. The writer needs to check the support that underlies his evidence, and this involves induction.

---

## *Test Yourself on* Applying Induction or Deduction

A. *Induction:* Below are five sets of factual statements, each followed by a conclusion induced from them. Consider the value of the conclusion in the light of the foregoing discussions. Is the conclusion a reasonable one? Why? Why not?

1. Richard was a colonel in the army. He is used to taking responsibility, engaging in long-range planning, dealing effectively with large numbers of subordinates, executing policy. Therefore, he would make a good business executive.

2. The last three times America suffered from terrific inflation, we had a Democratic president. It's obvious that the Democrats don't know how to run the domestic economy.

3. Margie's family is always calling on her for help, and I'll be involved in it. Look what happened to Fred after he married Miss Dooley! I'm not going to marry Margie.

4. I heard that Professor Brody always springs surprises when he gives exams. I'm not going to study for them.

5. The average temperature in Athens in the summer is 85 degrees. So I think I'd better take light cotton clothing on my trip.

B. *Deduction:* Below are five syllogisms. Make a visual representation of each and check the conclusions. Are they valid? After you have checked on the valid conclusions, ask yourself whether these valid conclusions are also true.

1. All cats are independent.
   No independent animal likes humans.
   Cats don't like humans. (*conclusion*)

2. Most Americans are friendly.
   Most friendly people are hospitable.
   Most Americans are hospitable. (*conclusion*)

3. All Irishmen like to drink whiskey.
   Ed Quinn likes to drink whiskey.
   Ed Quinn is an Irishman. (*conclusion*)

4. Violence is wrong.
   War is violence.
   War is wrong. (*conclusion*)

5. Some actors are out of work.
   Out-of-work people are usually a little desperate.
   Some actors are a little desperate. (*conclusion*)

---

## Errors in Thinking

Even reasonable people make errors when they think. So we must take the time to deal with some common forms of thinking errors called *fallacies.*

### 1. Post hoc ergo propter hoc

This fallacy is known by its Latin name, meaning "after this, therefore because of this." Do not think that because event *B* follows or comes after event *A*, event *A* was the cause of event *B*. The conclusion that Phyllis started to be unhappy after she married Norman is not necessarily a criticism of her marriage to Norman. Her unhappiness may have nothing to do with Norman *or* the marriage. It might be that her career has taken a critical turn and she is under great pressure at her job. Or it is possible that her health is deteriorating, something entirely unrelated to the marriage.

The need to avoid this fallacy becomes even clearer when we consider public questions.

This town started to deteriorate rapidly after Mayor Buckley was elected.

This conclusion is especially pernicious because the so-called evidence (the deterioration) is visible and on that account may seem convincing. But a moment's thought will show that the conclusion is false. Deterioration, especially in an urban setting, is not an instantaneous process; it takes time. Ignoring the general nature of the accusation, we can extrapolate from what we know that deterioration takes place in a number of separate areas—housing, transportation, an increase in crime, and so on—a complex of events that cannot be attributed to the mayoral term of one man; its seeds were no doubt planted long before Buckley's nomination. If anything, Buckley arrived in the middle of all this. He did not cause it.

## 2. Non sequitur

This Latin term means "it does not follow." This fallacy occurs when the writer either leaves out steps in the thought process or draws conclusions that do not follow from the premises.

He's the best teacher I've ever seen and he should be made Dean.

The conclusion doesn't follow. Is it a fact that very good teachers make very good deans? How so? And even if this were true, how many teachers has the speaker seen?

Kennedy's an aristocrat; that's why he's for the common man.

The conclusion doesn't follow because steps have been omitted in the writer's reasoning process; that is, he hasn't let the reader in on these steps:

1. Kennedy is an aristocrat.
2. His family owns a considerable fortune.

3. Among people of his class, it is an important value to do public service to the underprivileged.
4. His brothers carried on in this tradition.
5. That's why he's for the common man.

To avoid non sequitur, you should be sure that, in your papers, all steps in the thinking process are included.

### 3. Hasty generalization

This fallacy is a form of using insufficient evidence. For example, if you know a seventeen-year-old who refused to get a job when his father asked him to and an eighteen-year-old who wouldn't observe his mother's 2 A.M. curfew, you do not have enough evidence to conclude that young people today are a bad lot because they don't obey their parents. Such a conclusion makes a statement about millions of individuals on the basis of a couple of cases—a bad business. If your main proposition is based on such evidence, you would do well to reconsider the whole thing.

### 4. False analogy

Analogies are useful in clarifying certain points under discussion, but they are seldom enough to win an argument because *alike* does not mean *identical.* But they are useful. For instance, we call a vehicle that travels over interplanetary distances a *spaceship,* thus making an analogy between the craft and a seagoing vessel and between space and water. But these two likenesses have the power to explain space travel in only a limited way. For example, both a spaceship and an oceangoing vessel travel far distances through a uniform medium, and both must be built in such a way as to protect against that medium's leaking into the ship; both must carry sufficient supplies; and so forth. But the analogy doesn't hold up entirely: Spacecraft need to be entirely enclosed, carry their own oxygen, and begin their journeys with an enormously powerful rocket thrust.

Analogies are useful, then, in clarifying certain points under discussion, but they are seldom enough to win an argument. Be careful in your use of analogy not to make false ones.

## 5. Begging the question

In this fallacy, the writer or speaker assumes in his thesis the validity of something that really needs to be proven. To say *He's an idiot because he says stupid things* is neither explanation nor proof. The word *idiot* in this context means *someone who says stupid things*. Thus the original utterance means *He's someone who says stupid things because he says stupid things*. We should have to hear these so-called stupid things before we accept the declaration of idiocy. On the level of formal argument, a statement like *The crucially important hospital should be built* is a similar type of statement. That is because *crucially important* here simply means *should be built*. Thus the statement means *The hospital which should be built should be built*. We need to know why it should be built. Otherwise, the statement begs the question.

---

## Test Yourself on
### Recognizing Logical Fallacies

Examine each set of statements below and point out the logical errors in the thinking behind each.

1. Ever since those Hispanics moved into the neighborhood, the crime rate has gone up. They must be responsible.
2. Nowadays, it's a crime to waste food.
3. It's a vital necessity that everyone get out and vote on Election Day.
4. He'd make a great Secretary of Defense. He's spent all his life in the army.
5. My two little cousins don't like candy. I guess children don't like sweets.
6. It's Tuesday. I'd better not skip work today.
7. All I can say is, he wasn't an alcoholic *before* he married Gail!

8. Professors are like tiny pieces of toast: They should be buttered up and swallowed whole.
9. My aunt and uncle love to visit Russia. They must be Communists.
10. The movie I saw last night was wonderful. It should easily win an Oscar.

---

## Misplaced Modifiers

A misplaced modifier is a word, phrase, or clause that does not point clearly and directly to what it is supposed to modify. When using modifiers, be sure to place the word, phrase, or clause close to the word or words it actually modifies, for meaning changes with the placement of the modifier.

He *almost* had a heart attack every time he looked at his bank statement. (He almost had the attack—but not quite—every time he looked.)

He had a heart attack *almost* every time he looked at his bank statement. (He actually had the attack—sometimes, but not every time he looked.)

**1.** Be careful to place the adverbs *almost, even, hardly, just, merely, only, nearly,* and *scarcely* close to the words they modify. Misplacing words like *almost* and *only* occurs quite often in informal writing, but you should learn to be careful about their placement, because misplacing them can often confuse the reader badly.

**Misplaced Word**   I *only* told the jury what I had seen. (The choices here are three: *I only*—and nobody else—told the jury; *I told only* the jury—and nobody else; or I told the jury *only what I had seen.*)
**Revised**          I told the jury *only* what I had seen.
                     I told *only* the jury what I had seen.
                     *Only* I told the jury what I had seen.

**Misplaced**   I *nearly* went halfway to Canada.
**Revised**     I went *nearly* halfway to Canada.

**Misplaced**   I *almost* ate half the pie.
**Revised**     I ate *almost* half the pie.

**2.** Be careful to place modifying phrases close to the word or words they modify.

**Misplaced Phrase**   My history professor made it clear why wars take place *on Tuesday.* (The *wars* take place on Tuesday?)
**Revised**   *On Tuesday,* my history professor make it clear why wars take place.

**Misplaced Phrase**   Airlines serve martinis to passengers *in little bottles.* (The *passengers* are in little bottles?)
**Revised**   Airlines serve passengers martinis *in little bottles.*

**Misplaced Phrase**   Environmental groups protested the oil leaks *all over the country.* (Were there *oil leaks* all over the country?)
**Revised**   Environmental groups *all over the country* protested the oil leaks.

**3.** Be careful to place modifying clauses close to the word or words which they modify.

**Misplaced Clause**   Sid bought books for his library *that cost $19.04.* (Did his *library* or his *books* cost that much?)
**Revised**   Sid bought books *that cost $19.04* for his library. For his library, Sid bought books *that cost $19.04.*

**Misplaced ·Clause**   The paint job looked sloppy *which was not dry yet.*
**Revised**   The paint job, *which was not dry yet,* looked sloppy.

A special case of the misplaced modifier is called a *squinting modifier* because it looks in two directions at the same time; that is, it "squints."

**Squinting Modifier**   To be beautifully dressed *often* pleases my wife. (Is she *often pleased* or *often beautifully dressed?*)
**Revised**   It *often* pleases my wife to be beautifully dressed. It pleases my wife to be beautifully dressed *often.*

**Squinting Modifier**   Lucia said *when she was on her way* home she would stop and buy the vegetables. (Did she say it while traveling home? Or did she say that sometime on her way home she would stop?)
**Revised**   When she was on her way home, Lucia said that she would stop and buy the vegetables. (*Said* while on her way home.) Lucia said that on her way home she would stop and buy the vegetables. (She will *stop* on her way home.)

## *Test Yourself on*
## Revising Misplaced and Squinting Modifiers

Some of the following sentences contain well-placed modifiers; next to these, write C. Others, however, have misplaced or squinting modifiers; correct these, even if it means recasting the sentence.

1. _____ With this calculator, I can show you how to make a million dollars in twenty seconds.

2. _____ The sick patient wanted to live happily.

3. _____ The sunset that we loved completely stunned us.

4. _____ We made plans to leave over the weekend.

5. _____ Professors who teach rarely get rich.

6. _____ Subconsciously, Kathy wanted to become famous.

7. _____ Caesar was stabbed in the heyday of his glory.

8. _____ He just left for a minute.

9. _____ For Christopher's sake, I decided to go to California.

10. _____ The state penalizes those who commit murder for good reason.

11. _____ Robert DeNiro just arrived here last week.

12. _____ The father heard the news that his son had been born with joy.

13. _____ *True Confessions* appeals to readers with scandalous stories.

14. _____ Those who jog slowly develop heart trouble.

15. _____ The ugly face scared him that looked through the window.

16. _____ They told us at midnight the show would begin.

17. _____ I took a train to Waterbury that was going north.

18. _____ She was planting seeds in her garden that she had bought yesterday.

---

# Modifiers

In Part 1, we noted that adjectives and adverbs act to modify or further describe members of other word classes: nouns and verbs. Adjectives and adverbs, as well as determiners, are called modifiers. But the question of modification is a bit more complicated than you may have imagined from reading about it in Part 1. Here we shall discuss the complications by discussing other words that can act as adjectives and adverbs. These other words are called *adjectivals* and *adverbials*.

## Other Words Used as Adjectives: Adjectivals

Some words are nearly always used as adjectives: *old, young, happy, proud,* and so forth. But other words, ordinarily belonging to other parts of speech, can also act as adjectives. So, of course, can phrases. All are entitled to be called adjectivals.

### 1. Nouns used as adjectives

We looked into the *bear* cage. (modifies *cage*)
She was wearing her *party* dress. (modifies *dress*)
We went to the *baseball* game. (modifies *game*)

### 2. Verbs used as adjectives

A whole class of verbs can be commonly used as adjectives. These are the participles: the *-ing* forms (present participles), the *-d* or *-ed* forms (past participles), and the irregular past participles (*gone, broken, kept,* and so forth).

The *fleeing* suspect was caught by the police. (modifies *suspect,* the subject)
The *broken* arrow was useless. (modifies *arrow,* the subject)
He seemed *defeated.* (acts as predicate adjective)
The job was *finished.* (acts as predicate adjective)

### 3. Adverbs used as adjectives

The apartment *below* is mine. (modifies *apartment*)
The road *ahead* is closed. (modifies *road*)

### 4. Phrases and clauses used as adjectives

**Phrase** The men *in the truck* were tired. (modifies *men*)
**Phrase** The planes *flying overhead* are bound for Europe. (modifies *planes*)

**Clause** The people *who rented my house* will stay until August. (modifies *people*)
**Clause** I bought a Toyota, *which runs like a top.* (modifies *Toyota*)

## Other Words Used as Adverbs: Adverbials

Some words are nearly always used as adverbs: *often, soon, rarely,* and so forth. But other words, ordinarily belonging to other parts of speech, can also act as adverbs, as can phrases and clauses. All these are entitled to be called adverbials.

### 1. Nouns used as adverbs

I went *home.* (modifies *went*)
She arrived *yesterday.* (modifies *arrived*)

### 2. Verbs used as adverbs

Because he was in a hurry, he decided to eat *standing.* (modifies *to eat.*)
Peter played *to win.* (modifies *played*)

### 3. Phrases and clauses used as adverbs

**Phrase**   We are staying *at a hotel.* (modifies *are staying*)
**Phrase**   We were impatient *to leave for the theater.* (modifies *impatient*)

**Clause**   *Although we were tired,* we couldn't fall asleep. (modifies the whole of the main clause)
**Clause**   *When they saw the shark,* they were frightened.(modifies *were frightened*)

---

## Test Yourself on
### Recognizing Modifiers: Adjectivals and Adverbials

Identify each of the italicized words or word groups as either an adjectival or an adverbial.

1. We were going on a *holiday* trip.
2. We would arrive *in the afternoon.*
3. He went *home.*
4. *When he spoke softly,* we had to strain to listen.
5. He gave the apples to the man *in the raincoat.*
6. He was promoted to *plant* manager.
7. The books, *which cost $18,* were overpriced.
8. The man *who sent her the flowers* was in love with her.
9. He was a *broken* man.
10. They were a *defeated* team.
11. The *purring* cat likes his milk.
12. The man *in the gray flannel suit* looks like my brother.

---

## Number

See **Shifts.**

# Numerals

Whether your writing is formal or informal, the basic guideline in handling numerals is to be consistent in your usage: Either use numerals or spell the numbers out in words—do not mix the two. There are several basic rules for handling numerals in formal writing.

**1.** Spell out numbers that require no more than two words. In other cases, use numerals.

There were *seventy-five* cases of swine flu reported.
The population of New York City is less than *eight million.*

*but*

My federal tax refund amounted to *$88.37.*

*Note:* In business and technical writing, numbers from 10 up are often written as numerals.

**2.** In writing dates, addresses, percentages followed by %, page numbers, or the time of day followed by *a.m.* or *p.m.,* use numerals.

**Date**  October 19, 1926 *or* 19 October 1926
**Address**  55 East 9th Street, Apartment 7K
**Percentages**  Richard gets 1%, and I get the rest.

> *but*
>
> This bank pays 5 percent interest.

**Page Numbers**  See Chapter 3, page 112.
**Time of Day**  11:30 p.m. *or* 11:30 P.M., *but* three o'clock

**3.** Use numerals for quantities in scientific and technical writing.

The barometric pressure is *29.31.*
The specimen was *.37* centimeter in length.

**4.** It is appropriate to use in the same sentence a combination of words and numerals where such a combination will make your writing clear.

You may take only *six* 6-inch trout from this stream.
The cashier counted out *70* one-dollar bills.

**5.** Do not begin a sentence with a numeral that is not spelled out.

**Wrong** *250,000,000* is the approximate population of the U.S.S.R.
**Right** The population of the U.S.S.R. is approximately 250,000,000.

**Wrong** *6* miles from here there is a gas station.
**Right** *Six* miles from here there is a gas station.

*Note:* If your text includes a great many numbers or a mixture of whole numbers and decimals, it is preferable to use numerals for all the numbers.

---

## *Test Yourself on*
## Using Numerals Correctly

Each of the following sentences contains errors in handling numerals. Correct them.

1. 2,000 years ago, an important event took place in Palestine.
2. Including finance charges, this new car would cost you five thousand six hundred and thirty-eight dollars.
3. They live at nine-0-eight President Street, apartment three E.
4. Dennis drinks about 36 cases of wine every year.
5. The father is 40, the mother is 37, and their children are 12 and ten.
6. 3 years ago I owned a Volkswagen.
7. The average annual rainfall in the Mato Grosso district of Brazil is one hundred twelve point seven three centimeters.
8. On February second, nineteen twenty-two, he managed to publish a book of some seven hundred pages.
9. On page five, there is a good description of a corrupt man.
10. His author's royalties amounted to twelve percent of the price of the book.

11. I promised to pay him ninety-eight fifty-six on February twenty-third.

12. It's either the fourteenth of September or the seventeenth—the odds are thirty to one that I'll forget which.

13. Take your application to Room thirty-two; someone will be there by four p.m.

14. He was useful to the track team because he could run the four forty and could double in the ten thousand meters.

15. 9 years ago, I had an operation and was in the hospital for 3 weeks.

---

# Organization and Planning

Organization and planning are essential to good writing. An essay that is disorganized is incoherent, but achieving proper organization takes planning. This entry is devoted to both.

## Organization

An essay is commonly organized into three parts: an introduction, a main body, and a conclusion. The main body is the most important of these parts, for in it the writer treats the main ideas of the essay. The organization of the body of the essay is treated under **Unity, Paragraph Development,** and **Coherence.**

Here we are interested in introductions and conclusions, but before we take up these important items, let us consider a whole essay—including introduction, main body, and conclusion:

### My Disaster at Freshman Registration

[1] If you've ever wondered why you see so many prematurely gray-haired freshmen on this campus, this little story will answer your question.

[2] Bright and early on the first day of registration, I showed up at the Bursar's Office at 8 a.m. to pay my fees. The line at Window 1 snaked halfway around two corners to the lobby of the Administration Building. But I was patient (not to say in

shock). After a half-hour, I was at the promised land—the grilled window. I paid. They stamped my receipt. I was pushed out of the way.

[3] Suddenly, it dawned on me that I didn't know what to do next. I looked around, stupidly, I'm afraid. A passerby took pity on me. "Window 2 for your days and hours booklet," he snapped.

[4] So there I was, back in line. Another half-hour passed. There I was, back at the grill. I showed my receipt. They gave me—a *torn* booklet. I was shoved out of the way again. But the booklet might have been ripped into shreds for all I cared; the crazy abbreviations and symbols were nearly unreadable. How would I ever figure out how to register?

[5] This problem seemed small when I arrived at the main registration area in the gymnasium, because there it was literally a matter of survival. The physical contact here made the shoving at the Bursar's Office seem like love pats. Again, a friendly person intervened; that is, I found an adviser who explained that I needed to go to each departmental desk and register for courses one by one according to the days and hours I preferred.

[6] By this time, afternoon was crawling toward late afternoon. As I pondered my choice, I decided I'd better get cracking before dying of starvation (I'd missed lunch by now). So I ran to the English Department desk to register for Composition 101. But I was twenty yards away from that desk—without having registered—before I realized I didn't understand what they'd meant when they told me I'd been "closed out."

[7] I'll spare you the catalog of further horrors I endured that long day. You will learn whatever else you need to know about the registration experience by looking for me on campus. I'm the stooped, graying male freshman you see arriving for an 8 a.m. math class, the same one you see leaving after his 5 p.m. biology lecture.

The *introduction,* paragraph 1, opens the essay by proposing a challenge to the readers, and it does so in a humorous vein. It also tunes the readers in to the nature of what they are about to read: a little story. Further, it gives the tone of the piece and its main idea in brief.

The *main body* consists of paragraphs 2 to 6 and includes everything that actually happened; this portion of the paper is the centrally important part of what the writer has to say.

The *conclusion,* paragraph 7, ends the piece by returning to an idea presented in the introduction. It also gives a climactic end to the story by telling the reader the kind of schedule the poor freshman managed for himself—a long, ten-hour day.

The main body here is a little story—a piece of narration. Under **Paragraph Development,** other types of development are explained. See that entry to study more about how to handle a main body according to your specific purpose in writing a particular paper. For now, we will continue with more on introductions and conclusions and go on to planning an outline.

## *Introductions*

Introductions are important because they are the first words of yours that readers will see. Effective introductions perform a number of different tasks. Perhaps the most important is to catch the readers' interest and attention; right behind this come the tasks of identifying the subject and setting some sort of limit on it. A good introduction also sets the tone for the rest of the piece— it advises the readers how you, the writer, intend to treat the subject.

Here are a number of introductions, each identified by the method the writer employs:

### Using the Writer's Personal Experience

There was, I think, only a brief period in my life when I actually turned heads. It was the summer of my seventeenth year when, newly graduated from a private girls' school, I was in that transition stage between being an old child and a young woman, a state of half and half that men of all ages apparently find disarmingly erotic.

Anne Taylor Fleming, "In Defense of Flirting"

### Making an Unusual Statement

There are certain things an American is not permitted to hate. Americans may, without social ostracism or penalty of law, hate their partisan or ideological opposites. They may hate someone because of race or religion or class so long as they show selective decorum and speak in coded euphemisms.

Larry L. King, "Un-American Peeves"

### Offering a Strong Opinion
The current terrorist epidemic has mystified a great many people, and various explanations have been offered—most of them quite wrong.

Walter Laqueur, "Terrorist Myths"

### Stating and Illustrating the Main Idea
The dedicated baseball fan is a man who likes to kid himself. He'll get to a World Series game early, see a ballplayer yawning and take it as a sign of nervousness. He'll see a nervelessly relaxed body leaning against a batting cage and consider it merely feigned indifference. He'll watch an outfielder casually scratching his nose and count it as a tic. He's wrong. In fact, what looks like boredom on behalf of the people involved in the World Series is most often just that.

Jim Bouton, "A Few World Series Sinkers"

### Opening with a Challenge to the Reader
If you want your mate to stop guessing about your feelings and motives, you have to be prepared to reveal yourself.

Nena and George O'Neill, "Communicating with Yourself"

## *Conclusions*

A good conclusion to an essay leaves readers feeling that they have enjoyed a satisfying, rounded-off reading experience. It does this in one of the following ways:

**1.** By concluding with a reiteration, often in some varied form, of your thesis statement or main idea. A paper called "Abolish Big-Time Collegiate Sports" might end like this:

If big-time sports on campus were abolished, as I have suggested they should be, then perhaps some real sports enthusiasts could begin to engage in sports—myself, for example.

**2.** By concluding with a summary of your main points, thus reinforcing in the readers' minds the effective things you have said. A possible ending for "Nuclear Energy Versus Solar Power" might go as follows:

Nuclear energy presents us with the prospect of dangerous operation, deadly waste products, and sinister accidents, but the sun—as we have known all along—is an endless source of pleasure, enduring and powerful.

**3.** By making a climactic point. This type of conclusion is effective when you present a series of points in ascending dramatic order and finish with a particularly high note.


## Planning

Planning an essay—or even a five-hundred-word theme—begins with note-taking, jotting down ideas as you ask questions about your subject. Say it's "freshman registration." What time did I get there? *Awful. Arrived at eight in the morning.* Then what happened? *Got on line at Bursar's Office to pay fees.* Next? *Didn't know what to do—had to get on line again to ask!* Ask enough questions, and you may wind up with a list that looks something like this:

1. Awful. Arrived at 8 in the morning.
2. Got on line at Bursar's Office Window 1 to pay fees.
3. Had to line up again—find out what to do next!
4. Closed out of English.
5. Had to ask what "closed out" means.
6. Found out I needed to go to Window 2 for days and hours booklet.
7. Days and hours booklet torn.
8. Couldn't read it, anyway.
9. Entered registration area and was shoved and pushed for five minutes before I found an adviser.
10. Lost my pack of computer cards.
11. Finally got classes that begin at 8 and end at 6, four days a week.


### *Outlines*

The ultimate tool for planning an essay is an outline, and although the notes above do not exactly constitute an outline, you couldn't start to make an outline without them, and very little effort will enable you to make an outline from the notes. They have, embedded within them, just what you need for *controlling* and *directing* the way your theme will proceed.

For one thing, a quick glance at the notes tells you that there is a main point here—registration is a shocking, traumatic experience for an uninformed and inexperienced freshman. Furthermore, the fact that two areas are mentioned—the Bursar's Office and the registration area—provides a way of dividing the essay and beginning to organize an outline:

I. The Bursar's Office
   A. Got on line to pay fees
   B. Got on line again for booklet
      1. booklet torn
      2. couldn't read it
II. The registration area
   A. Got pushed and shoved before finding adviser
   B. Got closed out of English
      1. Found out what "closed out" means
      2. Missed lunch
   C. Got laborer's 8-6 schedule

This outline would help you to control your writing. It is an aid in keeping your plan in mind, indicates the order in which you discuss things, and manages to suggest the relative importance of the two places on the day of registration, by assigning a greater proportion of space to one (registration area) than to the other.

In order to become competent at making useful outlines, you should know something about the formal principles of outlining and the different types of outlines that can be used.

## Types of outlines

The three types of outlines most commonly employed are the topic outline, the sentence outline, and the paragraph outline. In a *topic outline,* each entry is a word or a small group of words. In a *sentence outline,* which has the same basic structural pattern as the topic outline, the words are replaced by complete sentences. In a *paragraph outline,* there are no divisions, headings, and subheadings, as in the others, but only a list of paragraph topic sentences. Some writers feel that the paragraph outline is most suitable for short papers, and the others for longer papers. A writer using a sentence outline is likely to keep in closer touch with the points because of the fuller information contained in sentences.

Whatever you do, decide beforehand which kind of outline you plan to use, and then follow its requirements systematically: Use *only* sentences in the sentence outline; be sure you have topic sentences for the paragraph outline. And check your outline to be sure that it is consistent with the principles that apply to all outlines.

Here are samples of each kind of outline, for a paper on "The Energy Crisis in Oil and Two Alternate Sources of Power":

**Topic Outline**
I. The Arab oil embargo of 1973
   A. Shortage of oil
   B. Dwindling of resources
II. Alternative of nuclear power
   A. Expensive
   B. Dangerous
   C. Likely to run out
III. Solar power
   A. Inexpensive
   B. Not dangerous
   C. Limitless supply
   D. Needs technology

**Sentence Outline**
I. The Arab oil embargo of 1973 pointed up the need for America to find alternate sources of fuel.
   A. The embargo produced a shortage of oil.
   B. It reminded us that all our fossil fuel resources are limited.
II. Nuclear power as an alternative, though widely favored, is not likely to be the answer.
   A. It's very expensive—both for new plants and fuel processing.
   B. It's very dangerous.
   C. It's also likely to prove a limited resource.
III. Solar power is probably a more attractive alternative.
   A. It's relatively inexpensive except for startup costs.
   B. It's easy to handle and not dangerous.
   C. The supply is limitless.

**Paragraph Outline**

1. The Arab oil embargo of 1973 pointed up the need for America to find alternate sources of fuel, by creating a shortage of oil and reminding us that oil was in any case in very limited supply—a dwindling resource.
2. Nuclear energy is widely favored as an alternative source of power, but it has many serious drawbacks.
3. Solar power is probably a more attractive alternative because it is cheap, limitless in supply, and relatively inexpensive.
4. It may be that solar energy will not be adopted because of industry's resistance to high startup costs for such a program.

### Testing the outline

Use the following criteria to be sure that your outline is logical and consistent:

**1.** Use a conventional form of notation. The following example is a useful one; it is rarely necessary to subdivide more than is shown:

I. . . . . . . . . . . . . . . . .
  A. . . . . . . . . . . . . . . .
    1. . . . . . . . . . . . . . . .
      a. . . . . . . . . . . . . . .
      b. . . . . . . . . . . . . . .
    2. . . . . . . . . . . . . . . .
  B. . . . . . . . . . . . . . . .
II. . . . . . . . . . . . . . . . .

**2.** Be sure that your outline covers your subject adequately. The major headings in your outline should include enough material to satisfy the expectations provoked by your subject. For example, consider these two outlines:

THE FEDERAL GOVERNMENT

| **Inadequate Material** | **Adequate Material** |
|---|---|
| I. Congress | I. Congress |
| II. The Executive Branch | II. The Executive Branch |
|  | III. The Judiciary |

Obviously, the outline on the left shows the writer's failure to consider the entire subject; of course this is a simple example, but checking your outline against this criterion of completeness can save you a great deal of trouble.

**3.** Be sure that your outline is in logical order. All the heads and subheads in your outline indicate parts. No category of head or subhead, therefore, can have only one part—if the essay or part is brief enough to be considered one part, it doesn't need to be outlined. Every outline must have at least two main headings, and wherever you divide one of these (I, II), you must divide it into at least two parts. If a I has an A, it must have a B. If an A has a 1, it must have a 2, and so forth.

Moreover, the order of your parts (the progression from I to II to III) must follow some consistent principle: chronology is one, cause and effect another. Do not mix your principles.

**Consistent Time Order**
  I. Selecting the date
 II. Inviting the guests
III. Preparing the menu
 IV. Cooking the food
  V. Setting the table

**Mixed Order**
Crime
  I. Its increase since Vietnam (time order)
 II. Its causes (cause and effect order)
III. Robbery versus rape (order by classification)

If your outline fails to meet this criterion, you are probably uncertain of your whole approach and need to reexamine your central idea or thesis statement.

**4.** Be sure to cast groups of headings and subheadings in parallel grammatical form. This will ensure that the parts of the outline are clearly related to one another. Notice in the sentence outline on page 186 that I A and I B are parallel (in B, the pronoun *it* stands for *the embargo* ), but that they are not parallel with II A, II B, and II C—which are parallel with one another. (*Note:* It is only due to the nature of the subject that III A, III B, and III C are parallel with the same group under II; in most cases, they need not be and will not be parallel.)

## *Test Yourself on*
### the Principles of Outlining

A. Using one of the manageable titles given at the end of **Subjects for Essays** (p. 276A), construct three outlines for it: a topic, a sentence, and a paragraph outline.

B. Choose one of the topics on page 276B, give it a manageable title, and construct a sentence outline for it.

# Paragraph Development

Adequate development is one of the three criteria for an effectively written paragraph. (For the other two, see **Unity** and **Coherence.** Also discussed under **Unity** is the important idea of the *topic sentence:* if you are not familiar with the topic sentence, read **Unity** before reading further here.)

A paragraph that is adequately developed is one that gives reasons, details, illustrations, or examples to fully support its topic sentence. The failure to give full development to every topic sentence leads to a series of short, choppy statements—not paragraphs—and leaves readers with the impression of a hasty and ill-thought-out composition.

The United Nations, which was established to maintain peace, does not do so. Since 1945, there have been many wars—Korea, the Middle East, and Vietnam, to name just a few.

Besides, the United Nations is an instrument for propaganda. The Russians use it constantly for this purpose.

Obviously, this writer opposes the United Nations, but the first "paragraph" gives inadequate development to the topic sentence because not enough examples of the U.N.'s failure are given. Similarly, the second "paragraph" fails to be specific enough; it doesn't give examples of *how* the Russians use the U.N. for propaganda.

With nuclear energy, there is still the possibility of accidents. One big one in Iowa in 1962 caused three deaths and a permanent shutdown.

Moreover, there is also the problem of waste materials. Some of those waste materials have toxic effects for as long as 150,000 years!

The one example given in the first fragment is unpersuasive. Has there been only one? If not, how many? The emphatic exclamation point in the second fragment does not hide the fact that the fragment is undeveloped. What is being done now with waste materials? Why is it inadequate? The fragment is badly in need of development.

---

## *Test Yourself on*
## Developing Fragmentary Paragraphs

Each of the following sets of sentences is badly in need of further development. Develop each.

1. The more money you make, the more money you spend. When your income is low, you yearn for more—but learn to be restrained. As soon as your salary rises, however, you begin to give in to your desires.
2. Television tends to make us passive. The reason for this is that we have nothing to *do* as television viewers. It's all done for us.
3. Woodworking is not as difficult as it appears. The first thing you need is a reliable set of tools.

---

Development is not a haphazard process, but one that depends upon your topic sentence; that is, it depends on the nature of the subject you are dealing with in your paragraph. Therefore, it is important to be clear about what you're writing and to try to determine the best way to express and develop your thought. Most well-constructed paragraphs follow one or another of the following basic developmental plans, chronological, spatial, or logical (also called expository).

## Chronological Order

Use chronological order wherever time and sequence are important. In the example that follows, the author achieves clarity by constant reference to time, date, and season in an orderly manner.

The *Terra Nova* sailed from London 15th June 1910 and from New Zealand 26th November. She was fearfully overloaded; on deck, as well as the motor-sledges in their huge crates, there were 30 tons of coal in sacks, $2\frac{1}{2}$ tons of petrol in drums, 33 dogs, and 19 ponies. She rode out a bad storm by a miracle. "Bowers and Campbell were standing upon the bridge and the ship rolled sluggishly over until the lee combings of the main hatch were under the sea . . . as a rule, if a ship goes that far over she goes down." It took her thirty-eight days to get to McMurdo Sound, by which time the men were in poor shape. They had slept in their clothes, lucky if they got five hours a night, and had had no proper meals. As soon as they dropped anchor they began to unload the ship. This entailed dragging its cargo over ice floes which were in constant danger of being tipped up by killer whales, a very tricky business, specially when it came to moving ponies, motor-sledges and a pianola. Then they built the Hut which was henceforward to be their home. Scott, tireless himself, always drove his men hard and these things were accomplished in a fortnight. The *Terra Nova* sailed away; she was to return the following summer, when it was hoped that the Polar party would be back in time to be taken off before the freezing up of the sea forced her to leave again. If not, they would be obliged to spend a second winter on McMurdo Sound. Winter, of course, in those latitudes, happens during our summer months and is perpetual night, as the summer is perpetual day. The stunning beauty of the scenery affected the men deeply. When the sun shone the snow was never white, but brilliant shades of pink, blue and lilac; in winter the aurora australis flamed across the sky and the summit of Mount Erebus glowed.

Nancy Mitford, "A Bad Time," from *The Water Beetle**

*Reprinted by permission of A.D. Peters & Co., Ltd.

## Spatial Order

Use spatial order when it is necessary to describe physical reality and the spatial relationships between persons,
things, or parts of things. A spatial ordering can proceed
from inside to outside, top to bottom, up to down, and so
forth. This description of a turtle crossing a road is a
classic one.

The sun lay on the grass and warmed it, and in the shade under
the grass the insects moved, ants and ant lions to set traps for
them, grasshoppers to jump into the air and flick their yellow
wings for a second, sow bugs like little armadillos, plodding
restlessly on many tender feet. And over the grass at the roadside
a land turtle crawled, turning aside for nothing, dragging his
high-domed shell over the grass. His hard legs and yellow-nailed
feet threshed slowly through the grass, not really walking but
boosting and dragging his shell along. The barley beards slid off
his shell, and the clover burrs fell on him and rolled to the
ground. His horny beak was partly open, and his fierce, humorous eyes, under brows like fingernails, stared straight ahead. He
came over the grass leaving a beaten trail behind him, and the
hill, which was the highway embankment, reared up ahead of
him. For a moment he stopped, his head held high. He blinked
and looked up and down. At last he started to climb the embankment. Front clawed feet reached forward but did not touch.
The hind feet kicked his shell along, and it scraped on the grass,
and on the gravel. As the embankment grew steeper and steeper,
the more frantic were the efforts of the land turtle. Pushing hind
legs strained and slipped, boosting the shell along, and the
horny head protruded as far as the neck could stretch. Little by
little the shell slid up the embankment until at last a parapet cut
straight across its line of march, the shoulder of the road, a
concrete wall four inches high. As though they worked indepen-
dently the hind legs pushed the shell against the wall. The head
upraised and peered over the wall to the broad smooth plain of
cement. Now the hands, braced on top of the wall, strained and
lifted, and the shell came slowly up and rested its front end on
the wall. For a moment the turtle rested. A red ant ran into the
shell, into the soft skin inside the shell, and suddenly head and
legs snapped in, and the armored tail clamped in sideways. The
red ant was crushed between body and legs. And one head of
wild oats was clamped into the shell by a front leg. For a long
moment the turtle lay still, and then the neck crept out and the
old humorous frowning eyes looked about and the legs and tail

of immortality is thus more than mere denial of death, and grows out of compelling, life-enhancing imagery of one's involvement in the historical process. This sense of immortality may be expressed *biologically,* by living on through one's sons and daughters and their sons and daughters, extending out into social dimensions (of tribe, organization, people, nation, or even species); *theologically,* in the idea of a life after death or of other forms of spiritual conquest of death; *creatively,* through "works" and influences persisting beyond biological death; *naturally,* through identification with nature, with its infinite extension into time and space; or *transcendentally,* through a feeling-state so intense that time and death disappear.

Roberty Jay Lifton, "The Struggle for Cultural Rebirth,"<br>*Harper's*, April 1973

But who, then, is the desirable man—the patron who will cajole the best out of the writer's brain and bring to birth the most varied and vigorous progeny of which he is capable? Different ages have answered the question differently. The Elizabethans, to speak roughly, chose the aristocracy to write for and the playhouse public. The eighteenth-century patron was a combination of coffee-house wit and Grub Street bookseller. In the nineteenth century the great writers wrote for the half-crown magazines and the leisured classes. And looking back and applauding the splendid results of these different alliances, it all seems enviably simple, and plain as a pike-staff compared with our own predicament—for whom should we write? For the present supply of patrons is of unexampled and bewildering variety. There is the daily Press, the weekly Press, the monthly Press; the English public and the American public; the best-seller public and the worst-seller public; the high-brow public and the red-blood public; all now organised self-conscious entities capable through their various mouthpieces of making their needs known and their approval or displeasure felt. Thus the writer who has been moved by the sight of the first crocus in Kensington Gardens has, before he sets pen to paper, to choose from a crowd of competitors the particular patron who suits him best. It is futile to say, "Dismiss them all; think only of your crocus," because writing is a method of communication; and the crocus is an imperfect crocus until it has been shared. The first man or the last may write for himself alone, but he is an exception and an unenviable one at that, and the gulls are welcome to his works if the gulls can read them.

Virginia Woolf, "The Patron and the Crocus,"<br>from *The Common Reader*

## 5. *Process analysis*

Process analysis is a method of separating some complex whole into its component parts—usually a mechanical process. A paragraph that explains in detail how something functions or how a machine is put together is filled with explanatory power. Process analysis is also useful in giving directions on how to do something, and paragraphs using this method of development frequently employ chronological or spatial order.

These solitary wasps are beautiful and formidable creatures. Most species are either a deep shiny blue all over, or deep blue with rusty wings. The largest have a wing span of about four inches. They live on nectar. When excited, they give off a pungent odor—a warning that they are ready to attack. The sting is much worse than that of a bee or common wasp, and the pain and swelling last longer. In the adult stage the wasp lives only a few months. The female produces but a few eggs, one at a time at intervals of two or three days. For each egg the mother must provide one adult tarantula, alive but paralyzed. The mother wasp attaches the egg to the paralyzed spider's abdomen. Upon hatching from the egg, the larva is many hundreds of times smaller than its living but helpless victim. It eats no other food and drinks no water. By the time it has finished its single Gargantuan meal and become ready for wasphood, nothing remains of the tarantula but its indigestible chitinous skeleton.

Alexander Petrunkevich, "The Spider and the Wasp,"
*Scientific American*, August 1952

The three absolute acts of the tragedy are first the entry of the bull when the picadors receive the shock of his attacks and attempt to protect their horses with their lances. Then the horses go out and the second act is the planting of the banderillos. This is one of the most interesting and difficult parts but among the easiest for a new bull fight fan to appreciate in technique. The banderillos are three-foot, gaily colored darts with a small fish hook prong in the end. The man who is going to plant them walks out into the arena alone with the bull. He lifts the banderillos at arm's length and points them toward the bull. Then he calls "Toro! Toro!" The bull charges and the banderillero rises to his toes, bends in a curve forward and just as the bull is about to hit him drops the darts into the bull's hump just back of his horns.

*By-Line: Ernest Hemingway*, ed. William White

### 6. *Causal analysis*

This method too separates something into its component parts, but here the something is some specific event or other human situation, and the aim of the writer is to suggest the causes that produced some particular result.

We are the first society in which parents expect to learn from their children. Such a topsy-turvy situation has come about at least in part because, unlike the rest of the world, ours is an immigrant society, and for immigrants the *only* hope is in the kids. In the Old Country, hope was in the father, and how much family wealth he could accumulate and pass along to his children. In the growth pattern of America and its ever-expanding frontier, the young man was ever advised to Go West; the father was ever inheriting from his son: the topsy-turviness was built-in from the beginning. In short, a melting pot needs a spoon. Kids' Country may be the inevitable result.

> Shana Alexander, "Kids' Country,"
> *Newsweek*, December 1972

Now, failure to uphold the law is no less corrupt than violation of the law. And the continuing shame of this country now is the growing number of Americans who fail to uphold and assist enforcement of the law, simply—and ignominiously—out of fear. Fear of "involvement," fear of reprisal, fear of "trouble." A man is beaten by hoodlums in plain daylight and in view of bystanders. These people not only fail to help the victim, but, like the hoodlums, flee before the police can question them. A city official knows of a colleague's bribe but does not report it. A pedestrian watches a car hit a woman but leaves the scene, to avoid giving testimony. It happens every day. And if the police get cynical at this irresponsibility, they are hardly to blame. Morale is a matter of giving support and having faith in one another; where both are lacking, "law" has become a worthless word.

> Marya Mannes, "The Thin Gray Line,"
> *McCall's*, January 1964

---

## *Test Yourself on*
## Understanding Methods of Paragraph Development

A. Which method of development would be most suitable for making a paragraph out of each of the following topic sentences? Give reasons. Then select one topic sentence and develop it into a paragraph.

1. Marijuana is not more harmful than alcohol, though my parents seem to think so.
2. The Guggenheim Museum, from the outside, looks like a bomb shelter.
3. Unexpected things happen to freshmen on this campus.
4. Television commercials don't care what they do as long as they sell, sell, sell.
5. Intelligence is the capacity to face what you do not know how to handle.
6. There are three kinds of English teacher on this campus.
7. Lung cancer is a result of certain environmental pressures on the respiratory system.
8. My troubles with mathematics began in 1982.
9. The secret to treating raw wood to look like fine furniture finishing is patience.
10. Foreign cars and American cars differ in crucial ways.

B. Write three separate paragraphs using the topic sentence below. In the first, explain *why* this change has taken place. In the second, explain *how* these attitudes have changed. Finally, in the third, compare and contrast two sets of attitudes toward teachers: the ones you had in high school and the ones you have now.

*My attitudes toward teachers have changed since I came to college.*

---

## Parallel Construction

Wherever grammatical structures—words, phrases, or clauses—are repeated, we have a parallel construction.

**Words**  Jenny *whispered* in David's ear, *touched* his arm, *winked* at him, then *walked* away. (parallel verbs)
*Impetuously, bravely, daringly,* Colin drove to the hoop and stuffed the ball through. (parallel adverbs)

**Phrases** *To think clearly, to act ethically, to love completely —*
these were Dierdre's goals. (parallel infinitive phrases)

**Clauses** *When you have learned who you are, when you have
experienced the world, when you have come to respect others —*
then you are entitled to be called an adult. (parallel adverbial
clauses)

The advantage of parallel construction is that it binds
ideas together and allows readers to grasp each point
because they have been prepared for the second and
third by the *form of the first.* You may not want to use
parallel construction to the extent that it is used in the
above examples, but ineffective writing results when you
*begin* to use parallel construction and then abandon it.
You must be sure to either use it or avoid it—and not use
it partly, as in the following examples:

                                    1            2                  3
**Partly Parallel** Melissa was *bright, beautiful,* and *a person
who had great consideration for others.* (1. single-word adjective; 2. single-word adjective; 3. noun + adjective clause)
**Revised** Melissa was *bright, beautiful,* and *considerate.*

                                                          1
**Partly Parallel** The Governor favored *a revised income tax*
             2                                 3
*schedule, simplifying the criminal code,* and *less money for
judges of the State Supreme Court.* (1. adjective, compound
noun phrase; 2. gerund phrase; 3. adjective + noun + prepositional phrase)
**Revised** The Governor favored *a revised income tax schedule
a simplified criminal code,* and *a lowered salary for State
Supreme Court judges.*

The problem with the partly parallel examples above is
that they set up an expectation in the mind of the reader
and then don't fulfill that expectation. The result is
confusion.

In order to avoid incomplete parallels, you should
make sure that whatever grammatical construction follows the word *and* (or any of the other coordinating
conjunctions) in your sentence construction also precedes it. If you have a construction like *. . . and a policeman,* you would need a noun to parallel *a policeman*

before the word *and* (*a doctor and a policeman*). Similarly, if one of your sentences contained ... *and which
always haunted him,* you would need the same kind of
construction *before* the word *and* (*which always followed him and which always haunted him*).

---

### *Test Yourself on*
### Filling in the Other Side of *and, but,*
### *or* Constructions

What could go on the other side of the words *and, or,*
and *but* in each of the following examples?

1. ... and snake oil.
2. ... and whose mother came from Italy.
3. ... and that hasn't been seen since.
4. ... but who thinks of himself as a gentleman.
5. ... and lovely.
6. ... or to live longer.
7. ... but never wanted to live there.
8. ... but hates whiskey.
9. ... and tries everything.
10. ... or went alone.

---

### *Test Yourself on*
### Making Constructions Parallel

Now that you have had some practice in making the
sides of coordinating conjunctions parallel, try your skill
at whole sentences. First locate the coordinating conjunction in each of the following examples. Then, if the
constructions on either side of the conjunctions are not
parallel, revise the sentences to make them parallel. If
the sentence is correct, write C beside it. Make sure you
underline all parallel constructions, whether or not the
sentence is correct.

1. _____ The purpose of this meeting is to review past procedures, recognize what we have to do in the future, and so that we can get to know each other better.

2. _____ This term I learned math, biology, and how to write a term paper.

3. _____ My mother is neat, patient, and a person who is filled with pride.

4. _____ Bob liked falling in love and to write poetry.

5. _____ She was happy but nervous.

6. _____ Whenever I visit my relatives, I'm nervous, exhausted, and I feel like I am disoriented.

7. _____ Traveling in Italy makes you aware of art and the food is wonderful for your taste buds when you eat there.

8. _____ Having a sprained ankle and then to try to walk is murder.

9. _____ Joking with my friends, swimming in the lake, and horseback riding in the woods—those are the things I like to do on my vacation.

10. _____ At the party, I spoke to a sociologist, a detective, a stockbroker, and this man who repaired television sets.

11. _____ Because of excessive welfare spending, poor accounting practices, and the fact that we borrowed and borrowed and borrowed, New York City experienced a financial crisis.

12. _____ My professor told me to go slowly with the material rather than trying to learn all of it at once.

13. _____ It was decided by the committee that we would hold a Memorial Day picnic and increase our dues.

14. _____ People who don't travel widely but want to enlarge their experience need to learn about other people in another way.

15. _____ The rules for graduate students apply neither to you nor me.

---

# Parentheses

*Parentheses* is the plural of the word *parenthesis. Parentheses* signifies *both* curved marks: (   ). Parentheses are used to set off material that is not absolutely essential to complete the meaning of the sentence pattern but that supplements or further explains a part or parts of that sentence. We call such material *parenthetical elements;* these elements can be appositives or other nonrestrictive phrases or clauses.

But since parentheses, commas, and dashes can all be used to set off parenthetical material, you should first note the difference between these marks when they are used for this purpose.

*Dashes* are used either to set off material that is emphatic or to set off material you decide to emphasize. In other words, using dashes gives emphasis; your material should match the emphasis given.

My friend Lewis—*who drove his pickup into the lake last night*—is a complete madman.
What happened last night—*if you believe him*—was an accident.

*Commas* are used to signal that the parenthetical material is more nearly a part of the sentence than if the material were set off by dashes or parentheses—that the material interrupts the flow of thought only slightly.

The signs of the storm, *lightning and thunder,* frightened him.
You can, *if you wish,* rent a cheaper model.

*Parentheses* signal that the enclosed material is not emphatic and that its nature is supplemental.

Channel 4 is owned by the National Broadcasting Company (*a subsidiary of the Radio Corporation of America*).
Most students pay heavy tuition charges (*though there are a few exceptions*).

As you can see, the choice of which marks to use can be a matter of taste. Nevertheless, the following general rules are good guidelines.

**1.** Use parentheses to set off material that is not essential to complete the meaning of the sentence and that is unemphatic and supplemental. Such material may include words, phrases, whole sentences, or even several sentences.

1. At that time, the vice-president (Garner) had very little power.
2. At that time, the vice-president (Garner, a gruff old man from Texas) had very little power.
3. At that time, the vice-president had very little power. (Garner, a gruff old man from Texas, understood this well.)
4. At that time, the vice-present had very little power. (Garner, a gruff old man from Texas, understood this well. It was, perhaps, Garner's understanding of the situation that later prompted Lyndon Johnson, his fellow Texan, to try to raise the status of the office.) He presided over the Senate, a largely ceremonial post, and greeted visiting dignitaries from abroad.

Note that in the third example, a full sentence is enclosed within the parentheses. In such cases, *the period comes before the closing parenthesis.* Note that there *is* a space before the opening parenthesis, but there *is no* space between the opening parenthesis and the first word or between the period and closing parenthesis.

Another point about punctuation with parentheses: *where the parenthetical material is a part of the sentence, the period goes outside the closing parenthesis.*

At that time, the vice-president was Garner (a gruff old man from Texas).

*Note:* Do not use parentheses for essential material.

**Wrong** The men were dog tired; the lieutenant (*therefore*) called a halt to the march.
**Wrong** I'm going to keep on taking that examination (*until I pass it*).

**2.** Use parentheses to set off cross-references and figures denoting life-span.

It will become clear later (*in Chapter 7*) that James Joyce (*1882–1941*) was not exactly kind to his brother.

---

## *Test Yourself on* Using Parentheses Correctly

Some of the sentences below have parenthetic material correctly set off by dashes and commas; next to these sentences, write C. However, some of the sentences should have parentheses *instead* of the commas or dashes; change these. In addition, where you see essential material enclosed within parentheses, eliminate those parentheses.

1. _____ I think, if you don't mind, I'll take my nap now.

2. _____ Charley—a good friend of mine—left for California yesterday.

3. _____ The power of the media—with their enormous audience—is hard to overestimate.

4. _____ We whizzed along the highway, all of us on our bicycles, enjoying the breezes and the sunshine.

5. _____ The author—authors?—of Genesis spoke the stories with reverence.

6. _____ I won't go to the party (unless you come with me).

7. _____ He had (probably) a logical mind.

8. _____ The magician—a most amazing sleight-of-hand artist—had us all on the edges of our seats.

9. _____ Then it rolled through the grating, my last coin, and I was flat broke.

10. _____ He was born in 1235, or somewhat earlier, and died about forty-five years later.

---

## Passive Voice

See **Voice.**

## Period

The period, which is sometimes (especially in British usage) called the _full stop,_ is a mark of end punctuation. It signals the end of a _declarative_ or mildly _imperative_ sentence and is used in most abbreviations. (Spaced periods ( ... ) also have special uses; see **Ellipsis.**)

**1.** Use a period to end declarative and imperative sentences. A declarative sentence makes an assertion; an imperative sentence issues a command.

I am going to the movies tonight. (Declarative.)
Go to the movies tonight. (Imperative—this one a very mild command.)

_Note:_ For strongly imperative sentences, consider using the exclamation point. Example: _Get out of my sight!_

**2.** Use a period after an abbreviation.

Mr. Buckley          Ms.
Dr. Brody            U.S.
Ph.D.                a.m.

# Person

See **Verbs** and **Shifts.**

# Possessives

See Nouns, Pronouns; **Apostrophe, Case,** and **Pronoun References.**

# Pronoun References

A pronoun sometimes does its work by referring back to another word or group of words. What the pronoun refers back to is called its *antecedent.*

The following guidelines will be useful to you in making sure that your pronoun references are clear and consistent.

**1.** Pronouns must *agree* in person and number with their antecedents.

**A.** In referring to persons, places, and things, use pronouns that agree in person and number.

I saw *John* yesterday; *he* seemed depressed.
The *dog* wagged *its* tail.
When I saw the *Smiths* yesterday, *they* were on *their* way to the movies.

**B.** Use a singular pronoun in referring to antecedents like the following: *any, anybody, anyone, each, every, everybody, everyone, either, neither, man, woman, person, nobody, none, someone, somebody.* In informal writing, we frequently find plural pronouns referring to some of these, but formal usage requires the singular.

**Formal**   *Everybody* has *his* dreams.
**Informal**   *Everybody* has *their* dreams.

**Formal**   Mathematics requires *each* of us to use *his* intellect.
**Informal**   Mathematics requires *each* of us to use *our* intellect.

C. In the case of a collective noun used as an antecedent, use a singular pronoun if you are thinking of the group as a unit; use a plural pronoun if you are thinking of the members separately.

The *team* raised *its* batting average by ten points.
The *team* came through when *their* fans began urging *them* on.

D. When two or more antecedents are joined by *and*, *or*, or *nor*, the following rules apply: (1) When two or more singular antecedents are joined by *and*, use a plural pronoun; (2) when two or more singular antecedents are joined by *or* or *nor*, use a singular pronoun; (3) when one of the antecedents joined by *or* or *nor* is singular and one plural, use a pronoun that agrees with the nearer of the two.

1. *Tom* and *Lisa* did *their* work together.
2. Neither *Lisa* nor *April* has *her* hat on.
3. Neither the *conductor* nor the *musicians have* held *their* rehearsal.

---

## *Test Yourself on* Pronoun Agreement

Make all the pronouns in the following sentences agree with their antecedents according to the principles of formal usage.

1. Anybody who knows their music would know the Rolling Stones.

2. The committee did their work in private.

3. Neither the new professor nor the first-year students knew his way around the campus.

4. Anybody who likes their morning coffee cold is peculiar.

5. When the team scored a touchdown, the band raised its instruments to play.

6. Everybody has a right to their own opinion in politics.

7. If a drugstore or a supermarket opened in our neighborhood, they would do well.

8. Neither of them could do their homework in the middle of all that noise.

9. Every cook thinks their recipes are best.

10. None of the students in biology could identify the specimens under their microscope.

---

## More on Pronouns

**2.** Do not use pronouns ambiguously. *Ambiguous* means "able to be understood in more than one way." Therefore, an ambiguous pronoun reference occurs whenever the pronoun you use can refer back to more than one antecedent.

**Ambiguous**  My father told my brother that *he* had to go to Boston. (Who had to go? the father or the brother?)
**Clear**   My father said to my brother, "I have to go to Boston." My father said to my brother, "You have to go to Boston."

**Ambiguous**  When Donna looked at Lisa, *she* blushed. (Who blushed? Donna or Lisa?)
**Clear**   When she looked at Lisa, Donna blushed.
**Clear**   Donna blushed when she looked at Lisa.
**Clear**   Lisa blushed when Donna looked at her.
**Clear**   When Donna looked at Lisa, Lisa blushed.

**3.** Do not use pronouns with remote references. A pronoun that is too far away from what it refers to is said to have a remote reference (or antecedent).

**Remote**   As for the Concorde, we did everything we could to stop the plane from landing at Kennedy Airport, including sending people out to picket the field and writing letters to our congressmen. *It* is obscene. (The *it*, referring to the airplane, is too far away, too remote, from its antecedent, *Concorde.*)
**Revised**   As for the Concorde, *it* is obscene, and we did everything we could to stop the plane from landing at Kennedy Airport, including sending people out to picket the field and writing letters to our congressmen.

**Remote**   Billy gave up smoking and, as a result, temporarily gained a lot of weight. *It* was very bad for his health.

**Revised**   Billy gave up the smoking *that* was very bad for his health and, as a result, temporarily gained a lot of weight.

**4.** Do not use pronouns with faulty broad reference. A pronoun used with broad reference is one that refers back to a whole idea rather than a single noun. When the pronoun refers back to more than one idea, it has a faulty broad reference. The vague use of *this, that,* and *which* most frequently results in faulty broad references.

**Faulty Broad Reference**   He planted a line of tall shrubbery to stop people from looking into his garden. *That* is not easy. (What is not easy? the planting or stopping the people?)

Sometimes a loosely used *this* or *that* can be made clear by converting the pronoun to a determiner and using a noun to make things clear.

**Revised**   He planted a line of tall shrubbery to stop people from looking into his garden. *That job* is not easy. (Now the *job* refers clearly to the *planting.*)

**Faulty Broad Reference**   He spent his time getting help with his income tax forms, *which* his wife considered unfair. (What does she consider unfair? that he spends his time that way? that he gets help? or does she consider the forms unfair?)

In faulty references involving a *which* clause, it is sometimes necessary to recast the sentence, getting rid of *which*.

**Revised**   His wife considered it unfair that he spent his time getting help with his income tax forms.

Now we can see that what the wife considers unfair is the way in which he spends his time.

Despite the fact that writers are prone to errors of broad pronoun reference, the use of the broad pronoun reference is not prohibited. Frequently, such references are perfectly appropriate—where they are perfectly clear.

I'll take the cash to the bank. *That's* the safest thing.
We need to save money. *This* is the only way to stay solvent.

**5.** Do not use pronouns with implied antecedents; that is, do not let the pronoun refer to a noun or a whole idea that is absent from the sentence. The vague use of *it, you, they,* and *them* most frequently causes this error.

**Implied Antecedent**   *It* says in my notebook that China has the biggest population.
**Revised**   My notebook says that China has the biggest population.

**Implied Antecedent**   I could have supplied the answer if I had thought about *it.*
**Revised**   I could have supplied the answer if I had thought about the question.

**Implied Antecedent**   In some colleges, *you're* not permitted to live off campus.
**Revised**   In some colleges, students are not permitted to live off campus.

**Implied Antecedent**   *They* have mostly an agricultural economy in Southeast Asia.
**Revised**   The economy in Southeast Asia is mostly agricultural.

**Implied Antecedent**   I go to Yankee Stadium because I like to watch *them* play.
**Revised**   I go to Yankee Stadium because I like to watch the Yankees play.

## *Test Yourself on* Pronoun References

Some of the sentences below have perfectly clear pronoun references; next to these, write C. Others, however, have faulty pronoun references; correct these, even if you have to recast the sentence.

1. _____ The Montreal Canadiens were soundly beaten by the Boston Bruins on their home ice last night.

2. \_\_\_\_ He carried a briefcase, which looked as if it had cost him a hundred dollars.

3. \_\_\_\_ During the Civil War, they struggled over the question of slavery.

4. \_\_\_\_ The idea that Fred broached to Eddie was one that he had thought of some years earlier.

5. \_\_\_\_ For the first time in months, we went up to the farm last weekend; we cleaned out the barn, pruned the apple trees, and swam in the creek. It was wonderful.

6. \_\_\_\_ Driving through Yellowstone, you are likely to see a bear.

7. \_\_\_\_ Alice's mother died when she was twenty-three.

8. \_\_\_\_ Arthur and Hilda came to the wedding in a horse-drawn carriage, which somewhat amused the other guests.

9. \_\_\_\_ Bill and Joanna are broke, but Arthur is rolling in it.

10. \_\_\_\_ Stuart started out to study medicine because society needed them.

11. \_\_\_\_ A great many service professionals do not offer their clients a touch of humanity but only a rule for efficient living. It is a great necessity.

12. \_\_\_\_ Lee stole things because he had no other way of earning a living, and he went to jail for it. It was a shame.

13. \_\_\_\_ I dropped a pebble in the gas tank and heard no splash. That proved we were out of gas.

14. _____ I never buy clothes at Barney's because they are expensive.

15. _____ Petit balanced himself 1,200 feet above the ground, which is a hard thing to do.

---

# Question Mark

The question mark is used to end a sentence that asks a direct question.

Where is Malcolm going?
He asked where Malcolm was going. (indirect question)
*Did he* ask where Malcolm is going? (a direct question, indicated by the italicized phrase)

Question marks can also convert declarative sentences into questions.

Betty went to the football game? (Imagine this sentence spoken with the emphasis on *football.*)
Dinitia loves David? (emphasis on *David*)
Colin and Frances are getting married? (emphasis on *married*)

An imperative sentence may also be converted into a question.

Pass the sugar?
Give you the newspaper?

A question mark is used between parentheses to indicate the writer's uncertainty about some detail.

My mother was born in 1893(?) and died in 1972.
Shakespeare was born in 1564 on April 23(?).

It is also permissible, for emphasis, to place a question mark after each question in a series.

Did you tell him you loved him? get interested in his work? try to work out your differences?

Note that this example constitutes a single sentence

and that there is no mark of punctuation or capital letter following the question marks. For treatment of the question mark in quotations, see **Quotation Marks.**

---

## *Test Yourself on*
### the Use of the Question Mark

A. Convert each of the following into questions by placing a question mark in the proper place; in some, you may have to change the pronouns.

1. Marshak ran the school.
2. Give me your pen.
3. Take off your coat.
4. George likes apples.
5. Fred likes parties.

B. Some of the following sentences are properly punctuated with question marks and some are not. Next to the correct sentences, write C. Supply question marks in the others where needed.

1. _____ He asked me if I would go to the ball game with him.

2. _____ He asked me, "Would you come with me to the ball game."

3. _____ Did he take you seriously read your paper give you a tutoring session grade you fairly.

4. _____ He mentioned to me—did I understand him correctly—that he was going to Scotland next summer.

5. _____ He was born in 1882 (  ) and must have been about thirty-five (  ) when the Great War began.

# Quotation Marks

Quotation marks (" ") always appear twice: once at the beginning of the quoted material, once at the end. *Note:* Don't forget that second pair; proofread your paper to make sure you haven't omitted the second pair, because confusion always results when you do forget.

Quotation marks are used in the following cases:

**1.** Use quotation marks wherever you quote directly someone's *written or spoken* words.

Declaring themselves openly in awe of that period, Quinn and Dolan wrote: "In the sixth decade of the twentieth century America entered its middle age, and discovered its youth." They conceived of this discovery as violent, radical, dangerous.

"Well," Norman said, "I wouldn't be surprised if Nancy took off for California and surprised us all."

The first example offers a quotation of someone's (in this case Quinn and Dolan's) *written* words. In the second example, a writer quotes what *Norman* has *said* about *Nancy.* Take careful note of the position of the quotation marks and the position of the other punctuation marks *in relation to the quotation marks.*

**2.** Although you use a pair of regular (double) quotation marks (" ") to enclose direct quotations, use a pair of single quotation marks (' ') to enclose a quote within a quote.

"Frankly," Lillian said, "Richard answered my inquiry with 'no comment, I'm busy.' "
Louise said, "The answer Donald gave was 'I don't know.' "

**3.** Quoting dialogue, conversation between two or more people, requires certain special conventions: (1) Use a separate paragraph when reporting each person's speech; (2) include in the same paragraph such phrases as *he said, she replied,* or *he answered;* (3) punctuate according to the practice in this sample passage; note especially that the first word of a quotation is always capitalized if the quoted material itself is a full sentence.

The policeman came running up to me, and I could tell he was furious.

"Do you own this robot?" he asked.

I was startled. "I never saw him before in my life!"

"Then how come," said the policeman, "he just winked at you?"

Sure enough, the robot's green-lit eye was blinking at me. "I think he's just friendly," I replied.

"He just leaked oil on my shoes," said the policeman, menacingly.

"Am I my robot's keeper?" I pleaded.

**4.** Use quotation marks for titles of short stories, essays, short poems, songs, articles from periodicals, book chapters, or other parts of books.

"The Cask of Amontillado" (short story by Poe)
"Soldiers Home" (short story by Hemingway)
"Politics and the English Language" (essay by Orwell)
"The Heavy Bear" (poem by Delmore Schwartz)
"Yesterday" (song by the Beatles)
"Nefarious Times We Live In" (magazine article)
In Chapter 4, "The Myth of the Poet," the author examines a modern dilemma.
Modern socialism is attacked in Part 2, "The Return."

**5.** Use quotation marks to give special emphasis to a word or a phrase or where you speak of a word *as* a word.

Johnny had a "system" for beating the dealers in Las Vegas.
He had a "hands-off" attitude.
A "bad dude" is slang for a "splendid chap." (*Note:* Italics may also be used in cases like this one.)

**6.** Do *not* use quotation marks for indirect quotations. An indirect quotation is one that reports what a speaker said but not necessarily in the speaker's exact words.

David asked Dinitia why she wanted to earn a Ph.D. (indirect)
David asked Dinitia, "Why do you want to earn a Ph.D.?" (direct)

Paul said that he liked my book. (indirect)
Paul said, "I like your book." (direct)

## Summary on Quotation Marks with Other Punctuation

**1.** Place commas and periods *inside* quotation marks.

**With Direct Quotation**   "I wanted to quit early," he said, "but I couldn't think of an excuse." (The only mark *outside* is the one used to separate *he said* from what follows those words.)

**With Commas Used for Emphasis**   Police work is an example of a "high-risk occupation," and policemen are paid accordingly.

He had "the common touch."

**2.** Place colons and semicolons *outside* quotation marks.

He had "the common touch"; consequently, people in all walks of life responded warmly to him.

Tom said that to have a good time he needed the right "equipment": congenial company, enough leisure, and peace of mind.

**3.** Place question marks and exclamation points inside quotation marks if they are actually part of the quote; place them outside if they are not.

She leaned out the window and shouted "Fire!"
Did you say "I don't know"?

*Note* that although the exclamation point in the first example applies to "Fire" and the question mark in the second applies to the whole sentence, neither sentence takes any additional punctuation marks at the end.

## Misuse of Quotation Marks

Quotation marks should not be used for the following purposes:

**1.** Do not make a practice of overusing quotation marks for emphasis.

**Inappropriate**   The cowboys in the movie were strong "men."
**Inappropriate**   I thought Al was a "wise guy."
**Inappropriate**   People like Richard are a "dime a dozen."

The first example needs no quotation marks around *men* (or *strong*) to convey its message; the quotation marks in the third example just point up a tired expression which should not have been used in the first place, and the quotation marks in the second are better left out too—though the expression *wise guy* is also trite by now.

**2.** Do not use quotation marks as an excuse to include an unacceptable slang expression in a piece of formal writing. If the slang expression is appropriate, use it without quotation marks; if it is not, do not use it at all.

**Inappropriate** At that point, President Ford simply "flipped out" and pardoned Nixon.
**Inappropriate** Most of the patients at the clinic are children who have "gone ape."

**Appropriate** He was displaying a common twentieth-century *hangup:* paranoia.
**Appropriate** The carnival atmosphere can only be described as *raunchy.*

**3.** Do not use quotation marks to excuse using a word that does not say precisely what you mean.

**Imprecise** My sister used to "get" me about the braces on my teeth.
**Precise** My sister used to *tease* me about the braces on my teeth.

**Imprecise** The cards in the library are kept in a wooden "box."
**Precise** The cards in the library are kept in a *card catalog.*

---

## *Test Yourself on* the Use of Quotation Marks

A. Some of the following sentences contain direct and some indirect quotations. Change the direct quotations to indirect ones, and change the indirect quotations to direct ones.

1. The student said that he considered me one of the best professors in the English Department.

2. "Judy's ceramics are elegant," said Mark.
3. Matt said, "In my opinion, Donna's a talented actress."
4. Fred said the policeman asked him why he was speeding.
5. Marian told Jean she wanted to see her over Easter.
6. Henry reminded Mike that they were brothers.

B. Some of the following sentences have quotation marks correctly placed. Next to them, write C. The others need quotation marks in one place or another. Supply them.

1. _____ We read a short story called The Killers and our professor said that Hemingway, the author, had been an adolescent loner.

2. _____ In the poem Sailing to Byzantium, what is the significance of the line The salmon-falls, the mackerel-crowded seas?

3. _____ When we say that a recording has a lot of wet, we mean that it contains many echo effects.

4. _____ In a moment of frenzy, Vito wrote: Elephants can be housed in a car garage just as well as in a regular cage.

5. _____ That song Silverbird is a winner.

6. _____ Part 2 of his book is called An Analysis of Urban Problems.

C. Place quotation marks correctly in each of the following sentences.

1. You made a fool of me, Margaret said, and I won't forgive you for it. The name of my article is not Childhood Reams but Childhood Dreams.

2. She had written: I don't care for the climate in the tropics, but when I saw her in Chicago she said, I'm looking forward to visiting Puerto Rico for the second time.

3. Can you lend me a hundred dollars? she asked timidly. Slapping his hand down hard on the table, he replied, I think not, madam. I never saw you before in my life.

4. Imagine, he said, that you are in a strange environment and you are surrounded by alien creatures. What thoughts go through your mind as you try to integrate yourself into this scene? he went on.

5. She said to me, He smirked, you're a loser, and I was startled, to say the least.

6. Who said so? I asked.

---

# Résumé Writing

A résumé (pronounced *rez-uh-may*), also called a data sheet or a vita, is an abbreviated account of your career—education, work experience, personal information, and references—usually prepared for the purpose of applying for jobs.

Prospective employers appreciate a one-page typed document similar in form to the sample résumé below. (If your particular career is long enough to warrant an extra page, don't hesitate to extend the résumé; be sure, however, that the pages are neatly stapled together and that your name and identification are typed across the top of the second page, e.g., "John Williams, Résumé. Page 2.")

Before you begin, it is wise to make a scratch sheet and systematically list everything in the course of your adult life that might be relevant; include whatever you possess by way of skills—the ability to drive a car, run various types of business or farm machinery, swim, play baseball, and so forth. You may not want to list all your skills on the résumé, but you may find that some are worth listing for the particular job you intend to apply for. Don't be modest: list everything; you can always eliminate what seems insubstantial or frivolous.

# Sample Résumé

Marion Leopold
7 Eccles Street
New York, New York 10014

Home telephone:(212) 987-3794

PERSONAL INFORMATION

Date of birth: September 8, 1960
Marital status: single; dependents: none
Height: 5'2"  Weight: 115 lbs.
Health: excellent
Physical handicaps: none

EDUCATION

B.A., New York University, June 1982, Magna Cum
Laude

> Major: psychology (60 credits, including
> statistics and psychometrics)
> Related studies: sociology; laboratory in
> social work (20 credits)

Special skills: fluent in spoken and written
Spanish; play piano; hold New
York State Chauffeur's License;
familiar with FORTRAN computer
language

WORK EXPERIENCE

1980-present: Continuously employed part time;
full time summers

Washington Square Center for
Psychological Counseling, New York

Duties: administered TAT and
Stanford-Binet Tests; conducted
intake interviews; research and
recording of patient follow-up
studies

1979-1980:   Part-time employment

Greenwich Village Neighborhood
Counseling Office, New York

Duties: Conducted initial interviews with counseling clients, including the elderly; led group sessions devoted to problem solving

1978–1979:    Full-time employment (nights)

The Open Line Clinic, New York

Duties:    Telephone hot-line counselor; night supervisor

Summers, 1976, 1977, 1978: Full-time employment

Camp Four Winds, Orono, Maine

Duties: counselor, dramatics counselor, waterfront supervisor

REFERENCES

Dr. Harvey Kaplan, Director
Washington Square Center for
  Psychological Counseling
42 West 10th Street
New York, New York 10011

Professor Sarah Gage
Department of Psychology
New York University
New York, New York 10003

Professor Barbara Comen
Department of Sociology
New York University
New York, New York 10003

Dr. Frederic Tuten
Greenwich Village Neighborhood
  Counseling Office
33 Bank Street
New York, New York 10014

## *Education*

In this section, you have the opportunity to include whatever honors you have earned during your school years and to emphasize your significant skills. You may type up several résumés, in fact, listing different skills appropriate to particular (different) jobs you are applying for. Of course, you have the option of listing in this section neither skills nor honors.

### Work experience

This section usually begins with your present employment and works its way backwards in reverse chronological order. Notice that Marion's duties on each of her jobs are carefully and clearly spelled out.

### A note on the form

You may, if you prefer, vary this form somewhat by changing the order of the first three sections (*personal information, education, work experience;* some authorities think employers prefer to see *work experience* before anything else); but the *references* usually come at the end.

Some job counselors think that the applicant's name and address and phone number should be centered for easier visibility. Whatever you choose to do, it is important to see that the information is separated and clearly organized for easy reading.

# Run-On Sentences

A run-on or fused sentence is the name given to an error in punctuation where one or more periods are omitted between sentences (or independent clauses).

My Aunt Bea is a great cook she always provides the food at big family dinners.

The writer of this sentence has failed to recognize that there are two independent clauses in the construction:

My Aunt Bea is a great cook

**and**

she always provides the food at big family dinners.

The run-on sentence is a serious error because it confuses and disorients a reader. Equally serious is the error known as the comma splice or comma fault. This error occurs when the writer separates the two clauses with *only* a comma:

My Aunt Bea is a great cook, she always provides the food at big family dinners.

In both the run-on sentence and the comma splice there is not enough punctuation to link the sentences. There are four ways to punctuate two independent clauses correctly.

**1.** Use a period:

My Aunt Bea is a great cook. She always provides the food at big family dinners.

**2.** Use a comma followed by a coordinating conjunction (*and, but, or, for, so, nor, yet*):

My Aunt Bea is a great cook, *and* she always provides the food at big family dinners.

**3.** Use a semicolon, which would provide enough stopping power to properly separate the clauses but would also indicate that the two clauses are closely related and belong together in the same sentence:

My Aunt Bea is a great cook; she always provides the food at big family dinners.

**4.** Use a semicolon followed by a conjunctive adverb (*anyway, besides, consequently, finally, furthermore, however, instead, meanwhile, moreover, nevertheless, otherwise, subsequently, therefore, thus,* and so forth). The conjunctive adverb acts to relate the two clauses more precisely:

My Aunt Bea is a great cook; *therefore,* she always provides the food at big family dinners. (Note how this additional word brings the clauses into closer relation.)

*Note:* There is usually a comma following the conjunctive adverb, but the strong linkage between the clauses is provided by the semicolon.

### *Test Yourself on*
### Linking Independent Clauses with a Coordinating Conjunction

Try linking the pairs of sentences below with a comma followed by one of the coordinating conjunctions: *and, but, or, nor, for, yet, so.*

1. Charles was head of the Honors Committee. He carried out his duties with high purpose.

2. He couldn't increase the speed of the car. There was a state trooper waiting at the exit.

3. Carla couldn't type. The paper was due the next morning.

4. Foreign policy was a pressing issue. The President knew he had to attack it.

5. He could take the train to Boston. He could stay later and take the air shuttle.

6. He had no money for the bus. He decided to walk.

7. In many ways she annoyed him. He thought he wanted to date her.

8. He thought she was kind. She had done him many favors.

9. The snowmobile was dangerous. He planned to go up the mountain in it.

10. Baseball players work a very long season. They are well paid for it.

11. Roller skates are ugly. They are fun to ride.

12. Prince Charles and Lady Diana are getting married. They are very much in love.

## *Test Yourself on*
## Linking Independent Clauses with a Semi-colon and a Conjunctive Adverb

Try linking the pairs of sentences below with a semi-colon. After you have done so, look at the list of conjunctive adverbs given above and see if the addition of one of those might create a better relation between parts. *Remember:* A comma follows a conjunctive adverb, but the strong link is made by the semicolon.

1. Lucia Ann had confidence in her ability to write. She sat down and wrote a book.
2. Painters have the urge to arrange form, line, color, and mass. They paint pictures working with these principles.
3. Free speech is a precious part of our heritage. We have a whole tradition of freedom and liberty.
4. He had just changed the spark plugs and the points. The car was in good running condition.
5. Arthur's tax refund came on July 25. On August 1, he began his European vacation.
6. His father wrote that he could no longer pay Tom's tuition. Tom had to get a part-time job.
7. Linsey's first novel was well received. Her second work received even greater recognition.
8. Shut the windows during a heavy rainstorm. Your apartment will be flooded.
9. The muscles in his legs were crying out with pain. He pressed on, walking and limping up the trail.
10. He knew he should stay at home and write his paper. He dressed up and went to the dance.

Let us return for a moment to the sentence with which we began this discussion:

My Aunt Bea is a great cook she always provides the food at big family dinners.

A fifth way to correct this run-on sentence is to change one of the independent clauses to a dependent clause— and separate the clauses with a comma.

*Because my Aunt Bea is a great cook,* she always provides the food at big family dinners.

The addition of the word *because* changes the independent clause to a dependent clause and makes a comma the correct punctuation to separate it from the main (independent) clause.

---

### *Test Yourself on*
### Recognizing and Correcting Run-On Sentences and Comma Splices

Some of the sentences below are run-on sentences or comma splices and some are correct. Next to the correct sentences, write C. Correct the other sentences by one or another of the methods discussed in this entry.

1. \_\_\_\_ I love to swim, there is no better exercise.

2. \_\_\_\_ I had to be in California on the 18th, therefore I decided to leave New York on the 12th.

3. \_\_\_\_ Crime does not result from the inborn tendency of individual criminals; rather, it is a complex social problem, having to do with social environment and economic status.

4. \_\_\_\_ Rick Cerone didn't get a base hit, the Yankees won the ball game.

5. _____ Because she had always been careful about money in her youth, she could look foward to a secure old age.

6. _____ The term *arson* should apply to a fire that someone has set even if the fire isn't set deliberately the results are the same.

7. _____ Potential students are no longer flocking to colleges the job market no longer requires so many college graduates.

8. _____ America's oil reserves are nearly depleted what we need now is her reserves of goodwill if we are to solve the energy crisis.

9. _____ Marriages are not made in heaven, divorces are not made in courts.

10. _____ He looks like my brother, he talks like my enemy.

## *Test Yourself on*
## Proofreading to Catch Run-On Sentences and Comma Splices

Read carefully the following paragraphs, and wherever you see a run-on sentence or comma splice, correct it.

Hospitals can really be depressing, it's depressing seeing all those sick people in beds. Of course, some of them get well and go home with their families, but it's depressing knowing that some of them will die in those beds. It doesn't matter hospitals are still depressing places.

The white walls are gloomy, the beds are small and narrow. Some nurses are snobbish and make your stay impossible with their aloofness some of them are so nice you hate to leave. But doctors are so busy that they have no time for you personally, they treat you like an experiment most of the time. As for the food, it too is depressing it's supposed to make you healthy but it really makes you sick just to look at it, even the way it's prepared, the way it looks, causes that depressed feeling.

Some people enter the hospital with a minor illness by the time they have been there a few days, they have a major problem, remember the movie *Hospital* they had it right.

Of course, if you think your stay in the hospital is depressing, you should wait until you leave and get the bill *that's* really depressing!

---

# Semicolon

The semicolon (;) is a mark of internal punctuation that is equivalent to a period in its power to bring an independent clause to an end.

**1.** When it is used to separate independent clauses, it can be used with or without the conjunctive adverb (words such as *nevertheless, moreover, thus, subsequently, consequently, therefore,* and others; see **Conjunctions** for a longer list of these words).

The car wouldn't run on regular gas; *therefore,* we filled the tank with unleaded.
Sid never liked home cooking; he preferred to eat out every night.

---

## *Test Yourself on*
## the Correct Use of the Semicolon

Each of the sentences below is poorly punctuated because it needs a semicolon for one reason or other. Some of those consisting of two independent clauses could also use a conjunctive adverb after the semicolon.

For each sentence, add one or more semicolons where needed.

1. My father thinks I'm lazy he'll only give me my allowance if I do chores around the house.

2. The news we heard on the radio was bad, we went out and got drunk.

3. We could have insisted they cancel the reservation and give us back our deposit so that we could go to another hotel, we could have stayed there without making a fuss and spent three miserable nights sleeping on lumpy mattresses and listening to the sound of the freight trains, or we could have gone quietly away and taken our sleeping bags out to the trailer park and camped underneath the beech trees by the lake.

4. The elevator shakes and rumbles as it goes up, the inspector says it's safe.

5. Christmas is only three weeks away, this year I don't care.

6. Professors care only about their own lectures, their students' producing a great deal of work for them, their status, and their vacations, students care only about snap courses, getting high grades however they can, and enjoying midwinter and summer recesses, administrators care only about budgets, reputations, and no emergencies.

7. He was given a long prison sentence, he had never been arrested before.

8. Six men were killed in an accident, the mine owners instituted stringent safety regulations.

9. I have a six-figure income and a house that's all paid for, I have investments in real estate and oil wells.

10. I exercise too hard and long, I get muscle aches.

---

**2.** The semicolon can also be used to set off items in a series if they are very long or contain other kinds of internal punctuation.

What he objected to in her character was that she was angry, willful and stubborn; that she had no capacity to develop or sustain a professional or vocational interest that would lead to her taking or holding a job; and that she was incapable of having easy relationships with either her peers, her family, or her neighbors.

We were divided into three groups: (1) those who could sing, dance, act, or play a musical instrument; (2) those who had carpentry or other technical skills; and (3) those who had some kind of business experience or advertising and public relations skills.

*Note:* Where you use quotation marks, the semicolon goes outside the closing quotation marks:

He thinks of himself as "progressive"; he voted for Nixon.
Tom said, "Stagecraft is vital to any study of Shakespeare"; he meant it, too.

For more on the semicolon, see also **Fragments** and **Run-on Sentences.**

## Sentence Length and Variety

Variation in the length and kinds of sentences you write helps to avoid giving your readers the impression of monotony. There are a number of ways to achieve this variation in sentence structure and length, but let us first consider what to avoid.

**1.** Avoid writing a series of short, simple sentences. Children write this way, but that is because their minds are not yet developed to the point where they can understand the relations between ideas.

**Weak** We went to the movies. It was a cowboy picture. We bought popcorn. It made noise. The other people were mad. They told us to stop.

**Revised** Because there was a cowboy picture playing, we went to the movies. We bought some popcorn, but we made so much noise eating it that the other patrons were angered and asked us to stop.

The series of weak sentences constitutes a simple example, of the kind a child might write, but there are occasions when more mature writers fall into the same pattern.

**Weak** The house was dark. We walked up the steps. We went through the door. There was a noise. We paused and listened. We decided it was only the wind.

**Revised** The house was dark as we walked up the stairs and through the door. There was a noise, and we paused to listen more carefully, but it was only the wind.

(For further information on combining short sentences into more complex structures, see **Subordination.**)

**2.** Avoid writing long, excessively compounded sentences. By this is meant sentences that join together, willy-nilly, a number of independent clauses using *and* or other coordinating conjunctions.

**Weak** We drove up to the park, but we saw that the gate had been locked for the night, and so we changed our plans and turned around and headed for Warrensburg.

**Revised** As we drove up to the park, we saw that the gate had been locked for the night. Changing our plans, we turned around and headed for Warrensburg. (First independent clause made into a subordinate clause by the use of *as*; third clause is made into a phrase; second and fourth clauses become main clauses of two separate sentences.)

**Weak** He was the faculty adviser of the campus newspaper, and he was a professor in the English Department, but he was never too busy with his duties to consult with students.

**Revised** The faculty adviser of the campus newspaper, who was also a professor in the English Department, was never too busy with his duties to consult with students. (First clause becomes a phrase which is the subject of the new sentence; second clause becomes a subordinate clause; third clause becomes the predicate of the sentence.)

The excessively simple pattern and the badly coordinated pattern have one thing in common—they both present regular independent clauses in the regular order of subject-verb and they present only one type of sentence—the declarative. To achieve variety, you must occasionally interrupt these patterns—by beginning or ending sentences with subordinate structures or by interrupting the sentence itself with an appositive.

## *Test Yourself on*
## Revising Sentences of Monotonous Length

A. Revise the following groups of short sentences.

1. Television commercials are annoying. They insult the intelligence. They waste one's time. They should be banned from the airways.
2. President Reagan is from California. He was an actor there. He was formerly Governor of California. He has brought many business leaders to Washington.
3. She wanted to be a doctor. She studied chemistry. She studied biology. She worked for good grades. She put in long hours. Her senior year arrived. She applied to medical school. She was accepted.
4. The doctor came. He took my temperature. He checked my heart. He took my blood pressure. He prescribed some medicine. Then he said I'd probably recover in a few days.
5. I needed a job. I looked at the want ads. I went to employment agencies. I even visited a number of factories and offices. I got very tired. But I finally landed a job.

B. Revise the following sentences: Eliminate excessive joining together of independent clauses by creating subordinate clauses and phrases.

1. The train entered the station, and I got ready to board but then I found I'd left my bag in the checkroom and I ran back inside the waiting room to get it.

2. *Star Wars* was a very successful movie and broke many box office records and this goes to show that science fiction adventure movies appeal greatly to the American public.
3. There are more than seven million American college students, and most of them believe that they need this education to get better jobs, but the job market is not encouraging for the hopes of these students, and some of them might do better in vocational training.
4. Members of the volunteer fire company are really dedicated and they give much of their time in public service, but they are not appreciated enough and often feel bitter because of this.
5. Soccer is the fastest growing sport in America and now as many as 70,000 fans turn out for one game, but if Pelé hadn't given the sport a boost, things might not have turned out so well for soccer.

## Achieving Sentence Variety

So far we have looked at what to avoid: a series of short simple sentences, and a sentence composed of many independent clauses strung together with coordinating conjunctions. Both types of sentence tend to produce monotony when used exclusively because both begin with the subject of the sentence. This is not a bad thing to do—more than half of your sentences will probably begin that way—but such a practice produces monotony when followed exclusively. Therefore, variety is achieved by changing the order of words in your sentences. Variety is also achieved by occasionally departing from the declarative sentence and using the question or the command. You should undertake these changes with great care, however, since altering the order of words in a sentence always involves a slight alteration of meaning. Choosing the proper alteration is a matter of carefully considering your subject matter and the meaning you want to convey. Here are the principal means of achieving sentence variety.

**1.** Vary the beginnings of your sentences.
Suppose you had one sentence that looks like this:

The miners worked purposefully in the tunnel and they were
  unaware of the storm outside.

**or two that look like this:**

The miners worked purposefully in the tunnel. They were unaware of the storm outside.

**In either case, you could produce variations looking like
these:**

*Working purposefully in the tunnel,* the miners were unaware of
  the storm outside. (beginning with a verbal phrase)
*In the tunnel,* the miners worked purposefully, unaware of the
  storm outside. (beginning with a prepositional phrase)
*Because the miners were working purposefully in the tunnel,*
  they were unaware of the storm outside. (beginning with an
  adverb clause)
*There* were miners working purposefully in the tunnel, unaware
  of the storm outside. (beginning with an expletive)
*But* the miners worked purposefully in the tunnel, unaware of
  the   storm   outside.   (beginning   with   a   coordinating
  conjunction)
*And* the miners worked purposefully in the tunnel, unaware of
  the storm outside. (Beginnings with coordinating conjunctions are perfectly acceptable, but usually the meaning of the
  sentence depends on something that has gone before.)

**2.** Reverse the usual order of subject-verb or subject-
verb-object. But to do this is to create a distinctly
emphatic order, and you should do so only where your
aim is to achieve such emphasis.

| **Subject-Verb** | **Verb-Subject** |
|---|---|
| The mouse ran up the wall. | Up the wall ran the mouse. |
| Mike's letter rested in the mailbox. | In the mailbox rested Mike's letter. |

| **Subject-Verb-Object** | **Object-Subject-Verb** |
|---|---|
| Joanna loves pizza. | Pizza Joanna loves. |
| I never saw him. | Him I never saw. |

**3.** Occasionally use a question or a command instead
of a declarative sentence, but only when it is appropriate
to do so.

**Imperative (command)** *Imagine a fine tapestry,* interwoven with various attractively colored threads, and you will have a picture of the diversity and beauty in the fabric of American life.

**Question** *What is the purpose of an education?* One purpose is to train the mind to perceive fine distinctions.

---

## *Test Yourself on* Achieving Sentence Variety

Revise the following sentences by revising their beginnings.

1. The car had broken down the night before, and they had to take the bus to school.
2. The Republican Party held a fund-raiser at the Holiday Inn, and it attracted a surprising number of young people.
3. His grades were poor, and his scholarship money was almost gone, and he knew he had to do something.
4. The rescue team worked all night at the site of the cave-in, and they were unable to stop for dinner.
5. Readers with lively imaginations read *The Hobbit* and project themselves into its adventurous moments.
6. Governments are less inclined to give in to hijackers' demands these days, but hijackings continue anyway.
7. He knew he would have to save money regularly for next year's tuition, and he opened a savings account and began to make regular deposits.
8. Nobody knew where the cat had gone, but everybody began searching furiously.
9. Big-time professional sports can accommodate very few athletes, but many American youngsters still dream of a career in the big leagues.
10. Inflation has made money worth less, and it is more expensive to live in the United States than it used to be.

# Shifts

When you begin a sentence by saying "He *begged* and *pleaded* for the loan and ..." the reader immediately tunes in to *begged* and *pleaded* as verbs in the past tense. The reader's expectation is that if any other verb appears in the sentence, it too will be in the past tense. So that if the sentence is completed with "... *asks* the bank officer to have some sympathy" (present tense verb), the reader will be shocked, disappointed, and confused because you have *shifted* gears.

It is not easy, but it is absolutely essential, to maintain the kind of consistency that is missing in the above example. In fact, both beginning and experienced writers shift gears in a number of different ways. A writer should understand that achieving consistency requires consistent proofreading—until they are sure they are incapable of producing the various kinds of shifts.

Reread carefully the sentence you have just read (beginning with "A writer"). Notice that the sentence begins with a *singular* subject, *writer*, but that after the dash the second and fifth words, *they*, are plural pronouns. Here we see another kind of shift, a shift in *number*. We can also see shifts in *tense* (as in the first example given in this entry), *person, mood, voice,* and *point of view*. Below is a discussion of each kind of shift.

## Tense

Perhaps no other shift is so annoying to a reader as this one, because a verb carries not only meaning but a sense of time, and the writer who uses verb tenses inconsistently interferes with the reader's sense of a consistent time pattern.

**Inconsistent**   In the movie *It's My Turn*, Jill Clayburgh *plays* a mathematics professor. She *went* to her father's wedding and *had met* there Michael Douglas, who *played* a former baseball player. Eventually, after a series of delightful romantic adventures, they *get* together.

**Consistent**   In the movie *It's My Turn*, Jill Clayburgh *plays* a mathematics professor. She *goes* to her father's wedding and *meets* there Michael Douglas, who *plays* a former baseball player. Eventually, after a series of delightful romantic adventures, they *get* together.

**Inconsistent**   When I *go* to the seashore for my vacation, I *went* to the beach right away because I *loved* to swim. I *see* the lifeguard and I *asked* him it if *was* all right to swim. *Jaws makes* me frightened to go in the water.

**Consistent**   When I *went* to the seashore for my vacation, I *went* to the beach right away because I *love* to swim. I *saw* the lifeguard and I *asked* him if it *was* all right to swim. *Jaws made* me frightened to go in the water.

## Person

The English verb system recognizes three *persons:* the first person (*I* refuse, *we* refuse), the second person (*you* refuse [both singular and plural]), and the third person (*he, she,* or *it* refuses, *they* refuse). Most shifts in person occur because writers use the second person (*you*) carelessly. But that is not the only problem.

**Inconsistent**   *People* shouldn't expect to be dependent all their lives. *You* have to take care of *yourself* in adult life.

**Consistent**   *People* shouldn't expect to be dependent all their lives. *They* have to take care of *themselves* in adult life.

**Inconsistent**   When *you* have a cold, *one* should get plenty of rest and drink fluids.

**Consistent**   When *you* have a cold, *you* should get plenty of rest and drink fluids.

## Number

Errors in consistency can happen when writers begin with a singular noun and shift to a plural pronoun—or vice versa.

**Inconsistent**   The American *medical student* abroad *has* special problems because *they* have to do *their* work in a foreign language.

**Consistent**   American *medical students* abroad *have* special problems because *they* have to do *their* work in a foreign language.

**Inconsistent**   Business is so good at the U.S. Time Company that *no* one loses *their* job there.
**Consistent**   Business is so good at the U.S. Time Company that *no one* loses *his* job there.

**Inconsistent**   *Lawyers* have an easy life, because every time *he* goes into court *he* makes a fat fee.
**Consistent**   *Lawyers* have an easy life, because every time *they* go into court *they* make fat fees.

## Voice

Once you have begun to use the active voice in a sentence, do not shift to the passive voice, and vice versa. (See also **Voice**.)

**Inconsistent**   We *leave* for the beach at 8 o'clock, *swim* from 9:30 to 11, and lunch *is eaten* at 12.
**Consistent**   We *leave* for the beach at 8 o'clock, *swim* from 9:30 to 11, and *eat* lunch at 12.

**Inconsistent**   *Dig* a hole for the seeds, *drop* them in and cover them with loose soil, and then the ground *is lightly watered.*
**Consistent**   *Dig* a hole for the seeds, *drop* them in and cover them with loose soil, and then *water* the ground lightly.

## Mood

Do not shift from the indicative to the subjunctive mood, or vice versa. Maintain consistency by sticking with one or the other, bearing in mind that in formal writing the subjunctive is preferred where it is called for. The indicative mood is used for statements of fact or other kinds of assertions or questions; the subjunctive mood is used for statements contrary to fact or those expressing possibility or potential.

**Inconsistent**   If I *were* a rock star and I *was* making a lot of money, I'd give a lot of free concerts.
**Consistent**   If I *were* a rock star and I *were* making a lot of money, I'd give a lot of free concerts.

**Inconsistent**   The Red Cross representative prefers that the donations *be* given by check and that the amounts *are* entered on their special form.

**Consistent** The Red Cross representative prefers that the donations *be* given by check and that the amounts *be* entered on their special form.

# Point of View

A point of view is a position from which an observation is made; it is also the place from which an idea springs. You should be consistent in making your observations from the same place (point of view) and should be sure the reader knows whose ideas belong to whom—that is, that the place the ideas come from is consistently named.

### Inconsistent Observation

Lying facedown on the pavement, I could see the collected debris of the day—cigarette butts, candy wrappers, odd bits of paper—*and then came the sound of the ambulance and I could see it approach.* (Obviously, the writer could not see the ambulance if he were lying facedown on the pavement.)

### Consistent Observation

Lying facedown on the pavement, I could see the collected debris of the day—cigarette butts, candy wrappers, odd bits of paper—*and then came the sound of the ambulance and I knew it was getting closer.*

### Inconsistent Assignment of Ideas

Most people understand that animals need space in which to live. Malin Himes, the anthropologist, says that the acquisition of such space is connected to the amount of power the animal has. How we fight for space—and thus gain the necessary power to get it—is determined by our cultural training. The current conflict between Russia and the United States over outer space exemplifies this idea. (The reader does not know to whom the ideas in the third and fourth sentences belong.)

### Consistent Assignment of Ideas

Most people understand that animals need space in which to live. Malin Himes, the anthropologist, says that the acquisition of such space is connected to the amount of power the animal has. *Himes asserts* that how we fight for space—and thus gain the necessary power to get it—is determined by our cultural training. *Himes offers as an example of this notion* the current conflict between Russia and the United States over outer space.

## *Test Yourself on*
## Correcting Shifts

Correct all the unnecessary shifts you find in the sentences below. Some are correct as they stand; next to these, write C.

1. _____ People need to be praised when we work hard and accomplish our goals.

2. _____ Tommy argued with his counselor about the curfew and asks him to make an exception.

3. _____ He goes up to the cashier's window and asked for three tickets.

4. _____ Anybody who cares about his health can have themselves examined by a doctor twice a year.

5. _____ According to Quinn, Shakespeare is the greatest writer in English. Shakespeare takes in all points of view.

6. _____ My wife said she was thirsty and would I please get her a glass of water.

7. _____ We arrive in London on Tuesday, leave for Paris on Thursday, and then the rest of the week is spent in Rome.

8. _____ Johnny Carson is known to all because he sparkles on television every night.

9. _____ Every basketball player has their own way of driving to the hoop.

10. _____ He went to the movies, sees *King Kong,* is terribly frightened, and was afraid to go home.

11. _____ Finally, we added the icing, and then it was baked for fifty minutes.

12. _____ Barry said that he liked Lorna and would she care to have dinner with him.

13. _____ From the top of the Empire State Building, the people looked like toy figures, strutting mechanically along, smoking their cigars.

14. _____ I was told that cigarette smoking would ruin my lungs and that you should give it up if you wanted to avoid heart trouble, too.

15. _____ Wagner recommended that admissions standards be raised and students warned about their poor preparation for college.

## Specific/General

See **Diction.**

## Spelling

Most readers think of misspelling as a sure sign of inadequate writing. The impression is well-nigh impossible to dispel, but there is hope for poor spellers. For the way you spell is surely a habit and one that you can change. The spelling problem can be divided into two parts: (1) you and (2) English spelling.

### You

The burden of improving your spelling rests squarely on you; a teacher cannot help much in your discarding the old habit and taking on the new. Only an increased consciousness that improvement is possible and a disciplined approach can help. To begin, take note of the following suggestions on how to proceed and design your program based on them or something similar.

**1.** Be aware when you are in doubt about the spelling

of a word. If you are *not* aware of your doubts, you cannot dispel them by consulting a good dictionary and will continue to make the same mistake.

**2.** When you have found the correct spelling of a word, don't try simply to memorize it. Hand–brain practice is necessary. Try to visualize the word before you write it out. Then write it out correctly several times. After you've been able to write the word correctly three times, construct five sentences using the word in each. This practice will reinforce your new spelling habit.

**3.** Keep tabs on the words you misspell; make a list of them and keep the list handy. Notice if there are types of words that you persistently misspell and work through the rule that applies to the group.

**4.** Don't reserve certain words for writing and others for speaking. Try to use your whole vocabulary in both speaking and writing. This is useful because the correct pronunciation of words often helps you to visualize the correct spelling—but not always.

**5.** Proofread everything you write at least once for spelling errors alone.

**6.** Develop your own special methods to help you in this process. Some students use flash cards, others tack lists of troublesome words on the walls of their rooms. Be creative. There are many ways to approach the problem.

### *English spelling*

You will no doubt misspell a few words because you habitually pronounce them wrong.

| | | |
|---|---|---|
| accident*al*ly | NOT | acciden*tl*y |
| mathe*m*atics | NOT | math*m*atics |
| heigh*t* | NOT | heigh*th* (by analogy with *eighth*) |
| dis*as*trous | NOT | disas*tero*us |

The dictionary will help you by giving the correct pronunciation of such words. Beyond a few dozen of these words, English pronunciation and spelling are notoriously eccentric. Therefore, you must use pronunciation cautiously. You cannot analogize too much, because in English *through* and *bough,* for example, as well as dozens of other analogous spellings, are not pronounced the same way.

The first place to begin your disciplined study is with the following rules and notes.

## Rule 1: *ie* and *ei*

Memorize this famous jingle:

> *i* before *e*
> except after *c*
> or when sounded like *a*
> as in *neighbor* or *weigh.*

| *i* before *e* | *ei* after *c* | *ei* as in *neighbor* and *weigh* |
|---|---|---|
| achieve | deceit | freight |
| cashier | receive | reign |
| believe | ceiling | sleigh |

| **exceptions** | **exceptions** | **exceptions** |
|---|---|---|
| either | financier | sleight |
| neither | species | height |
| seizure | | eider |
| sheik | | |
| leisure | | |
| weird | | |

---

## *Test Yourself on*
## *ie* and *ei*

Complete the spelling of the following words by using either *ie* or *ei* in the blank spaces.

1. fr____nd
2. conc____ve
3. bel____f
4. ach____vement
5. exper____nce
6. rec____ving
7. th____r
8. f____ld
9. effic____ncy
10. conven____nce

| | |
|---|---|
| 11. aud____nce | 16. sl____gh |
| 12. dec____t | 17. w____ght |
| 13. misch____f | 18. forf____t |
| 14. p____ce | 19. v____n |
| 15. y____ld | 20. h____nous |

## Rule 2: Final Silent -*e*

**1.** Final silent -*e* is usually dropped before adding a suffix that begins with a vowel.

argue—arguing          dare—daring
baste—basting          give—giving
charge—charging

**2.** Final silent -*e* is usually retained when adding a suffix that begins with a consonant.

arrange—arrangements      hate—hateful      like—likeness
love—lovely              sore—soreness     sure—surely

Note the following exceptions:
**A.** Final silent -*e* is retained after soft *c* (as in *dance; color* has the hard *c*) and soft *g* (as in *rage; glove* has the hard *g*) when adding suffixes beginning with *a* or *o*. Because *c* and *g* are generally hard before *a, o,* and *u,* we keep the silent -*e* in order to keep the consonant soft.

charge—charging—chargeable
stage—staging—stageable
slice—slicing—sliceable

**B.** In some words, the final silent -*e* must be retained before the suffix -*ing* in order to prevent mispronunciation or ambiguity of meaning.

singe—singeing (to scorch; retains *e* to prevent confusion with *sing—singing.*)
dye—dyeing (to tint; retains *e* to prevent confusion with *die—dying.*)

**C.** Final silent -*e* is retained when the suffixes *ye, oe,* or *ee* precede the suffix -*ing*.

| | |
|---|---|
| free—freeing | shoe—shoeing |
| hoe—hoeing | tree—treeing |
| see—seeing | eye—eyeing |

---

## *Test Yourself on*
### Final Silent -*e*

Complete the spelling of the following words by using an *e* to fill in the blank space in each. If no *e* is needed, leave the space blank.

1. mov____ing

2. prov____ing

3. mov____ment

4. peac____able

5. chang____able

6. liv____ly

7. manag____ment

8. sens____ible

9. realiz____ation

10. ton____al

11. receiv____ing

12. bor____ing

13. bor____dom

14. car____ing

15. car____ful

16. dy____ing (to tint)

17. rang____ing

18. rag____ing

19. troubl____some

20. bar____ness.

---

## Rule 3: Final -*y*

Followed by a suffix other than one beginning with the letter *i*, final -*y* is usually changed to an *i*.

marry—marriage     beauty—beautiful     busy—business

When the suffix begins with an *i*, retain final -*y*.

cry—crying     enjoy—enjoying

**Some exceptions**

| | |
|---|---|
| day—daily | lay—laid |
| pay—paid | say—said |

### *Test Yourself on*
### Final -*y*

Complete the spelling of the following words by using either *y* or *i* or *ie* to fill in the blank spaces.

1. occup____ing
2. lonel____ness
3. anno____ing
4. pl____s
5. turke____s
6. fr____s
7. plo____s
8. repl____ing
9. cr____s
10. pra____s

11. theor____s
12. stor____s
13. bur____ing
14. histor____s
15. histor____'s (belonging to history)
16. accompan____ing
17. opportunit____s
18. happ____ness
19. modif____ing
20. def____ance

## Rule 4: Final Consonants and Doubling

A final single consonant is doubled when adding a suffix that begins with a vowel under the following conditions:

    a. when it appears after a single vowel, as in *allot,* or ends a monosyllabic word, as in *bat* or *run.*
    b. when it is the final consonant of a word stressed on the last syllable, as in *preFER.*

Without *both* these conditions, the consonant is *not* doubled.

| | |
|---|---|
| beg—begging | equip—equipping |
| begin—beginning | forGET—forGETTing |
| comPEL—comPELLing | ship—shipping |

## Note 1: Noun plurals and third person singular, present tense verbs

A. When a noun ends in a sound that allows a pronounceable final -s, *add* -s to form its plural. For verbs having this capacity, add -s to form the third person singular, present tense.

| Nouns | Verbs |
|---|---|
| stone—stones | trust—trusts |
| pill—pills | know—knows |
| drawer—drawers | hope—hopes |

**Some Exceptions**

| | |
|---|---|
| tomato—tomatoes | veto—vetoes |
| buffalo—buffaloes | echo—echoes |

B. When a noun ends in a sound that does not allow a pronounceable final -s, add -es to form its plural. For verbs without this capacity, add -es to form the third person singular, present tense.

| Nouns | Verbs |
|---|---|
| lunch—lunches | pass—passes |
| tax—taxes | wish—wishes |

C. To form the plural of a noun ending in *y* preceded by a consonant, change the *y* to *i* and add -es. For a verb with the same ending, do the same to the third person singular, present tense.

| Nouns | Verbs |
|---|---|
| company—companies | carry—carries |
| party—parties | fly—flies |

D. When a noun ending in *y* is preceded by *a, e, o,* or *u,* form the plural by adding -s. For a verb with the same ending, do the same to form the third person singular, present tense.

| Nouns | Verbs |
|---|---|
| day—days | buy—buys |
| boy—boys | pay—pays |
| toy—toys | enjoy—enjoys |
| key—keys | |

E. Certain nouns borrowed from other languages

frequently form their plurals by retaining the plural form
of the original language.

alumna—alumnae          datum—data
alumnus—alumni          penomenon—phenomena
basis—bases

However, good writers have tended to anglicize some
of these and dictionaries frequently list two plural forms.
See what your dictionary says is the acceptable plural
form of each of these:

beau      focus      index      radius      stadium

### Note 2: Suffixes to preserve hard c

To preserve the hard sound of *c*, words ending in that
letter add a *k* before a suffix ending in *e, i,* or *y.*

panic—panicked—panicking
mimic—mimicked—mimicking
traffic—trafficked—trafficking

### Note 3: Four special words and the eed sound

A. *Supersede* is the only word in English that ends in
-*sede.*

B. Exceed, proceed, and succeed are the only words
in English ending in -*ceed.*

C. Thus all other words in English ending in the -*eed*
sound are spelled -*cede.*

accede          precede
concede         recede
intercede       secede

---

### Test Yourself on
### Spelling Rules 1–4

Complete the spelling of the words with blanks in the
example below by filling in the blank spaces according to
one or another of the rules or notes explained in this
section. Some blanks do not need filling in.

1. she is occasional____y absent

2. the Sh____k of Araby

3. a sens____ible commit____ment

4. pro____ to jail; do not pass go; do not collect 200 dollars.

5. he perc____ved a sunset

6. cake top____ing

7. I like the ic____ing

8. the c____ling is cracking

9. the professor counsel____ed me

10. the water is boil____ing

11. a terrible argu____ment

12. he stud____ed hard

13. he went swim____ing

14. he was stop____ing me from drop____ing my

 p____ce of cake

15. the lovel____ness of the flowers

16. it is occur____ing often

17. a bus____ness appoint____ment

18. standing around ey____ing girls

19. attorn____s work in courthouses

20. my brother is dy____ing

## Word Lists

One or both of the following lists of words may be useful to you in working on your spelling problem.

## 1. Words that sound alike but mean different things (homophones)

The following pairs of words sound alike or look somewhat alike, but are spelled differently. Of course, their meanings are different, too. To master this list, you should write out sentences, using each word correctly in a number of different ways.

After each word is an abbreviation indicating the part of speech to which it belongs (*n.* for *noun; v.* for *verb; adj.* for *adjective; adv.* for *adverb; prep.* for *preposition; conj.* for *conjunction; pro.* for *pronoun; poss.* for *possessive; contr.* for *contraction*). This is followed by a definition.

**accept**   *v.* to receive
**except**   *prep.* not included
**except**   *v.* to leave out

**advice**   *n.* counsel; information offered
**advise**   *v.* to give advice or counsel

**affect**   *v.* to have an effect on; to influence
**effect**   *n.* the result of some action
**effect**   *v.* to accomplish or execute

**all ready**   *pro. + adj.* all are prepared
**already**   *adj.* at or before this time

**all together**   *pro. + adj.* all in the same place
**altogether**   *adv.* entirely

**allusion**   *n.* a reference
**illusion**   *n.* a false impression

**altar**   *n.* a special place for religious ceremony
**alter**   *v.* to change

**always**   *adv.* constantly; at all times
**all ways**   *determiner + n.* in every manner

**ascend**   *v.* to rise or go up
**ascent**   *n.* a movement upward
**assent**   *n.* an agreement
**assent**   *v.* to agree

**assistance** *n.* help given
**assistants** *n.pl.* helpers

**beside** *prep.* by the side of
**besides** *prep.* and *adv.* in addition to

**boarder** *n.* a person paying for subsistence in someone's house
**border** *n.* a boundary

**born** *v. (always passive)* given birth to
**borne** *v. (always active)* carried; given birth to

**breath** *n.* air inhaled or exhaled
**breathe** *v.* to inhale and exhale

**canvas** *n.* a heavy, coarse cloth
**canvass** *v.* to search for, examine, or solicit

**capital** *n.* a city that is a seat of government; an upper-case letter; money
**capital** *adj.* principal; first-rate; upper-case
**capitol** *n.* a building used by a legislature

**choose** *v.* to select
**chose** *v. (past tense of choose)* selected

**cite** *v.* to quote; to charge with an offense
**site** *n.* a place or location
**sight** *n.* the faculty of seeing

**coarse** *adj.* rough; not refined
**course** *n.* school subject; a way or a path

**complement** *n.* something that completes
**compliment** *n.* praise

**conscience** *n.* part of the mind that rules on moral questions
**conscious** *adj.* awake or alert

**council** *n.* a deliberative body
**counsel** *n.* advice given; a lawyer
**counsel** *v.* to give advice

**descent** *n.* a downward movement
**dissent** *n.* disagreement
**dissent** *v.* to disagree

**desert** *n.* a dry, barren area of land
**desert** *v.* to abandon
**dessert** *n.* final course of a meal

**device**   *n.* something contrived
**devise**   *v.* to prepare, originate, or make a contrivance

**do**   *v.* to perform
**due**   *adj.* with *to* specifies the cause of something; owing

**dual**   *adj.* twofold
**duel**   *n.* a formal fight between two people

**eminent**   *adj.* famous
**imminent**   *adj.* about to happen

**envelop**   *v.* to enclose
**envelope**   *n.* a paper container used for mailing

**extant**   *adj.* still existing
**extent**   *n.* the degree of something

**farther**   *adv. and adj.* usually refers to distance
**further**   *adv. and adj.* usually refers to time, quantity, or degree

**formally**   *adv.* in a formal manner
**formerly**   *adv.* at an earlier time

**forth**   *adv.* forward; onward; out
**fourth**   *adj. or adv.* the one following the third

**human**   *adj.* pertaining to people
**humane**   *adj.* compassionate or kindly

**idle**   *adj.* not occupied or employed; *v.* to spend time in idleness
**idol**   *n.* a likeness of something, usually a god, for worship

**ingenious**   *adj.* resourceful, clever
**ingenuous**   *adj.* showing innocent or childlike simplicity

**its**   *poss. pro.* belonging to it
**it's**   *contr.* it is

**know**   *v.* to understand, recognize, have experience of
**no**   *adv.* expressing the negative
**now**   *adv.* at the present time

**lead**   *n.* (pronounced *led*) the metal
**lead**   *v* (pronounced *leed*) to show the way, to conduct
**led**   *v.* (past tense of *lead*) showed the way; conducted

**loose**   *adj.* not tight
**lose**   *v.* to misplace; to be defeated

**maybe**   *adv.* perhaps
**may be**   *v.* possibly may exist or happen

**moral**   *adj.* relating to right or wrong
**morale**   *n.* the mental or emotional condition of a person or group

**passed**   *v.* past tense and past participle of *pass*
**past**   *n.* an earlier time
**past**   *prep.* at the farther side of

**peace**   *n.* not war
**piece**   *n.* a part of

**personal**   *adj.* relating privately
**personnel**   *n.pl.* a group of persons employed

**principal**   *n.* chief; head of a school; capital owned; *adj.* most important
**principle**   *n.* rule or doctrine

**prophecy**   *n.* a prediction
**prophesy**   *v.* to predict

**quiet**   *adj.* not noisy
**quit**   *v.* to depart from or out; resign
**quite**   *adv.* rather; almost completely

**respectfully**   *adj.* showing deference
**respectively**   *adv.* each in the order given

**right**   *adj.* correct or suitable
**rite**   *n.* a ceremony or ritual

**stationary**   *adj.* fixed, or immobile
**stationery**   *n.* paper for writing or typing

**than**   *conj.* a comparative term
**then**   *n. or adv.* indicates time

**their**   *poss. pro.* belonging to them
**there**   *adv.* a place; also used as expletive at beginning of sentences
**they're**   *contr.* they are

**to**   *prep.* indicates direction
**too**   *adv.* excessively; overly much
**two**   *n.* the number

**weather**   *n.* climate
**whether**   *conj.* expresses alternatives

**were**   *v.* past tense plural of *to be*; also subjunctive form
**we're**   *contr.* we are
**where**   *adv. or pro.* indicates place or position

**who's**   *contr.* who is or who has?
**whose**   *poss. pro.* belonging to whom?

**your**   *poss. pro.* belonging to you
**you're**   *contr.* you are

## 2.  Words that are troublesome to spell

The following list consists of words that are habitually troublesome to spell. The part or parts of each that are the sources of the trouble are printed in boldface or noted in parentheses, or both. The best way to use this list is to write sentences using each of the words; write as many as five sentences for each word, and in that way embed in your hand, eye, and brain the correct spelling of each word. Proceed gradually. If you do a mere five words a day, you will master the whole list by the end of the semester.

a lot of
abse**nce**
academy
**a**cceptable
**a**cceptance
**a**cce**ss**ible
acc**i**dental
acc**i**dent**ally**
acc**l**aim
acco**mm**odate
accomp**ani**ment
accomp**any**ing
acc**o**mplish
acc**u**mulate
accura**cy**
accu**r**ate (one *r*)
acc**us**tom
ach**ie**vement
ac**q**uaintance
ac**qui**re
actual**i**ty
actual**ly**
ad**m**ittance
adole**scence**

adole**scent**
advertising (no *e* after *s*)
advi**ce**/advi**se**
**a**ffect/**e**ffect
alle**vi**ate
al**l**otted
all**ot**ment (one *t*)
all right (2 words)
all together (2 words)
al**l**ready (one *l*)
alt**ar**/alt**er**
am**a**t**eur**
anal**y**sis
anal**yze**
a**nn**ual**ly**
ap**o**l**og**etic**ally**
ap**o**l**og**y
ap**p**arent
ap**p**lies
appre**ci**ate
appre**cia**tion
app**ro**p**ri**ate
arc**t**ic

argument (no *e* after *u*)
arguing (no *e*)
arise
arising
arouse
arrangement
article
athlete (no *e* after *h*)
attack (no *t* after *k*)
attempts
attendant
attended
audience
authority
autumn

bargain
basically
beauteous
beauty
becoming (no *e*)
before
beginner
belief
believe
beneficial
benefited (one *t*)
boundary
breath (no final *e*)
breathe
brilliance
burial
business
busing, bussing
busy

calendar
capitalism
career
careful (one *l*)
carried
carrying
category
cemetery
changeable

chief
children
Christian
choice
choose (double *o*)
chose
cigarette
clothes
coming (no *e* after *m*)
commercial
committee
communist
comparative
compatible
concede
conceivable
condemn
connotation
conscience
conscientious
conscious
consequently
continuously
controlled
controversy
convenience
correlate
criticism
criticize
cruelly
cruelty
curiosity
curious
curriculum

dealt
deceive
definitely
dependent
description
desirability (no *e* after *r*)
despair
detriment
devastating
device/devise

different
dilemma
disastrous (no *e* after *t*)
disciple
discipline
discrimination
disillusioned
dissatisfied
dominant

effect/affect
efficiency
eighth
eliminate
embarrass
emphasize
endeavor
environment
equipment (no *e* after *p*)
escapade
escape (no **x**)
especially
exaggerate
except
exercise
explanation
extremely

fallacy
familiar
families
fantasies
fantasy
fascinate
fictitious
foreigners
forty (no *u* after *o*)
forward/foreword
fourth
friendliness
fulfill
further

gaiety
government

governor
group
guaranteed

harass
height (no *h* after *t*)
heroes
heroine/heroin
hindrance (no *e* after *d*)
hospitalization
huge
humorist
humorous
hypocrisy
hypocrite

ignorant
imagine
immediately
immense
importance
incidentally
independence
indispensable
individually
industrious
initiative
intellect
intelligence
interrupt
irrelevant
irresistible
irritable
its/it's

jealousy
judgment (no *e* after *g*)

know/no/now

laboratory
laborer
laboriously
laid
leisurely

library
license
lieutenant
lightning (no *e*)
likelihood
literature
liveliest
livelihood
liveliness
loneliness
lonely
loose/lose
losing (no *e*)
loss
luxury

magazine
maintenance
maneuver
marriage
material
maybe/may be
meant
medieval
melancholy
millennium
miniature
minuscule (not *i*)
mischief
mischievous (no *i* after *v*)
moral/morale
morally
mysterious

narrative
necessary
ninety
noticeable
noticing (no *e*)
numerous

occasion
occurred
off/of
omit

opportunity
opponent
opposite
optimism

paid
pamphlets
parallel
parliament
paralyzed
passed/past
perceive
persistently
personal/personnel
phase/faze
phenomenon
piece
plausible
pleasant
politician
possession
precede
preferred
prejudice (no *d* before or
   after *j*)
presence
prestige
prevalent
procedure
proceed
profession (one *f*)
professor (one *f*)
pronounce
pronunciation (no *o* after *n*)
prophecy/prophesy
psychoanalysis
psychology
psychosomatic

quiet/quite

receive
recognize
recommend
referring

relieve

remembrance

reminisce

resources

rhythm

ridicule

roommate


scene

schedule

seize

sentence

separate

sergeant

shepherd

significance

sophomore

stabilization

strength

studying

substantial

subtle

subtly (no *e*)

succeed

succession

sufficient

summary

suppress

surprise

susceptible

suspense

symbol

synonym


technique

tendency

than/then

their/there/they're

themselves

therefore

thorough/through

thought

to/too/two

transferred

tremendous

tried

tries

tyranny


undoubtedly

unnecessary

unusually

useful

useless

using


vacuum

valuable

varies

various

vengeance


warrant

weather/whether

weird

where/were

whose/who's

woman/women

write

writing


yield

your/you're

---

## *Test Yourself on*
## Catching Spelling Errors by Proofreading

Proofread carefully each of the following paragraphs. There are six spelling errors in the first and seven in the second. See if you can find and correct them all.

1. In order to achieve one's academic goals, one must lead a disciplined life as a student. The arrangment of one's time is of first importance. The student should set aside regular hours for studing: so many hours per week for reading, so many for writing papers, so many for gainful employment, and so on. It helps if the same hours are set aside for each activitie, for the mind is best trained by regularity. Nor should liesure time be neglected; a balanced life is best for any kind of achievement. Discipline also requires that the student appear promptly for confferences with instructors and that he, in fact, be mature enough to ask that instructors meet with him. Reaching one's academic goals thus requires discipline *and* maturity.

2. Most of us, when we see on the calender that Christmas is approaching, are paniced if we haven't completed our shoping. To avoid that sinking feelling in the pit of your stomach, take a few tips from me. (1) Inteligent gift givers will feel that old urge at the first sign of a nip in the air; begining with the first fall frost, start buying. (2) Paralell with an early start should go a slow start: buy one gift at a time, leaving that long list at home and crossing off names as you go. If you will heed these two simple rules, you will save money—prices are usually lower *before* the season starts—and the anxiety of the Christmas rush. Instead, you'll have given yourself the gift of peace.

---

# Study and Examination-Taking Skills

To acquire and retain study skills, you should be aware that studying requires some of the same virtues the rest of this book has been urging on you, that is, the virtues of organization, clarity, concreteness, logic, and concentration. In this entry, we will try to show you how to apply and develop these virtues as they affect your study and examination-taking skills.

# Preparation

First, although some of us can study anywhere and at any time of the night or day, most of us would benefit from having a fairly quiet and well-lighted place that we can use on a more or less regular basis. Keep with you the materials you will need: texts, pencils and pens, highlighting magic markers, paper and notebook.

But the most important thing you must bring to your study sessions is *concentration*. Some of us have the capacity to concentrate for long periods of time without taking a break; some of us have such poor concentration that we can barely read for five minutes without feeling itchy. The latter group should take heart; you can easily increase your concentration time by practice. First, read and concentrate for as long as you can in a study session without fidgeting and looking for some distraction. Note how long a time this concentration lasted. If it lasted, say, five minutes, all good and well. Continue the five-minute pattern for a week. Beginning the second week, add two minutes to that five to make seven. Go at that rate for another week. Keep adding minutes week by week. By these means, you will soon find yourself concentrating for half an hour or more without the strain you felt that first week. *Then,* don't be afraid to take little breaks. Psychologists are certain that these are as natural and refreshing as any other ordinary shift in attention during ordinary activity. Trying to push yourself without building up the strength can only result in defeat by self-scolding or some other form of psychological punishment.

Most of us, however, do not concentrate for hours on end—only some manageable period of time: half an hour, an hour, what-have-you.

An immense aid to concentration is the setting of proper goals for a study period. Try to clear your mind of long-range goals, like getting an A in the course or getting into medical or graduate school. For any single study session, your goals must be more modest: the complete comprehension of a chapter of a text or a set of related ideas, such as the causes of the French Revolution or the meaning of the concept of I.Q. With immediate, concrete, and attainable goals like these, you will be much less likely to get yourself into a stew with worry, the real enemy of concentration. For during any one study period, you cannot realize a long-term goal. You must be patient and realize that mastery of the small, concrete goals will lead to achievement of the large ones.

Next, you must understand how recent psychological research into study phenomena can help you to become a more efficient student.

For example, most studies indicate that the student processes information best by (1) organizing it into small and manageable segments, (2) attempting to understand only small and manageable numbers of facts or ideas at any one time, and (3) eliminating the temptation to cram.

The last item first: cramming is not productive because it is done under stress. The pressure to do well and the pressure of not enough time are, together, defeating to the crammer. If you absolutely *must* cram, you should try hard to resist the temptation to cram *everything* into your brain: settle for the broadest possible outlines of ideas or information.

Better yet, avoid it altogether. Instead, start becoming a more efficient student by *proper scheduling*. Make a chart of the week's hours—168 of them—by means of columns for days and boxes for hours. *Divide* the week into periods for sleep, travel, meals, part-time work, study—and don't forget recreation: Drudgery is not the answer. Now, see if you can arrange to study at the same hour every day. This will aid in concentration and retrieval of information because you will approach these similar hours with all your conscious and unconscious forces ready for the assigned activity. Naturally, you will need to assign different blocks of time for different kinds of study; written work or creative work requires larger blocks of time than the ordinary study of texts.

Finally, you should not attempt to master more material than the mind can manage at any one session. Most of us can keep in mind about seven items at a time but have trouble with more. In order to do this and to *keep* what you have learned, it is important that you not keep it—the material learned—sealed off from the rest of what you know and can remember. Thus it is important to relate what you master to as much of your other mental contents as you can. For example, if you are studying French history and want to remember the dates of the Franco-Prussian War (1870–1871), you should try to link the dates and the event to American history: Probably you know that the American Civil War ended about five years before the Franco-Prussian War. Similarly, when you undertake to master French nouns, not only should you recognize that the word *oncle* (uncle) is cognate with the English form of *uncle* but also you should make up a French sentence, using *oncle,* to associate it with the other French words you've already mastered: *Mon oncle n'est pas content.*

Furthermore, you should be advised that *periodic review—reinforcement*—is an important aid to memory. Don't bury what you know by failing to look at it from time to time. Look at your lecture notes a few hours after you've taken them. Look at the notes on your reading the morning after you've taken them. These procedures will be much more profitable to your memory than if you wait until an examination is coming up before doing your review. Protect your investment in study time: don't let your material slip away.

## Reading

Everything we learn, we learn by analogy: *something* is there to assist us, a model, a fragment of similar information, an idea. That is why it is important when you read college texts that you do it in an organized way so that you can begin with a model or an analog, however fragmentary. Thus students are well advised not to begin by plunging into a text with a close reading.

First, *skim* the chapter or section. Examine the boldface or italicized subheads. Get into your mind the general area of study; prepare yourself with that fragment or analogy to which you can hook on those numerous concrete details. The goal in skimming is to gain a *general* idea of the author's organization and major ideas. You might, in skimming, go through a process like the following:

1. What does the chapter title mean? Can you relate the subject to anything else you know?
2. Read the first few paragraphs and then the last few: Frequently, these summarize the major ideas. What are they, roughly? Say them aloud to yourself, in your own words.
3. Skim the chapter from heading to heading, subhead to subhead. Can you feel what the author's getting at? How he's proceeding?
4. Look a little more carefully at any maps, diagrams, charts, graphs, tables, pictures, or schematics. Do these add anything to your first grasp?
5. Pause and think over what you've learned so far. See if you can tell yourself in your own words what the major idea or ideas are.

As soon after your skimming as possible, read carefully through the chapter or section with a view toward grasping the ideas or groups of related ideas and understanding the concrete details out of which these ideas arose. Follow a procedure something like the following:

1. As you read, try to distinguish the main ideas from the supporting evidence or ideas. To help you, stop after a paragraph or a group of related paragraphs to be sure you've understood them and have been alerted to any special terms the author uses or highlights in a special typeface or color. Remember that every discipline proceeds by *naming* its concepts. If you want to master psychoanalysis, for example, you must master terms like *unconscious, transference,* and *Oedipus complex.* The special language of a subject *is,* in a sense, the subject.
2. Examine the structure of the chapter as if it were a graphic guide to the author's ideas. Notice what happens as the author goes through explanatory steps, pauses for diagrams, or shifts his focus through extended analogies. Every once in a while, skip to the

summary at the end or the introductory paragraphs at the beginning: How are you doing in understanding the ideas related there? If you are lost, go back and read a bit more carefully the section or sections you don't quite grasp.

3. After reading a section or sections, start annotating in the margins and highlighting with magic marker. Take the section or sections under your review and see if you can repeat the main and supporting ideas in your own words. Relate what you've learned to anything else you know. Integrate.

When you have done this, after a short period of time has intervened, do a quick review for reinforcement's sake. Check your underlinings and annotations, the special terms, the graphic material. Whatever seems foreign or unfamiliar needs rereading. Make a rough reading outline, a set of notes in outline form. Practice from head to hand is another form of reinforcement.

## Taking Notes and Using Them

Going into a lecture or class discussion *cold*—without having done the assigned reading for that class—is an inefficient mistake. It robs you of that model we spoke about a moment ago and thus hampers you in grasping the material to be had from the class hour.

The aim in taking class notes is (1) to reinforce what you have learned in your own reading and (2) to integrate your instructor's view of the material with your own. You *can* listen (and/or make a classroom contribution yourself) and take notes at the same time—*if* you're prepared. If not, you'll waste time writing down every word spoken, when in fact what you want is to take down main and subordinate ideas in such a way that they appear so in your notes. Thus you should block out the main ideas in larger script, the subordinate ones in smaller. Underline special terms. Above all, do not try to write down everything. First, it can't be done; second, it's unnecessary. If you do miss something, leave a space in your notebook that you can fill in later. Later, you can consult a fellow student to fill in the gaps or even ask the instructor. If you've read the material of the lecture or class, you should have even less trouble filling in. Within hours of taking notes, go over them for a quick skimming review, taking time to highlight what needs it with a special marker.

The acquisition of a "great" set of notes is useless unless they are profitably employed. Notes should be periodically reviewed; short study sessions should be set aside solely for this purpose. There are few better ways to reinforce what you know *and,* not incidentally, slowly and carefully prepare you for examinations. If you don't want your notes to seem as foreign to you as a brand-new subject would be, keep up a process of periodic review and revision.

## *Test Yourself on* Improving Study Skills

Get together with two other students in one of your classes. Let the three of you read a chapter of the text, each in his or her own study session. Then get together again, and taking turns, each of you should present his or her version of the chapter's main and supporting ideas along with a definition of key terms. See which of you came nearest the mark in mastering the chapter's materials. Do the others have a way of reading that can help you? After discussing the chapter's contents, discuss study methods.

## Taking Examinations

Taking an essay examination involves some of the same skills we have been seeking to acquire in pursuit of effective writing. That is, your instructor will expect you to use standard English, organize your ideas properly, and support them with effective examples or details. Although it is obvious that you cannot be as careful when you are under the pressure of time in an in-class examination as you can be when you've taken an assignment home, you can nevertheless follow the same procedures as when writing any other essay—with modifications.

## Before the examination

No matter how much time you allot for preparation for the exam, you will need to do three things in order to assure that you are adequately prepared: (1) you will need to organize your notes and other materials (your reading notes, your class notes, your annotated texts, and any Xeroxed or Rexographed materials your instructor has handed out); (2) you will need to review this material in a coherent way; and (3) you will need to test yourself. By fulfilling these needs, you will strengthen your memory and mastery of the course material and increase your ability to apply what you know in the contexts of the questions you are likely to be asked on the examination.

As you begin the process of studying, you should first organize your materials in such a way that you can review them in manageable units. During this process—a period of time before the examination, remember, not the night before—you should reread your texts, reread your notes, reread Rexographed materials, all the time striving to grasp main ideas and the supporting details that make them alive. Recite these ideas and details to yourself. Pick out supporting details that are particularly effective in illustrating main ideas.

As you go on, allow time to examine all your material in different contexts: cause and effect, advantage and disadvantage, analysis and synthesis, and so forth. If you are studying electricity for a physics course, for example, you will want to understand resistance, voltage, amperage, and related terms. Thus if you are asked to analyze electricity into its component parts, you can use these terms to do so. If you are asked to take these terms and make them into a whole, you can define electricity through their use: a synthesis. Make up possible test questions in several categories: questions that ask you to define terms, analyze events or effects, describe a process, and so forth—questions that use the materials of the course in more ways than one. This flexibility of thought will prepare you for giving answers in a variety of ways.

The last part of your preparation should be devoted solely to practicing for the test by testing yourself. Take each unit of knowledge separately and make up a question or questions for it. Actually write the answers. Check them against your material and see where your memory or information needs strengthening. Write a tough and accurate definition of every key term you have met with in your reading. For courses in the sciences and mathematics, do a tough series of calculations, one each for every type of math problem or chemistry quantification in the course. For history, it is clear that you will need to know the causes and effects of various events and their sequence in time. For psychology and sociology, you will need to test yourself on terms like *acculturation* and *learning theory*. For literature courses, you will want to examine yourself on characters, themes, imagery, style.

## During the examination

Regardless of how much time you are allotted for an in-class essay examination, you will do best if you proceed in an orderly manner. That is, you should work as if you were at home preparing to write an essay: plan, write, rewrite.

The first thing to do in the examination room is to read the question or questions carefully—several times—until you are sure you understand them. (If there are more than one, you should decide how much time to spend on each; perhaps the instructor has marked each with a point value to help you with this decision. Obviously, you will want to spend more time on the questions that have the higher point values.) Now ask yourself what the questions ask of *you*: Are you being asked to summarize? analyze? synthesize? compare and contrast? comment on a quotation (interpret)? You would do well to try to answer the question precisely rather than take it as an opportunity to write down everything you know in the *general area.* For example, one of the questions instructs you to *define "socialism" and say to what extent the definition fits one of the Western and one of the Eastern bloc nations.* Analyzing the question, we can see that it contains clues on how to answer. First, you would need to *define* socialism exactly. A socialist system is one in which the producers possess both political power and the means of producing and distributing goods. The answer also requires that you apply this theory to one Western nation and one Eastern one. Here you should proceed to choose a pair: the United States and Poland, Britain and Rumania, or some other pair.

In responding to this question, it will not do either simply to *name* the countries that appear to be socialist in intent or to comment on the desirability of living under a socialist system. These considerations are ir- relevant. The instructions ask you to *analyze* the politi- cal systems of two nations and to see if (*interpret* whether) they fit the theory of socialism.

Once you have read the questions carefully and have allotted the proper time for each, proceed as follows for each one.

Reach back in your memory for the general outline of the material you are being questioned on. Jot it down on a piece of scratch paper or in the back of the exam booklet. Now bend that material to fit the question. As you prepared for the test, you took the material and placed it in several contexts; now call on your prepara- tion to give you the proper context. Jot down in scratch form several good supporting ideas. Order your material. What should you write about first? Should you go from most important to least important idea—or the reverse? Should you use time or spatial order? Now try to con- ceive of a cover or thesis statement.

A well-conceived thesis or cover statement can mean a great deal to an essay answer. First, it helps you, the writer, to organize the answer; it helps you to avoid padding, for with the thesis statement to guide you, you will not write what does not apply to that thesis state- ment, what does not illustrate or support it. Second, the thesis statement guides the reader (who grades your paper) and instills in him or her a sense that you have a firm and controlled grasp of your material.

Thus your opening statement should address the question precisely by presenting your thesis statement. Here, from an examination in political science, is a question followed by a tentative thesis statement. After you have read both, evaluate the thesis statement. Is it a good one?

### Question

Given that in American presidential politics an incumbent is rarely defeated for reelection, how would you account for the overwhelming defeat of President Carter by Ronald Reagan in the 1980 election? Be specific in citing the factors that seem to you to have been most important in causing Carter's defeat.

### Tentative Thesis

In order to understand the 1980 presidential election, one must understand the historic position of Democrats and Republicans in American politics. In times of stress, the American electorate invariably turns conservative and therefore elects Republicans.

This tentative thesis says not a word about what the question asked for: specific factors that were instrumental in causing Carter's defeat. Instead, it rambles on about "the historic position" of Democrats and Republicans. No doubt there is *some* truth in the statement, but the question doesn't ask for whatever truth the examinee has at his disposal; rather, it asks for a specific response.

Here is a more concrete and responsive thesis for the question:

Carter's defeat was probably caused by a combination of the following factors: (1) the public's perception of him as an indecisive leader; (2) the soaring interest and inflation rates between 1976 and 1980; (3) Carter's ineffectiveness in obtaining the release of the Iranian hostages; (4) the public perception that American prestige in the world was declining, especially in the face of OPEC and Russian pressures; (5) the electorate's belief that Reagan's toughness and certainty would cause a reversal of our foreign and domestic troubles.

As you can see, it may be that one or more of the writer's reasons (causal factors) are either wrong or weak, but she has surely written a statement directly to the point and one that will be of enormous assistance as she writes the whole essay.

Now the writer can proceed from (1) to (5) with examples and illustrations to construct a forceful and well-organized essay.

The efficient examination writer will always leave time—however limited—for a last look before handing in his booklet. Since you cannot be as careful in revising here as you would be under ordinary circumstances, it is doubly important that you do so. During this phase of the work, you should first check to fill in omitted words and phrases, lost during the heat of the writing battle. Correct here any passages that are illegible, misspellings, or other grammatical errors. Fill in a passage with a late thought or two—a sharper example or illustration. (Place the word *insert* clearly in a margin and direct the reader to an insert page at the back of the book.) Cross out what seems irrelevant or padded.

You can influence graders in your favor by writing clearly, concisely, and in an orderly manner; you can influence them against you by writing off the top of your head without direction or specificity or by (inevitably if you have no direction) padding—no matter how truthful or knowledgeable your padding may be.

---

## *Test Yourself on*
### Taking Examinations

A. Evaluate an examination you have previously taken. Take careful note in the margins of where you went wrong. Notice your strengths and weaknesses as an examination writer. Now go back to your notes and reanswer questions that were poorly dealt with until you feel certain that your new examination would receive a better grade than the old.

B. Give your notes to a student who is unfamiliar with the course. Ask him to create an examination for you. Take it with watch in hand. Ask him to grade it. If you receive a poor grade, go over the examination as suggested in A above.

# Subjects for Essays: Choosing and Limiting a Topic

## Choosing a Topic

The only time selecting a subject may become a problem for you is when you are asked to select one. (If you are assigned a subject, the problem doesn't come up.) Your best course of action then is to choose a subject that interests you, one that captures your imagination and that you either know or want to learn more about.

The place to begin is in your personal experience—in the things that have happened to you, the things you have done, the beliefs you hold, the skills and special interests you have nurtured.

Student writers who think they have nothing to say are much mistaken. *Everybody has something to say.* In fact, we might define being human as the state of having something to say. The trouble is that we are not always aware of what we have to say until we've begun to look for it. That is why you should begin with experience; there is the great repository of writing materials, and questions are the entree to this great storehouse.

What do I like and dislike? Whom have I known that would be of interest to others? What interesting places have I seen? What books and articles have I read that have provoked me? What movies and television shows have impressed me—one way or another? What do I do in my spare time? About what aspects of life in my community, town, or country am I passionately concerned? Are there wrongs that I think should be righted? social inequities that stick in my craw?

Questions like these will generate subject matter for essays, and if you generate the concrete details that make these subjects come alive, the essays will be interesting.

Sometimes these questions, this examination of the range of your personal experience, will lead you directly to a usable specific subject. But often the result will be a wide generalization. For example, the answer to one of the questions above ("What do I like?") might be "television comedy." Television comedy is simply too wide a generalization on which to base a 300- to 500-word essay. In any case, you would have to give specific examples of television comedy in your essay in order for it to be an effective piece of writing. Your task, then, when your experience suggests a widely general topic, is to narrow it down to a manageable specific one. Instead of "television comedy," you would have to come up with an essay topic like "The Humor of Archie Bunker in 'Archie Bunker's Place.'"

---

## Test Yourself on
### Generating Subject Matter

A. Examine your taste in television fare. Are there specific types of shows you like and watch consistently? Make a list of them. Now see if they are related. Make a list of five essay titles—possible writing assignments—suggested by the list. Examples might be such titles as "The Basic Plot of the Situation Comedy," "Will Anybody Shoot J. R. Again?" and "The Appeal in Watching Game Shows."

B. Make a list of places or buildings you've seen and been impressed by recently—or even during the past few years. Ask yourself what features of these natural or man-made environments appeal to you most or interest you most. Now make a list of five essay titles, possible writing assignments, suggested by those places. Examples might be such titles as "A Barn with a Gambrel Roof" or "A Campsite in Glacier National Park."

---

## Limiting a Topic

Subjects should "fit" the size of the paper or essay for which they are intended. If you were assigned to write a three-volume book, you might very well choose "The Life of George Washington" as your subject. Since you are unlikely to be given such an assignment, better forgo that subject. In fact, for the size of the assignment you are likely to be given—say a paper 300 to 500 words—better forgo all subjects on that massive scale. You can't possibly do a creditable job in 500 words of writing on topics such as "The Causes of the Civil War" or "The Drug Culture in America." Short papers on subjects such as these can only wind up being filled with windy judgments and vague generalities.

To limit yourself, it is necessary continually to pare down a topic until it is manageable. It is not enough to go from "The Drug Culture in America" to "Marijuana Use in Chicago"—you must go further, for "Marijuana Use in Chicago" is quite as unmanageable in 500 words as is "The Drug Culture in America." Another problem with large topics like these is that they probably go beyond your own experience and would require considerable research before you could plausibly do a good job on them.

The process of limiting a topic involves successive narrowings from a general topic to a usable subject for a short theme.

Suppose you have chosen the general topic of "Sports Cars." Since you probably have no knowledge of the history of sports cars—and therefore wouldn't be able to talk about Bugattis and Reos—your first narrowing would take you to "Contemporary American Sports Cars." This may strike you as exactly right until you realize that it would be folly to try to talk about the dizzying number of makes and models available from American manufacturers nowadays.

Then you get a brainstorm: you decide to talk about your own sports car. This is a shrewd decision, but you realize further that "My Sports Car" is a subject that would certainly require more than the assigned 500 words, because of the complexity of the piece of machinery you own. Try talking about a 1968 Thunderbird—about its basic specifications, size, equipment, road-handling characteristics, and so forth, all in 500 words. Not possible. At this point, you see that *one* of the aspects of your own car would really do nicely, and you finally (and correctly) decide on "Acceleration and Deceleration in My Thunderbird."

This subject is not only the right size, it is also well within the bounds of your experience—so far within, in fact, that you are a great authority on the subject, probably the *only* authority.

You may find that your method of narrowing down a general topic requires less deliberation than the process above. Perhaps you will be able to proceed more quickly. Whatever the case, limiting a topic requires a disciplined effort to proceed toward the specific and manageable from the wide generalization.

---

## *Test Yourself on*
## Limiting a Topic

A. Below are listed five general topics and the manageable subjects derived from each. Provide the intermediate steps between them. Use the previous analysis as a model in arriving at each stage.

1. *Clothing fashions:* The Role of Designer Blue Jeans on Campus

2. *Education:* My Troubles at the Beginning of Biology [or some other subject] 101

3. *Television:* What Archie Bunker Hates Most

4. *Student self-government:* The Duties of the Student Senator at My School

5. *Urban decay:* Why My Family Left the City (the South Side of Chicago)

B. Write specific, manageable titles for five of the topics listed below.

1. Political parties
2. The United Nations
3. Basketball
4. Vacations
5. Water pollution
6. Kurt Vonnegut
7. Racial prejudice in the United States
8. The energy crisis
9. Television commercials
10. Farm-price supports

# Subject-Verb Agreement

In English, the problem of subject-verb agreement arises mainly in the present tense. To understand what it means, consider the verb *to play* and the forms of *play* in the present tense:

| Subject | Verb | Subject | Verb |
|---------|------|---------|------|
| I | play | we | play |
| you | play | you | play |
| he, she, it | plays | they | play |

The subjects in the left-hand column are all *singular;* the subjects in the right-hand column are all *plural*. All the verb forms are the same—except the third one in the left-hand column. It is a feature of the English language that whenever the subject is *he, she,* or *it,* in the present tense, indicative mood, the verb form that goes with it must end in *-s.*

He considers me his friend.
She tells me when to pick her up.
It seems like a nice day.

Most of us have no trouble when the subject is *he, she,* or *it.* The trouble starts when the subject gets more complicated.

My Aunt Vicky *plays* basketball on Friday nights.
My Uncle Joe and my cousin Lewis *think* she's a good player.

In these cases, once you have decided whether the subject is singular or plural, you can make the right choice. In the first sentence, you can think of Aunt Vicky as *she;* in the second, there is what we call a compound (and therefore plural) subject; therefore, the first sentence requires a verb with an *-s* at the end, and the second does not. In the first sentence, there is a singular subject and a singular verb in the third person. In the second sentence, there is a plural (compound) subject and a plural verb form.

For some, the subject-verb agreement problem arises from a common confusion; that is, they know that *plural* nouns end in -*s*, so they make the analogy that words ending in -*s*, even verbs that end in -*s*, are all plural. But of course this is not the case. The number of the verb ending in -*s* is always singular and when the subject agrees with the verb in *number* (singular subject/singular verb; plural subject/plural verb), there is no subject-verb agreement problem.

## *Test Yourself on* Subject-Verb Agreement

A. Change each of the sentences below by following the procedure of the example.

*Example:* Joanna's best *feature is* her eyes.
Her *eyes are* Joanna's best feature.

1. His main interest is guns.
2. Rock and roll records are my only hobby.
3. Our greatest need is dollars.
4. Many days of nonstop studying were the cause of his breakdown.
5. Too many drinks on an empty stomach were the cause of his drunkenness.

B. Change each of the sentences below by following the procedure of the example.

*Example:* They let me know when they want to take a break.
She lets me know when she wants to take a break.

1. They amuse themselves when they have no toys to play with.

He _____

2. This turns me off.

These _____

3. It seems to like being fed by the children.

   They _____

4. That forces the argument in another direction.

   Those _____

5. They happen a lot more often than you think.

   It _____

6. She frightens me when she talks like that.

   They _____

7. She seems to profit from the time she spends in the biology lab.

   They _____

## The Subject: How to Determine Number

You can begin to clear up the problem of subject-verb agreement by gaining an understanding of what number (singular or plural) to assign to certain subjects.

### Compound subjects

A compound subject consists of more than one noun or pronoun connected by *and* and therefore requires a plural verb.

*Rocco, Vito,* and *Danny* are brothers.
My *sister* Lucia *and I* are starting a rock band.

The use of *neither ... nor* or *either ... or* with a compound subject produces a singular subject when both individual subjects are singular.

Neither my father nor my mother *is* a Democrat.
Either biology or astronomy *is* required.

When one of the subjects is plural, use the verb that agrees with the closest one.

Neither my uncle nor my *aunts play* pool.
Either fruits or *cereal is* all right for breakfast.

When a compound subject consists of two items that are considered one unit, the subject can be thought of as singular.

*Ham and eggs is* my favorite dish.
*Stormin' Norman and Suzy is* my favorite rock group.

---

### *Test Yourself on*
### Subject-Verb Agreement with Compound Subjects and *either/or, neither/nor* Subjects

In some of the sentences below, the subject and verb agree. Next to these, write C. For the others, underline the complete subject and the verb and decide whether these are singular or plural. Correct the lack of agreement between subject and verb by changing one or the other.

1. _____ Either your father or your mother are responsible for the financial aid repayment.

2. _____ Charlie and Dick open their new bookstore next month.

3. _____ The professional and the rich man decides their own fates in the labor market.

4. _____ Coffee and donuts is fine for breakfast.

5. _____ Was the sofa and chair on sale?

6. _____ Either lung cancer or heart disease is the chief killer in the United States.

7. _____ Public transportation and welfare is the items needing reform in American cities.

8. _____ Neither Margaret nor Maureen think their kid brother is a failure.

9. _____ Air, water, the earth, and people are all being polluted.

10. _____ Neither George nor the Joneses plays bridge.

---

### Collective nouns as subjects

Such collective nouns as *army, audience, class, faculty, committee, team,* and *public* indicate a number of people, but they usually take singular verbs because they are thought of as units.

The *team is* in first place. (the team as one whole; not the separate players)
The *crowd was* on *its* feet.

Such collective nouns as *plurality, minority, mass,* and *majority* may take either singular or plural verbs, depending on how you use them.

A minority of students *are* Greek majors. (The minority consists of separate Greek majors—a plural number.)
A minority of students *is* a force to be reckoned with. (The minority is a political unit—a singular number.)

---

### *Test Yourself on*
## Subject-Verb Agreement with Collective Nouns as Subjects

In each of the following sentences, determine whether the collective noun subject refers to a single unit or a plural number of individuals. Then cross out the incorrect verb in parentheses.

1. In this course, the class (decide, decides) whether to have a final exam.

2. The jury (render, renders) a verdict of *not guilty*.

3. The majority of my stamp collection (is, are) valuable.

4. The majority of my stamps (is, are) valuable.

5. The Congress (vote, votes) into law a thousand bills every year.

6. A plurality of Democrats (vote, votes) for liberal candidates.

7. The Appointments Committee (settle, settles) the fate of the faculty.

8. The staff (organize, organizes) the summer program.

9. The mass of men (leads, lead) lives of quiet desperation.

10. The audience (applaud, applauds) the performance vigorously.

---

## Subjects modified by phrases and clauses

Sometimes the full subject of a verb is a whole string of words, consisting of the simple subject and its modifiers; these modifiers are frequently phrases, clauses, or both. But regardless of how many or what kinds of words intervene between the simple subject and the verb, the basic rule still holds: the verb must agree with the simple subject.

### Subject Modified by a Phrase
*Living alone in college dormitories* seems to encourage students' maturity.

The full subject is the italicized portion of the example. But the headword, *living,* is the simple subject; it is singular and agrees with the singular verb *seems.*

### Subject Modified by a Clause
*Students who butter up their professors* earn better grades than those who don't.

The full subject is the italicized portion of the example, but the headword, *students,* is the simple subject; it is plural and agrees with the plural verb *earn.*

We could take either of these examples and make the full subject longer and longer by adding more and more phrases and clauses, but the fact is that these long strings of words accompanying the simple subject are *modifiers;* and the verb never agrees with a word or words in the modifier—only with the simple subject.

The *music is* beautiful. (*Music* is singular; therefore *is* is also singular.)

The *music* of the *strings is* beautiful. (*Strings* is plural, but *strings* is part of the modifying phrase *of the strings;* the correct verb remains singular *is* because singular *music* is still the subject.)

---

### *Test Yourself on*
### Choosing the Correct Verb for Subjects Modified by Phrases and Clauses

Underline the simple subject of each of the following sentences. Then, ignoring the phrase or clause that modifies it, read the sentence to determine which of the verbs in parentheses agrees with that subject. Cross out the incorrect verb.

*Example:* Actors ~~who look like other actors~~ (hate, hates) to be reminded of the fact.

Actors who look like other actors (hate, ~~hates~~) to be reminded of the fact.

1. The passenger with a cowboy hat and boots in the aisle seat (look, looks) like my brother.
2. The patrons who are waiting in line behind the ropes (want, wants) desperately to be seated.
3. The purpose of the rules (is, are) to assure order.
4. The catch-22 in the examinations given by the Biology Department (lie, lies) in the large number of choices you are given.
5. The guard who stands at the doors of the museum (punch, punches) the tickets.

6. The difference between you and your cousins (appear, appears) to be that you are more comfortable away from home.

7. The smell of those fresh pastries (make, makes) my mouth water.

8. The progress of Jim's achievements in college (please, pleases) his parents.

9. Classes that meet late in the day (is, are) poorly attended.

10. Ed's affection for politics (distract, distracts) him from his real work.

---

## Special cases

**1.** Pronouns as subjects. All of the following are singular and take singular verbs:

| | | | |
|---|---|---|---|
| anybody | each | everyone | nobody |
| anything | either | everything | none |
| anyone | everybody | neither | no one |
| somebody | someone | something | one |

*Everyone* with an interest in ecology *opposes* offshore oil drilling.
*Each writes* well.
*Neither writes* brilliantly.

**2.** Words ending in *-ics* as subjects. Words like *mathematics, economics, politics,* and *dialectics* are singular when you are speaking of the subject as a whole— as *one* thing.

*Mathematics offers* us a way of looking at the world.
*Economics has* no solution to the problem of inflation.

Where these terms refer to a number or collection of ideas rather than a singular, academic subject, they take a plural verb.

Marx's *economics do* not apply in all societies.
Since 1968, my *politics have* changed considerably.

**3.** *One of those which/who.* Where you find this structure, the first verb you use must be plural, the second singular.

*One* of those *who sing* in the choir *is* my brother. (*Sing* agrees with the subject of the relative clause *who*—which agrees with *those* [plural]—and *is* agrees with *one*, the main subject.)

**4.** *There is, there are. There* is not usually a subject. That's the trouble. Whether you use *is* or *are* depends on what follows the word *there*.

There is something I want to discuss with you. (The subject here is *something*, which agrees with the singular *is*.)
There are reasons that I can't see you tonight. (*Reasons* is the plural subject here—agreeing with the plural verb *are*.)

**5.** *A number of, the number of. The number of* always takes a singular verb; *a number of* always takes a plural verb.

*A number of dogs are* playing in the garden.
*The number of dogs* playing in the garden *is* small.

**6.** *Part* and *portion*. These words, though they indicate a quantity, always take a singular verb, because each signifies a single unit or fraction.

*Part* of my time *is* spent loafing.
*Part* of my work *is* boring.
A *portion* of my salary *goes* into savings bonds.
A *portion* of cherries *is* fine for dessert.

**7.** Expressions such as *together with, as well as, in addition to, including.* A parenthetical expression introduced by phrases such as these does not affect the agreement of the subject and the verb.

The *truck cab* and the *trailer are* barreling down the highway. (The compound subject—*truck cab and trailer*—requires the plural verb *are*.)
The *truck cab*, together with the trailer, is barreling down the highway. (The subject is now *truck cab*—the parenthetical expression introduced by *together with* doesn't count—and the verb is therefore the singular *is*.)

## *Test Yourself on*
## Subject-Verb Agreement in Special Cases

For each of the sentences below, cross out the verb in the parentheses that does not agree with the italicized subject.

1. *Billiards* (is, are) a difficult game to learn.

2. *Economics* (involve, involves) a lot of statistics.

3. Joanna noticed that Bill's *trousers* (was, were) dirty.

4. *Gymnastics* (require, requires) a high degree of agility.

5. The *news* these days (depress, depresses) me.

6. Now that I have graduated, a *part* of my life's tasks (is, are) over.

7. A *portion* of these marbles (is, are) yours.

8. A *portion* of blueberry pancakes (is, are) served with butter and syrup.

## *Test Yourself on*
## Proofreading to Catch Subject-Verb Agreement Errors

Each of the following paragraphs contains five errors in subject-verb agreement. See if, by careful proofreading, you can catch them all.

1. Paris is a city that has something for everyone. There is the Louvre, gardens, restaurants, and—ah, yes!—cafés. These are the very center of outdoor life in this beautiful city. Rising up from the tables at cafés are talk of politics, art, love, the very stuff of sophisticated European life. One of those who sings the praises of Paris most loudly is my brother Lazare. Neither Lazare nor I are stinting in our praise, but he is a fanatic. Although I never fail to be charmed by a visit to the Louvre or a walk along the

beautiful Seine, I manage a quiet joy. Lazare, on the other hand, think that Paris not only has something for everyone but that all these "somethings" are for him.

2. Either my mother or my father are always pestering me about progress in my schoolwork. Their attitude is that I need to report improvement every semester. I tell them that living alone in dormitories have deepened my maturity and that I don't need their pressure. But neither of them will listen. The music of my grade reports are beautiful to them and they never forget to ask for those reports. Economics, my major, are a difficult subject for me, but even though I'm running a B+ in eco, you should hear my parents bellow when I report a B in advanced statistics. Neither my father nor my mother and her sisters (who also get into the act) understands that sometimes progress isn't measurable by grades alone and that I need to be left alone to make more progress as a human being.

---

## Subjunctive Mood

See **Verbs** and Part 1, Verbs.

## Subordination

Subordination is the technique of indicating that one idea is not as important as another. Consider these two ideas.

1. The rate of inflation in the United States is growing at a rapid pace.
2. Prices and wages are in an upward spiral.

Both ideas are interesting, but though we can be sure the two are related, there is nothing to indicate their *relative* importance. In a piece of writing whose thesis was that sentence 1 was more important than 2, we should rewrite the sentences like this:

Because prices and wages are in an upward spiral, the rate of inflation in the United States is growing at a rapid pace.

Of course, your thesis might be that the reverse is true and that sentence 2 is more important than 1. Then the two ideas would be expressed like this:

Because the rate of inflation in the United States is growing at a rapid pace, prices and wages are in an upward spiral.

In either case, however, it is important that you learn the technique of subordination and then go on to use it habitually in your writing.

Subordinate ideas may be expressed, as we did above, by putting them in the form of a dependent (subordinate) clause. They may also be put in the form of phrases or even single words.

Included in my wardrobe is a summer suit, *which is made of cotton.* (subordinate idea cast in the form of a dependent, subordinate clause)

Included in my wardrobe is a summer suit *made of cotton.* (subordinate idea cast in the form of a participial phrase)

Included in my wardrobe is a *cotton* summer suit. (subordinate idea made into an adjective)

Probably the most important technique of subordination is casting subordinate ideas into the form of subordinate clauses. Otherwise your prose can sound like the following childish and monotonous passage:

I went to the movies. I ran into my friend Charlie. The movie ran two hours. I hated it. Charlie wanted to sit up front. I wanted to smoke in the balcony. We sat in the third row.

Because these seven ideas are presented as seven separate sentences, they appear to be of equal importance. But of course they are not. Nor would it be much help to string them together with *and* or *but* or other coordinating conjunctions. In fact, you should avoid such strings at all costs. What is needed is subordination—reducing the less important ideas and highlighting the more important ones. One possible way of revising the passage is this:

I went to the movies, where I ran into my friend Charlie. The movie, which I hated, ran for two hours. Although I wanted to smoke in the balcony, Charlie wanted to sit up front and we sat in the third row.

You might disagree over whether this is the best way to revise the passage, but you would surely agree that this change is for the better.

In practicing subordination, you should be wary of two errors that are likely to crop up.

**1.** Don't subordinate the more important idea. Where you have two ideas and want to subordinate one of them, do not haphazardly make your choice. That is, do not subordinate one of the ideas without thinking through the problem and deciding what you want to stress. What you want to stress will, of course, go into the main clause.

Ali won the fight.
Ali was tiring at the end.
Although Ali won the fight, he was tiring at the end. (Are you just subordinating the first of the two ideas because it is the first one your eye fell on, or do you really want to stress the fact that Ali was tiring rather than that he won the fight?)

I break out in hives.
I eat strawberries.
Whenever I break out in hives, I eat strawberries. (In this case, subordinating the first of the two ideas because your eye fell on it first results in an absurdity.)
Whenever I eat strawberries, I break out in hives. (Of course, this is in keeping with the more probable sequence of events.)

**2.** Don't use the wrong subordinating conjunctions.
Be sure to use the correct subordinating conjunction whenever you *do* subordinate.

**Poor** *While* my English professor is not Woody Allen, he does have a good sense of humor.
**Better** *Although* my English professor is not Woody Allen, he does have a good sense of humor.

**Poor** I read in the paper *where* the Bee-Gees are making a comeback.
**Better** I read in the paper *that* the Bee-Gees are making a comeback.

**Poor** My final exams, *what* I have to take next week, have me scared.
**Better** My final exams, *which* I have to take next week, have me scared.

## *Test Yourself on*
## Subordination

A. Combine each of the following groups of sentences into one or two effective ones by using the techniques of subordination.

*Examples:* 1. I ran into the water.
It was cold.

When I ran into the water, it was cold.

2. James Joyce was an Irish novelist.
He did all his writing in exile in Europe.
He wrote five books.
*Dubliners* was a book he wrote.

James Joyce, an Irish novelist who did all his writing in exile in Europe, wrote five books, including *Dubliners*.

*Note:* Not every student will combine the groups in exactly the same way. Several ways are possible.

1. Marylea has a lovely blue shirt.
The shirt is cotton.
She likes to take it to the beach.
She likes to walk around with it.
2. My television set is broken again.
I paid four hundred dollars for it.
It happens.
I get furious.
3. Air pollution is a problem.
The problem affects us all.
The problem affects us if we live in the country.
The problem affects us if we live in the city.
4. We left Cleveland.
It was raining there.
We arrived in Chicago.
Chicago surprised us with its sunlit beauty.
5. My friend's name is Chris.
He is English.
He loves the United States.
He occasionally longs to return to London.

6. Some crimes are against the person.
   These crimes are increasing.
   These crimes must be dealt with.
   These crimes must be dealt with firmly.
7. It was early.
   It was a Sunday.
   It was morning.
   The streets were deadly quiet.
8. Promises are made.
   These promises are sincere.
   Promises can be broken.
   The breaking is easy.
9. It rains.
   My roof leaks.
   The roof tiles are loose.
   They were never repaired by the former owner.
10. Paul Klee was a painter.
    He was a Swiss.
    His paintings look like drawings.
    The drawings are made by children.

B. Revise the following sentences through the effective use of subordination.

1. My hair is drying. I'll read a book.
2. I eat too much pastry and I gain a lot of weight.
3. A whole set of encyclopedias came in the mail and I didn't order it.
4. You see a rainbow across the meadow and you know there's been a recent rainstorm.
5. Jerry was unpacking but Noella was cooking supper.
6. She was frightened of air travel and she got on the plane for Paris.
7. Her exams were over, so she could afford to relax.
8. She had enough money and she had enough time and she needed a change of scenery, so she went out to California to visit Craig.
9. The car is a symbol of his virility, so he spends a lot of time polishing it to a high luster.
10. He likes working in the darkroom, so he does his own printing.

# Thesis Statement

Thesis statement is the name give to a central idea when it is written out as a sentence. A thesis, or theme, is simply the stand you take on an issue or the main point you want to make about a subject.

*The Decline of American Cities,* for example, is not a thesis statement but a title. In fact, it isn't a sentence, and a thesis statement must be a complete sentence. "My subject is the decline of American cities" is not a thesis statement, either, but an announcement to the reader of what your subject will be—a job done better by a title. (Notice that it is not an improvement to write "My *thesis* is the decline of American cities.") "The decline of American cities is deplorable" is also not a thesis statement, because it needs no essay to support it; it is a fairly obvious statement of fact. A reader would be as interested in reading an essay about it as he would be in reading one that supports the statement "Hank Aaron holds the major league home run record."

You need an effective thesis statement in order to control your writing. A poorly worded thesis statement guarantees a poorly constructed, badly focused, and uninteresting piece of writing. In order to be sure that you have a thesis statement that will help control your writing, you should pay attention to the following criteria of a good thesis statement:

**1.** An effective thesis statement is limited or narrowed down from a larger statement. The idea is to give yourself a manageable, *limited* piece of territory to cover. "College teachers go too fast for the average college student" is a very broad statement that would take you into too large a territory. For example, you would have to talk about more than one college teacher and would also have to deal with whatever is an "average college student." The territory can be scaled down considerably if this topic is changed to "Professor Lucia John goes too fast for her math students." You can see how this limits the territory to one professor in just one class and how it provides real material in the form of actual students. Here are two more examples of large and narrower statements:

**Large**   Our tax burdens are too great.
**Narrower**   Federal tax rates penalize people for being single.

**Large**   Baseball is fun.
**Narrower**   Nothing matches the excitement of a low-scoring baseball game between evenly matched teams.

2.   An effective thesis statement is singular. More than one major idea in an essay is too many. If you have too many major ideas, you will write diffusely, your essay will wander all over the territory, and the reader will lose track of what he or she is supposed to be following. "The United Nations has not fulfilled its original purpose of keeping world peace; it's used for narrow political purposes instead, and many countries neglect to pay their share of its upkeep—which is quite expensive." This is a mouthful—enough for at least two and probably three essays. Better would be either "The United Nations has not fulfilled its original peace-keeping purpose" or "The United Nations is used for narrow political purposes." Here are two more examples:

**Multiple**   The social life of a freshman at this college is very limited, the place is so big that you can get lost looking for a classroom, and besides, the professors are an unfriendly bunch.
**Singular**   A freshman at this college has a number of difficult adjustments to make.
The social life of a freshman at this college is very limited.
The professors at this college are an unfriendly bunch.

**Multiple**   Contributions to our mounting ecological problems will be made by the energy crisis, rapid increases in world population, and the plans for modern industrial development by the third-world countries.
**Singular**   The energy crisis is contributing to our mounting ecological problems.
Plans for industrial development by third-world countries will contribute to our ecological problems.
Rapid increases in world population will contribute to our ecological problems.

**3.** An effective thesis statement is concrete. A thesis statement that is limited and singular must also be concrete. An abstract or vague expression can ruin it.

**Vague**   The Pittsburgh Steelers are a great football team. (What does *great* mean?)

**Concrete**   The Pittsburgh Steelers are solid at every position. (that is, at quarterback, tackle, end, etc.)

**Vague**   Those who stop smoking care about their health. (What *aspect* of health?)

**Concrete**   Giving up smoking reduces the smoker's chances of contracting lung cancer. (Lung cancer is a concrete item to work with.)

---

## *Test Yourself on*
## Recognizing an Appropriate Thesis Statement

Place a check next to any of the following that seem to be strong and effective thesis statements. Rework the others.

1. Diabetes is a leading killer of Americans.

2. American movies are hung up on nostalgia for the fifties.

3. My Aunt Rose is a stylish dresser.

4. Punk rock is for punks.

5. Mathematics is an engineering student's most useful basic subject.

6. The difference between newspaper coverage and television coverage of the fire on 29th Street illustrates an important media principle.

7. *Hamlet* is a better play than *Macbeth*.

8. The rules for getting a candidate on the ballot for mayor in this town are unfair to those without funds.

9. Utilities in this country make a fortune in profit.

10. The life of a pro athlete is a poor model for youth.

11. Science and art have nothing to say to one another.

12. A person's hobby is the key to that person's character.

---

## Topic Sentence

See **Unity.**

## Transitions

Transition is the relating of one idea to the next as your essay proceeds from start to finish. Smooth transition contributes to the coherence of sentences, paragraphs, and essays. A tight organizational pattern is usually the best guarantee that you will achieve coherence. (For more on **Coherence,** see that entry.)

The necessity for coherence is based on your readers' need to be led from point to point in the writing by some familiar principle of order. In other words, readers need a solid bridge to get from sentence to sentence, paragraph to paragraph, idea to idea. When such bridges are absent, readers lose confidence in the writing and distractedly wander away from what they are reading.

Thus unless the organizational pattern is so powerful that the writing has exceptionally smooth flow from part to part, it is a good idea to use what are called *transitional devices* to establish points of reference, bridges for the readers' eyes and minds. These devices are also useful in that they establish the exact relationship between succeeding parts. In that sense they are useful in *saying* more, and saying is the essential function of expository writing.

The major transitional devices, sometimes used in combination, are the following.

## *Repetition*

Repeating a word or a phrase is a most common device. Sometimes a pronoun, referring back to a subject, will also do the trick, as will repeating a reference to an idea.

## *The whole sentence or brief paragraph*

A sentence can be used as a transition between different ideas following and preceding it. A brief paragraph can also serve as a transition between two longer paragraphs.

## *Standard transitional words or phrases*

All of these are good bridges and most are also useful in indicating relationships. A few of the large number available are listed below:

soon, later, at the same time, afterward, meanwhile, simul-
taneously, in a little while, subsequently
nearby, close by, there, here, at the other end
therefore, thus, hence, consequently
similarly, likewise, in the same way
on the other hand, however, but, nevertheless, still, yet, by
contrast
moreover, furthermore, finally, also, in addition
indeed, in fact, in other words

## *Test Yourself on* Making Effective Transitions

Each of the groups of sentences below could be made more coherent by the use of one or more transitional devices. Use either repetition (which will require a little rewriting) or standard transitional words and phrases.

1. He had given Tom a handsome wedding gift. He had offered him a well-paying job with the firm.
2. He stood in a small ravine. There was a running brook.
3. The country is running out of oil. Our coal supply is

low. Research and development for new energy sources are at a standstill.

4. He received a receipt for his tuition. He was able to register.
5. She wanted to go to the seashore. He preferred the mountains.
6. Reading stimulated his taste for mulling over in his mind the writer's great ideas. The notions gave him a sense of participating in some great enterprise. He was always reading.
7. Among his possessions were a sports car, a motorcycle, a boat, and a bicycle. He had no need to use public transportation.
8. Sam made his way through his classes by impressing on his teacher what a bright, personable young man he was. He made contacts with girls and impressed them, too.
9. After walking around downtown for an hour, she stopped and had dinner. She went to the movies.
10. He was graduated *summa cum laude.* He was able to pick and choose from a number of high-paying jobs.
11. She treated him shabbily, never letting him know from one minute to the next how she felt about him, breaking appointments, speaking rudely to him in public. He could find things about her to love.
12. She said she had known him in Chicago. He had never been to Chicago.

## Unity

Effective paragraphs possess a quality called *unity*. All the sentences in a unified paragraph are directed toward a single purpose: they supply specific details to illustrate, explain, or define a single generalization made somewhere in, but usually at the beginning of, that paragraph. This generalization is called the *topic sentence,* and it states what the paragraph is *about*.

Thus every unified paragraph is about one thing and pursues the one thing by organizing itself about its topic sentence. The three ways of placing the topic sentence are illustrated by the following sample paragraphs.

**1.** The topic sentence can be the opening sentence of the paragraph. Such a paragraph follows the deductive method of stating the generalization and then adding illustrative or supporting details.

In the folklore of the country, numerous superstitions relate to winter weather. Back-country farmers examine their corn husks—the thicker the husk, the colder the winter. They watch the acorn crop—the more acorns, the more severe the season. They observe where white-faced hornets place their paper nests—the higher they are, the deeper will be the snow. They examine the size and shape and color of the spleens of butchered hogs for clues to the severity of the season. They keep track of the blooming of dogwood in the spring—the more abundant the blooms, the more bitter the cold in January. When chipmunks carry their tails high and squirrels have heavier fur and mice come into country houses early in the fall, the superstitious gird themselves for a long, hard winter. Without any scientific basis, a wider-than-usual black band on a woolly-bear caterpillar is accepted as a sign that winter will arrive early and stay late. Even the way a cat sits beside the stove carries its message to the credulous. According to a belief once widely held in the Ozarks, a cat sitting with its tail to the fire indicates very cold weather is on the way.

Edwin Way Teale, *Wandering Through Winter*

Observations indicate that the different clusters of galaxies are constantly moving apart from each other. To illustrate by a homely analogy, think of a raisin cake baking in an oven. Suppose the cake swells uniformly as it cooks, but the raisin themselves remain of the same size. Let each raisin represent a cluster of galaxies, and imagine yourself inside one of them. As the cake swells, you will observe that all the other raisins move away from you. Moreover, the farther away the raisin, the faster it will seem to move. When the cake has swollen to twice its initial dimensions, the distance between all the raisins will have doubled itself—two raisins that were initially an inch apart will now be two inches apart; two raisins that were a foot apart will have moved two feet apart. Since the entire action takes place within the same time interval, obviously the more distant raisins must move apart faster than those close at hand. So it happens with the clusters of galaxies.

Fred Hoyle, "When Time Began"

**2.** The topic sentence can be the final sentence of the paragraph. Such a paragraph follows the inductive method by giving details first and allowing these details to lead up to the concluding general statement.

Television sells cars as if they were sex objects. It tells one-hour stories that wind up with all the pieces in the right places, the heroines and heroes clearly marked. It pictures the news only in pictures—as if there were nothing else newsworthy. It relegates "educational" programs to a special channel—as if educational material did not belong with the other material. And it's right to do so, because commercial television does everything it can to sell us illusions.

The sports pages have columns telling us how to hit a tennis ball and how to flog a golf ball. The slick magazines give us expert advice on how to sew, build furniture, repair cars, use tools, and redecorate our houses. Stirring books are printed every day with titles bearing the words "How To . . ." and television talk shows consistently feature people who are *experts*, people who have *accomplished* something. Thus it is easy to see that Americans value nothing so much as competence.

**3.** The topic sentence can be unstated but implied. This is a frequent tactic of narrative and descriptive paragraphs. In the example given below, the implied topic is *a description of the plant life at the edge of a concrete highway*.

The concrete highway was edged with a mat of tangled, broken, dry grass, and the grass heads were heavy with oat beards to catch on a dog's coat, and foxtails to tangle in a horse's fetlocks, and clover burrs to fasten in sheep's wool; sleeping life waiting to be spread and dispersed, every seed armed with an appliance of dispersal, twisting darts and parachutes for the wind, little spears and balls of tiny thorns, and all waiting for animals and for the wind, for a man's trouser cuff or the hem of a woman's skirt, all passive but armed with appliances of activity, still, but each possessed of the anlage of movement.

John Steinbeck, *The Grapes of Wrath**

## *Test Yourself on*
## Identifying Topic Sentences

What are the topic sentences in the paragraphs below? If you cannot find one expressed directly, consider the possibility that it may be implied.

**1.** While the relationship between loving and being loved is an intimate one, this is not to say that love is automatically reciprocated. Indeed, it may lead to feelings of revulsion if the individual's self-image is already irretrievably low: "Anyone who says he loves *me* must be either a fool or a fraud." Still a person is relatively likely to love someone who loves him. Indirect support for this generalization comes from a number of experiments in which persons are falsely informed that they are liked (or disliked) by other members of their group. This misinformation is enough to elicit congruent feelings in most of the deceived subjects. A similar kind of feedback often operates in the elaborate American game of dating. The young woman, for any of several reasons, may pretend to like her escort more than is actually the case. The man, hungry for precisely this kind of response, responds favorably and in kind. And the woman, gratified by this expression of affection, now feels the fondness she had formerly feigned. Falling in love may be regarded, in cases such as these, as a snowball with a hollow core.

Lawrence Casler, "The Thing Called Love Is Pathological"

**2.** The gallows stood in a small yard, separate from the main grounds of the prison, and overgrown with tall prickly weeds. It was a brick erection like three sides of a shed, with planking on top, and above that two beams and a crossbar with the rope dangling. The hangman, a greyhaired convict in the white uniform of the prison, was waiting beside his machine. He greeted us with a servile crouch as we entered. At a word from Francis the two warders, gripping the prisoner more closely than ever, half led, half pushed him to the gallows and helped him clumsily up the ladder. Then the hangman climbed up and fixed the rope round the prisoner's neck.

George Orwell, "A Hanging," from *Shooting an Elephant*

**3.** Money in England is august. What a fine, scrolled document an English banknote is, and how carefully one thinks before one parts with it. How noble and weighty is the English penny, compared with the equivalent American coin, which is a mere scrap of metal. Try and get hold of an English penny; weigh it in your hand; savor its medallion-like quality, and think how painful it is to spend it on a mere bus ticket or a visit to the lavatory. And then think of the flimsiness of American cash, and how glad one is, really, to get rid of it. It doesn't confer status on a man, the way cash does in England. Indeed, one discerns a strange sense of abasement in American financial quarters. The last thing an American banker would like you to think of him is that he might *deal* in cash. He deals in bonds, and he finances things, but he doesn't touch money.

Malcolm Bradbury, "Can We Bring Back the Old Fashioned Bank Robber?"

**4.** Anyone who has worked on a committee preparing a document to be signed by all fellowwriters knows some of the difficulties. Disagreements of opinion and emphasis can produce a voice that is hardly a voice at all. Constant qualification makes for weakness. The various writers, all too aware of their audience as real people, may try to anticipate hopelessly conflicting prejudices and objections. Everybody has a point he wants included, but what is worse, no one feels any personal responsibility for the tone of the whole. Nobody cares, really. Contrast the situation of the single writer alone at his desk, who can establish a single speaking voice and an ideal assumed reader to listen to it. Yet a great deal of modern prose is written, or at any rate rewritten, not at a lonely desk but around a table where everybody talks at once. The loss of personality almost inevitable under such circumstances should cause us anguish whenever, as so often happens, we have to read or write the prose of organization life. When we speak of official prose as *stuffy*, we are referring, I think, directly to this loss of personality. (Not that you need a committee to produce stuffiness....) Stuffiness may imply, by way of the stuffed shirt, that the speaker has no insides, no humanity. It is scarecrow prose. Other familiar metaphors also seem to recognize an emptiness within; thus we speak of the "inflated" language of officialese, the speaker in that case being filled with gas, or hot air.

Walker Gibson, Tough, Sweet, and Stuffy

**5.** The running styles were as different as the physical characteristics. Dick Crompton, a small Texan scatback, ran with sharp exhalations when he had the ball, *ah-ah-ah*, like piston strokes—a habit he had picked up in high school which he felt gave power to his run. He could be heard across the width of a field. The "Gasper" some of the players called him, and he was also nicknamed "Roadrunner"—after the quick-running desert bird of his home state.

Jake Greer also had a distinctive run—moving his spindly body in leaps like a high jumper moving for the crossbar, high, bouncy steps, and then he stretched out fast, and when he got to the defending back he feinted with his small high-boned head, sometimes with a tiny bit of toothpick working in it. Then he'd fly on past or off at an angle, his hands splayed out wide, looking back for the ball honing in to intercept his line of flight, and then he'd *miss* it—good moves but bad hands in those early training sessions, they said—and the shouts would go up, "Squeeze that thing, baby," "Hands, man, hands." Greer would circle back, stricken, staring into his big hands as if they had betrayed him as he bent down to pick up the ball. His face would remain long and melancholy, and when his signal came up again, Scooter McLean would shout: "Look like you want it, Al, come *on*, baby."

George Plimpton, Paper Lion

## *Test Yourself on*
## Achieving Unity in Paragraphs

Each of the three topic sentences printed below is accompanied by a set of statements. Each topic sentence together with its accompanying statements could be made into an effective paragraph were it not for one problem: some of the statements in each set are irrelevant to the topic sentence. In each set, eliminate the potential hurdles to unity and organize the rest into an effective paragraph. Slight alterations in the statements are permissible.

A. Basketball is a game requiring great physical skills and coordination.

1. Basketball players must be able to run backward as well as forward.
2. They must have good peripheral vision in order to see their teammates and their opponents.
3. In order to leap for the ball off the backboard, players must have excellent timing.
4. Timing is also important in passing and shooting—the exact moment counts in basketball.
5. In football, such skills and coordination are not necessary; there you need brute strength.
6. Basketball can be played anywhere.
7. The speed at which the game is played seems to be the factor that requires these skills.

B. Your chances of getting a summer job are best if you make a systematic search and present yourself as a useful worker.

1. Explore all the relevant sources for jobs: want ads, school placement agency, friends and relatives, and signs hanging in the windows of businesses in your hometown.
2. Begin your campaign early.
3. If you get the right summer job, you can earn as much as $2,500 over the summer.

4. If you are applying to a large corporation, show your professionalism by presenting a résumé.

5. The résumé should not be modest; it should list all the skills you possess.

6. Then decide on what kind of job you want and go after it.

7. In appearing for an interview, be on time and present a neat and businesslike appearance.

8. The vigorous job seeker will appear vigorous to an employer.

9. A summer job is not so tiring that you will not be able to have fun and work at the same time.

C. There are a number of reasons why it is difficult for most high school seniors to adjust to college life.

1. For one thing, they usually come to a large campus from a much smaller high school setting, and this change alone is unsettling.

2. College administrators should be forced to go to freshman registration and see what's involved.

3. Not only a big school, but big classes contribute to the freshman's unease.

4. Crowded together in a large lecture hall with hundreds of students, they miss the intimacy they enjoyed in high school.

5. Where they were once friendly with a small number of "teachers," they are now subject to the alienating presence of the "professor."

6. Moreover, going to college often involves a change of residence—from home with the family to a college dorm in another town—and this factor requires some adjustment.

7. Colleges should try to make this transition easier.

# Verbs

A verb is a part of speech that expresses either action or some state of existence or condition of being.

Dr. J. *sank* a jumper.
The Rolling Stones *played* a concert.
My Uncle Gene *eats* like a whole platoon of Marines.
The typewriter *sits* waiting.

After a while, I *felt* better.
Eddie *seemed* depressed today.
She *is* a princess.
They *were* startled.

The verbs italicized in the second set of examples above are called *linking verbs.* (See Part 1, Verbs, for more information about them.) The verbs italicized in the first set of examples above denote some kind of action. (See Part 1, Verbs, under the headings *transitive* and *intransitive* for information about them.)

What all these verbs have in common is the fact that each one not only carries a meaning but also indicates *time.*

1. I *begin* work at eight o'clock. (present tense)
2. I *am beginning* work at eight o'clock. (continuous or progressive present tense)
3. I *was beginning* work at eight o'clock. (continuous past tense)
4. Yesterday, I *began* work at nine o'clock. (past tense)
5. Every day this week, I *have begun* work before ten o'clock. (perfect tense)
6. Before that, I *had begun* work at eleven o'clock. (past perfect tense)
7. Tomorrow, I *will begin* work at twelve o'clock. (future tense)
8. I *will have begun* work by twelve noon. (future perfect tense)

Sentence 1 indicates action taking place in the present or action that is typical and ongoing (something like "I *always* begin work at eight o'clock—I have done so and I will do so in the future"). Sentence 2 says much the same, perhaps with a bit more urgency—the statement could be read as a kind of warning, that is, "You'd better say what you have to say to me now because I'll be too busy after eight: I am beginning work at eight o'clock." Sentence 3 might answer the question "What time were you beginning work last week?" Sentence 4, the simple past tense, indicates that the action took place in the past and was completed then. Sentence 5 suggests that the action was begun in the past and has continued on up to the present. Sentence 6 tells us that the action specified took place and was completed *prior* to some other time in the past, perhaps prior to the week spoken of in sentence 5. Sentence 7 indicates future time, and sentence 8 indicates an action that *will be* completed at or by some specific time in the future.

There are other important things to notice about these examples. First, you should notice that a verb can consist of more than one word. Second, you should notice that in all the examples there appear only four forms of the verb *begin:*

begin (stem, or present tense form)
began (past tense)
begun (past participle)
beginning (present participle)

These are called the *principal parts* of the verb. Knowing the principal parts of a verb and knowing the forms of the auxiliary (helping) verbs *be* and *have* will enable you to form any tense or form of that verb.

## Conjugation of *Be* and *Have*

The *conjugation* of a verb is a listing of its forms.

**Be**

*present tense*

| I am | we are |
| you are | you are |
| he, she, it is | they are |

*past tense*

| I was | we were |
| you were | you were |
| he, she, it was | they were |

*perfect tense:* have been
*past perfect tense:* had been
*future tense:* will be
*future perfect tense:* will have been

**Have**

*present tense*

| I have | we have |
| you have | you have |
| he, she, it has | they have |

*past tense*

| I had | we had |
| you had | you had |
| he, she, it had | they had |

*perfect tense:* have had
*past perfect tense:* had had
*future tense:* will have
*future perfect tense:* will have had

# Regular and Irregular Verbs: Principal Parts

Notice these principal parts:

| Present (stem) | Past | Present Participle | Past Participle |
|---|---|---|---|
| talk | talked | talking | talked |
| play | played | playing | played |
| freeze | froze | freezing | frozen |
| catch | caught | catching | caught |

Notice that in the case of the first two verbs, the past and the past participle simply add -*ed* (the two forms are the same). These are called regular verbs. The last two are *irregular*.

Irregular verbs in English do not form the past and past participle with -*ed*. The irregularities of these verbs must be studied and memorized; here is a list of some of the main irregular verbs, together with their principal parts.

| Present (stem) | Past | Present Participle | Past Participle |
|---|---|---|---|
| arise | arose | arising | arisen |
| bear | bore | bearing | borne |
| begin | began | beginning | begun |
| bind | bound | binding | bound |
| blow | blew | blowing | blown |
| break | broke | breaking | broken |
| bring | brought | bringing | brought |
| buy | bought | buying | bought |
| catch | caught | catching | caught |
| choose | chose | choosing | chosen |
| come | came | coming | come |
| creep | crept | creeping | crept |
| deal | dealt | dealing | dealt |
| do | did | doing | done |
| draw | drew | drawing | drawn |
| drink | drank | drinking | drunk |
| drive | drove | driving | driven |
| eat | ate | eating | eaten |
| fall | fell | falling | fallen |
| flee | fled | fleeing | fled |
| fly | flew | flying | flown |
| forbid | forbade | forbidding | forbidden |
| forget | forgot | forgetting | forgotten |

| Present (stem) | Past | Present Participle | Past Participle |
|---|---|---|---|
| freeze | froze | freezing | frozen |
| get | got | getting | gotten |
| give | gave | giving | given |
| go | went | going | gone |
| grind | ground | grinding | ground |
| grow | grew | growing | grown |
| hang | hung* | hanging | hung* |
| hold | held | holding | held |
| hurt | hurt | hurting | hurt |
| know | knew | knowing | known |
| lay | laid | laying | laid |
| lead | led | leading | led |
| lend | lent | lending | lent |
| lie | lay | lying | lain |
| lose | lost | losing | lost |
| mean | meant | meaning | meant |
| mistake | mistook | mistaking | mistaken |
| ride | rode | riding | ridden |
| ring | rang | ringing | rung |
| rise | rose | rising | risen |
| run | run | running | run |
| see | saw | seeing | seen |
| seek | sought | seeking | sought |
| send | sent | sending | sent |
| shake | shook | shaking | shaken |
| shine | shone/ shined | shining | shone/ shined |
| sing | sang | singing | sung |
| sleep | slept | sleeping | slept |
| slide | slid | sliding | slid |
| speak | spoke | speaking | spoken |
| spin | spun | spinning | spun |
| spill | spilt/ spilled | spilling | spilled |
| spit | spat | spitting | spat |
| spread | spread | spreading | spread |
| spring | sprang | springing | sprung |
| steal | stole | stealing | stolen |
| sting | stung | stinging | stung |
| stink | stank | stinking | stunk |

*The past and past participle forms are *hanged* when the word is used in the sense of *executed*.

| Present (stem) | Past | Present Participle | Past Participle |
|---|---|---|---|
| strike | struck | striking | stricken/ struck |
| swear | swore | swearing | sworn |
| swim | swam | swimming | swum |
| swing | swung | swinging | swung |
| take | took | taking | taken |
| teach | taught | teaching | taught |
| tear | tore | tearing | torn |
| thrive | throve/ thrived | thriving | thrived/ thriven |
| throw | threw | throwing | thrown |
| wear | wore | wearing | worn |
| weep | wept | weeping | wept |
| win | won | winning | won |
| write | wrote | writing | written |

## *Test Yourself on*
## Forming the Tenses of Irregular Verbs

A. Construct five sentences using the perfect tense of the following irregular verbs: *blow, drink, forbid, hang* (what is done to a picture on the wall), and *strike.*

B. Fill in the blanks in the following sentences with the correct form of the verb that is given in parentheses:

1. For almost twenty years, he had (awake) _____ early every Sunday because he had (sing) _____ in the church choir.

2. Every day he (drink) _____ coffee for breakfast, but on Saturday, out of deference to his wife, he (choose) _____ tea and then (lie) _____ around reading his paper before doing the grocery shopping.

3. On some of her birthdays, her children (bring) _____ her the same gifts she had (bring) _____ them on their birthdays. It was a family joke and whenever it happened she was always (shake) _____ with laughter and tears.

4. She (lay) _____ the package down on the table and, after she had (take) _____ off her hat, she (lend) _____ Susan a hand with her packages.

5. Every night after supper, Grandpa (spin) _____ a yarn about the old days in Colorado while the children's faces (shine) _____ with pleasure.

6. Suddenly, the dog (spring) _____ at him, but he (freeze) _____ for just a moment and the animal (flee) _____ through the bushes.

7. He had always (sleep) _____ on his side, but now with his leg injury he was (drive) _____ to flip over onto his back.

8. He had (teach) _____ for a number of years, but the whole experience had just about (grind) _____ him down and now

    he wanted to be (bear) ———————————
away into retirement.

9. The stories the newspapers had (write) ——————————— about their marriage and divorce were (forget) ——————————— but the whole unpleasant experience still (sting) ——————————— him.

10. He had (seek) ——————————— peace by buying a little cottage on the lake, but there new and vexing problems had (arise) ———————————.

## *Test Yourself on* Forming Principal Parts

In the boxes below, some principal parts are given; others are not. Fill in the blank spaces with the appropriate principal part. Find the part you need by looking at the forms already filled in.

|   | Stem | Past | Present Participle | Past Participle |
|---|------|------|--------------------|-----------------|
| 1 |      | kept |                    | kept            |
| 2 | lose |      |                    |                 |
| 3 |      | played |                  |                 |
| 4 | tell |      |                    | told            |
| 5 | pursue |    |                    |                 |

| | Stem | Past | Present Participle | Past Participle |
|---|---|---|---|---|
| 6 | love | loved | | |
| 7 | | | growing | grown |
| 8 | answer | | | |
| 9 | | dreamt/dreamed | dreaming | |
| 10 | | tried | trying | |
| 11 | | | asking | asked |
| 12 | | wanted | | |
| 13 | shave | | shaving | |
| 14 | walk | walked | | |
| 15 | | sewed | | |
| 16 | | | smoking | |
| 17 | | went | | |
| 18 | | hit | | |
| 19 | | | having | |
| 20 | build | | | |
| 21 | | | breaking | |
| 22 | | | | seen |
| 23 | | | | become |
| 24 | | rode | | |
| 25 | prove | | | |

## *Test Yourself on*
### Forming Tenses

Circle the form or forms appropriate to complete each of the phrases given.

*Example:* I will have *went,* (*played,*) *doing,* (*grown,*) *build*

> *I will have played* and *I will have grown* are correct.

1. I will have *went, played, doing, grown, build*
2. She was *giving, lose, wrote, prepared, saw*
3. They could have *became, run, saw, operated, driven*
4. We had *travel, happened, dreaming, walk, wish*
5. They will *going, believed, decided, grown, punish*
6. We are not *became, laughed, dance, jumping, buying*
7. They could be *want, follow, requested, teach, guess*
8. This property might have been *change, appraise, divide, rent, sold*
9. Complications could not have been *rule, testing, know, avoided, saw*
10. Many men should have *telephone, speaking, singing, talked, known*
11. The ordinary problem is *say, use, suggested, going, called*
12. My son John might have been *named, charge, singing, swearing, known*

# Using Verb Tenses Correctly

## *Present tense*

The present tense indicates action taking place at the present moment:

I *suggest* you go later.
He *suggests*\* we take a walk.
They *suggest* dinner and a movie.

The present tense is also used to indicate an action that is habitual or ongoing:

This dog *bites* people.
My mother *hates* bananas.
Lucia *loves* beautiful plates.

Another form of the present tense is called the progressive present tense. Used with forms of the verb *to be*, it denotes action that is *continuing*:

I *am suggesting* Reading, Writing, and Rhetoric for my freshman students.
He *is draining* the water out of the boat.

*Note:* Substitute *suggest* for the first verb and *drains* for the second in these sentences. Can you see what is gained or lost by the changes?

## *Past tense*

The past tense consists of a single form—the simple past:

I *suggested* the book.
I *wrote* my paper.

You should be careful to use the proper form of the past. This is not a problem with regular verbs (which end in *-ed* in both the past and the past participle) but it *is* a problem with irregular verbs:

---

\*Note the *-s* ending on this verb. See **Subject-Verb Agreement** for information about this ending.

**Wrong**  I *rung* the bell.
**Right**  I *rang* the bell.

**Wrong**  He *torn* his pants.
**Right**  He *tore* his pants.

## Perfect tense

The perfect tense uses the past participle with a form of
the auxiliary verb *have*. This tense denotes action begun
some time in the past and continuing up to and including
the present moment:

I *have written* a letter.
He *has played* basketball every day this week.

The problem in using this tense is that writers frequently use the auxiliary with the *past tense* instead of
the auxiliary with the *past participle*. Again, there is no
problem when the verb involved is a regular verb; there
*is* a problem where the verb is irregular:

**Wrong**  She *has wrote* her term paper.
**Right**  She *has written* her term paper.

**Wrong**  He *has rode* horses since he was a boy.
**Right**  He *has ridden* horses since he was a boy.

## Past perfect tense

The past perfect tense is used to denote the earlier of
two actions, both of which have taken place in the past:

Dana *discovered* [simple past tense] that he *had taken* the
wrong road. (past perfect tense for earlier action)
Bill *saw* that Joanna *had rearranged* the furniture. (The *seeing*
is later than the *rearranging*.)

## Future tense

Few problems are presented by the future tense. It is
formed by using the words *will* or *shall* with the present
stem of the main verb:

I *will go* tomorrow.
We *shall begin* Wednesday.

*Note:* In formal English, *shall* in the first person and *will* in the second and third person are used to express simple future:

I shall go to the library tomorrow.
Mary will go with me.

For more on this verb, see the "Glossary of Usage," **shall, will, should, would.**

### Future perfect tense

The future perfect tense is used to express the *earlier* of two actions, both of which will be completed in the future:

By the time I *arrive* in Oneonta, she *will have risen.* (*Arrive* here is used to denote the *future; will have risen* denotes the earlier of the two actions.)

Before I *leave* for the airport, he *will have packed* my bag. (The *leaving* must take place *after* the *packing.*)

---

## Test Yourself on
## the Correct Use of Tenses

Underline the verbs in parentheses that make the sentences correct.

1. The tournament will end soon and our team (will lose, will have lost) its chance for the championship.

2. By the time the police get here, the burglar (will be, will have been) gone for half an hour.

3. When Bill (entered, had entered) the room, he saw that Joanna (rearranged, had rearranged) the furniture.

4. I (learned, have learned) quite a lot about Shakespeare this year, and I am hoping to learn even more next year.

5. Fred was terrified that his dog (bit, had bitten) the policeman.

6. By my next birthday, I (will live, will have lived) for half a century.

7. Once I (finished, had finished) writing Volume 1, I (began, had begun) to worry about Volume 2.

8. The people we saw in the restaurant (acted, had acted) like clowns.

9. Lasagna (was, had been) my favorite pasta before I discovered macaroni.

10. When the game (ended, had ended), the stadium (closed, had closed).

11. The chairman (left, had left) the meeting before it (adjourned, had adjourned).

12. He (was brought up, had been brought up) on charges after we (discovered, had discovered) his misconduct.

---

## Some Problems with Verbs

### 1. Final -d or -ed

Some writers make the error of omitting a final *-d* or *-ed* from past tense or past participle verb forms. It is especially important that you beware of the problem in one-syllable words, where the *-ed* ending is not likely to be sounded (as in *blamed, dreamed, missed,* and so forth). The *-ed* ending is not so frequently forgotten in words of more than one syllable, such as *completed* or *departed,* but the error is occasionally made in two-syllable words. *Supposed* and *used* (as in *I used to go to church regularly* and *I was supposed to see my analyst today*) are especially likely to be pronounced or written incorrectly.

## *Test Yourself on*
## the Final -*d* Sound

A. Pronounce the following italicized words so that the sound of the final -*d* is clearly heard by other students in the room:

1. I am *tired.*
2. He is *prejudiced.*
3. After he *arrived.*
4. The store he *owned.*
5. The lesson she *learned.*
6. He *blamed* me.
7. The meat is *weighed.*
8. Vegetables are *preferred.*
9. The defendant is *judged.*
10. Students are *graded.*
11. The army *surrendered.*
12. My song was *played.*
13. The crowd *cheered.*
14. Drowning man *saved.*
15. My pay *increased.*
16. Food is *provided.*
17. Choice is *offered.*
18. Package is *received.*
19. My heart was *deceived.*
20. I am *relieved.*

B. In the passage below, some words have had -*d* endings removed and some are spelled correctly. Read the passage aloud and notice how the fact that you pronounce some endings (the ones that are there) influences your pronunciation of others (ones that are *not* there). Write in endings wherever they are needed.

Something was needed to cheer me up. I was tire and hadn't been to bed in two days. I thought I would never be rescue and I was worried that even my best friends would not have notice me gone. My foot hurt a lot from when I had slip down the side of the gully and I would have given anything for a little sip of water.

A bird start to chirp. I wish I was as happy as he was. I wish I had his wings!

The accident must have happen because I wasn't as young as I use to be. Still, I was only 23! Are people suppose to lose all their agility after the age of 19? It all weighed on my heart. Suddenly, I notice that the sky was getting very dark. If anybody look for me now, they would have a hard time seeing me. I try to move a little, to see if I could climb to the crest of the hill and make myself more visible. But it was no use. I wish I had climbed up there earlier, when I had more strength.

---

## 2. Sequence of tenses

If you are using two or more verbs in a sequence, either within a single sentence or in sentences that follow each other, it is important that you indicate precise time to the reader.

A. *Finite verbs* (forms expressing tense, person, number, and mood):

When the Judge *banged* his gavel, the courtroom *grew* silent. (Both verbs in the past—both actions took place at the same time in the past.)

Although I *have complained,* I *have received* no satisfaction. (Two perfect tenses: time started in the past and continuing up to the present, in both cases.)

He *said* that he *was* a Martian. (Indirect discourse; both tenses should match: here, the past.)

By the time I *hand in* my papers, I *will have finished* the term's work. (Correct sequence for use of future perfect.)

B. *Infinitives* (*to* forms)

Use the present infinitive to indicate action that happens at the same time as or later than the main verb, and use the present perfect infinitive (*to* + *have* + past participle) for action prior to that of the main verb.

Bill *needed* [past tense] *to forget* [present infinitive]. Bill *needs* [present tense] *to forget* [present infinitive].

He *would love to have charged* his purchase. (Present perfect infinitive used for time prior to main verb.)

C. *Participles*

To denote action happening at the same time as the action of the main verb, use·the present participle. To denote action that happened prior to that of the main verb, use the present perfect participle (present participle of *have* + past participle of verb).

*Jogging* along the main road, he *noticed* many other joggers. (The *noticing* and the *jogging* take place at the same time.)
*Having mastered* geometry, he *knew* he could tackle calculus. (First came the *mastering,* then the *knowing; having mastered* is the present perfect participle.)

---

### *Test Yourself on*
### Sequence of Tenses

Underline the correct verb form in the parentheses for the sequence of tenses in each of the sentences below.

1. Because the patient's heart has begun beating, the doctors believe that the danger to his life (diminished, has diminished).

2. (Having finished, Finishing) the painting, Edward walked away from the easel.

3. They had not expected (to go, to have gone) to California last summer.

4. Pamela plans (to publish, to have published) her novel next year.

5. Arthur thought William missed the point, that he (neglected, had neglected) important issues.

6. (Having been taught, Being taught) good manners by my parents, I did not yawn when he began to speak.

7. (Reaching, Having reached) Chicago, she knew she could drive to Montana.

8. When they (visited, have visited) Italy, they never ate a poor meal.

9. Allan regretted (being born, having been born) handsome instead of rich.

10. Beth wanted (to read, to have read) the books in sequence.

11. Dan insisted that he (once saw, had once seen) a drunken Irishman.

12. (Teaching English, Having taught English), she thought she knew grammar.

---

### 3. Could of, being that, would have/had

Never use the expression *could of*. It is an approximation of what some writers hear when they say *could have* or *could've*.

**Wrong**  He *could of* gone with me to the movies.
**Right**  He *could have* gone with me to the movies.

The same holds true for the forms *would of* and *should of* and any other *of*.

Never use the expression *being that* for *since* or *because*.

**Wrong**  *Being that* he was just a kid, I helped him across the street.
**Right**  *Because* he was just a kid, I helped him across the street.

Never use the expression *would have* in place of *had*.

**Wrong**  If he *would have* done well on his GRE's, he would have been admitted to graduate school.
**Right**  If he *had* done well on his GRE's, he would have been admitted to graduate school.

### 4. The subjunctive mood

The subjunctive mood expresses actions or states of being that are contrary to fact, wishful, imaginary, or not yet actualities. Current English usage has found substitute expressions for virtually all uses of the subjunctive:

If he *were* to leave    If he *leaves*
I imagine he *be* young    I imagine he *is* young.
I wish I *were* finished    I wish I *was* finished.

Nevertheless, there are a few circumstances in which the subjunctive is required usage.

### A. In contrary-to-fact propositions:

He was eating the pizza as if there *were* nothing else on his mind.
I wish you *were* here.

### B. Where clarity is urgently needed:

I insist that the barn *be* painted red. (Substituting *is* for *be* makes the sentence say something entirely different, i.e., that the speaker insists the color of the barn *is already* red.)

### C. In certain *that* clauses:

He moved that the meeting *be* adjourned.
The student asked that he *be* given an oral examination.
Is it right that a woman *suffer* just because she is a woman?
It is necessary that justice *be* done.

The subjunctive also persists in certain idiomatic expressions:

Peace *be* with you.
*Be* that as it may.
*Be* it ever so humble, there's no place like home.

---

## Test Yourself on
## the Correct Use of Verb Forms

A. In each of the sentences below, some form of *could,* *should, would,* or *being* is misused. Correct them.

1. If he would have gone earlier, he would have seen the pregame show.
2. Being that it had the best psychology program she could find, she went to Jefferson College.
3. I could of been a star.
4. She wasn't as alert as she should of been.
5. If he had gone earlier, he would of seen the pregame show.

B. For each italicized verb form in the sentences that
follow, supply the correct subjunctive form.

1. It is necessary that justice *is* done.
2. He was eating as if there *was* no tomorrow.
3. He suggested that their lunch date *is* postponed until
   the following week.
4. Is it right that a man *suffers* for someone else's crime?
5. My brother asked that he *is* given the car tomorrow.

---

# Underlining

See **Italics.**

# Voice

Most verbs can be used in either the active or the passive
voice.

**Active Voice**   John *saw* his son yesterday.

**Passive Voice**   John *was seen* by his son yesterday.

The subject of both sentences is *John.* In the first (active
voice) sentence, *John* is performing the action; in the
second sentence, *John* is undergoing the action.

In English, the active voice is more vigorous and more
emphatic than the passive voice. Beginning writers frequently find their sentences slipping into the passive
voice because they are not quite sure what they want to
emphasize.

**Passive**   These fancy jeans *were bought* by me at the Clothes
Barn.

**Active**   I *bought* these fancy jeans at the Clothes Barn.

These sentences convey the same information, but each
emphasizes a different thing. The passive emphasizes the
*fancy jeans* (because *jeans* is in the subject position in

the sentence) and the active emphasizes *I*. The passive sentence also requires two more words to say the same thing that the active sentence says. The passive sentence is also made awkward because of the *by me* phrase.

We emphasize that the active voice is the stronger and therefore the preferred choice because beginning writers, as well as more experienced ones, are frequently evasive in their use of the passive voice. The use of the active voice corrects this tendency.

### Evasion by a Beginning Writer
Tutoring help in algebra *is needed* by Al. (The sentence reads as if the writer were a little reluctant to mention Al's name, so he has delayed saying that name as long as possible.)

### Evasiveness Corrected by Using the Active Voice
Al *needs* tutoring in algebra.

### Evasion by a More Experienced Writer
It *has been decided* that your application *will not be considered* at this time. (The evasion here is that no decision-maker is named.)

### Evasiveness Corrected by Using the Active Voice
We *have decided* not to consider your application.

Of course, there are circumstances where the use of the passive voice is appropriate.

**1.** Use of the passive voice when the doer of the action is not known.

The making of bronze *was begun* in Southwest Asia around 2500 B.C.
A fire *was set* in an abandoned warehouse on Pier 88 this morning.

It is easy to see why the specific doer in the first of these examples—the person who began to make bronze—is not known. In the second, the opening sentence of a newspaper story, it is clear that the person who set the fire is unknown. Nor would this sentence be improved if the author had written something like "Somebody set a fire ..." or "A person or persons unknown set a fire...."

**2.** Use the passive voice when it is more important to emphasize the receiver than the doer of the action.

The vote on the Equal Rights Amendment *was* not *taken* until midnight.

My vegetable garden *was ruined* by the heavy rainstorm in April, but it *was replanted* in time to give us enough vegetables to last the summer.

In the first sentence, the vote on the amendment is much more important than those who voted. In the second, the rainstorm is unimportant compared to the garden (in the first clause), and the people who replanted it less important than the garden itself (referred to by the pronoun *it* in the second clause).

*Nevertheless,* you should beware of using weakly or evasively passive sentences in a consistent pattern in your work. Sentences such as "This class *was taken* by me last semester" and "My car *was smashed into* by a truck" can only make your writing weak and uninteresting.

---

## *Test Yourself on* the Appropriate Use of the Active Voice

A. Change each of the following passive sentences into an active one.

1. I was bored by the book.
2. Dr. Waldorn is respected by his patients.
3. Everyone on my block is annoyed by Joe's dog.
4. The rich and the famous are admired by most people.
5. The police are angered by disrespect.
6. Financial aid is hoped for by all students.
7. Milk cows are given special care by dairy farmers.
8. Paying bills in an inflationary economy is disliked by everybody.
9. Help is urgently needed by the earthquake victims.
10. Subway riders are exhausted by rush hour traffic.

B. Some of the sentences below use the passive voice appropriately. Next to these, write C. Where the passive voice is either weak or evasive, recast the sentence into the active voice.

1. _____ It is thought by my mother that I'm too young to drive.

2. _____ The Montreal Canadiens were badly beaten by the Boston Bruins at the Montreal Forum last night.

3. _____ Freedom was given to us by God.

4. _____ The ring was given to me for Christmas by my brother.

5. _____ Television is watched by more and more people in this country.

6. _____ Crime is feared more by people in the cities than by people in the country.

7. _____ The labels on canned foods are not read by shoppers in supermarkets.

8. _____ While the kids were being filled with Cokes at the fountain, the car was being filled with gas.

9. _____ It is forbidden to feed the animals.

10. _____ The victims of the two-car crash were taken to the hospital by ambulance.

11. _____ The fuse was ignited.

12. _____ Hot cereal was eaten for breakfast by Jake.

## Wordiness

Direct expression is best. Wordiness, the use of more words than necessary, defeats directness. A good rule is to use as few words as possible but as many as necessary to say what you mean. Below are listed some of the writing faults that cause wordiness; discussed under each heading are ways of making your writing more economical.

## Redundancy: The Elimination of Deadwood

Redundancy means "needless repetition." Examine your writing carefully to make sure you are not being redundant.

**1.** Transform your clauses into phrases and your phrases into single words wherever possible. What you eliminate is called *deadwood*.

**Unnecessary Clause** The professor, *who teaches mathematics,* was angry.
**Revised** The professor *of mathematics* was angry.
**Revised** The *mathematics* professor was angry.

**Unnecessary Phrase** She was lovely *in appearance.*
**Revised** She was lovely.

**Deadwood** After the concert had come to a close, we went to dinner.
**Revised** After the concert, we went to dinner.

**Deadwood.** I am learning the skill of how to do the work of the job.
**Revised** I am learning how to do the job.

**Deadwood** The driver of the truck was angry.
**Revised** The truck driver was angry.

**2.** Eliminate *twofers* from your writing. A *twofer* is the use of two words that mean virtually the same imprecise thing where a single more accurate word, or one of the pair, will do.

**Twofer** He was a *real* and *true* friend.
**Revised** He was a *genuine* friend.

**Twofer** The *light* and the *brightness* were dazzling.
**Revised** The *sun* was dazzling.

**Twofer** I had a lot of *love* and *regard* for her.
**Revised** I *cared* for her very much.

**Twofer** She gave me a *warm* and *friendly* smile.
**Revised** She gave me a *friendly* smile.

**3.** Eliminate words that needlessly repeat what you have already said. *He made revised changes in his book* has a needless repetition. The sentence should read either *He made changes in his book* or *He revised his book.*

**Repetitious**   A hermit is someone who is isolated by himself.
**Revised**   A hermit is someone who is isolated.

**Repetitious**   The animals' roars were audible to the ear.
**Revised**   The animals' roars were audible.

**Repetitious**   Her shawl was a deep red in color.
**Revised**   Her shawl was deep red.

**Repetitious**   The assignments he gave were several in number.
**Revised**   He gave several assignments.

**4.** Do not use several words where one will do. Eliminate from your writing such long-winded (and by now hackneyed) expressions as *in this day and age* or *in this modern world* (*today* will do); *it should be noticed* (*notice* will do); and *as far as _____ is concerned* (where your subject fits in the blank space; eliminate this construction and just use the noun).

---

## *Test Yourself on* Eliminating Redundancies

The following sentences all contain some kind of redundancy. Correct each one by eliminating the redundancy.

1. John is an expert in the field of urban government.
2. Professor Buckley referred back to the Civil War.
3. The snow which fell yesterday is melting into water today.
4. At 9 a.m. in the morning, the driver started to drive toward Cincinnati.
5. As soon as he started to look for a job, he connected up with a large corporation.
6. I'm going to repeat again what I said a moment ago.
7. As far as reading is concerned, I would say that it is a difficult thing for me to do.

8. Most students spend the majority of the hours in each school day attending classes for which they are registered.

9. Although he seemed to be a warm and friendly man, I didn't care for him or like him for some reason.

10. It was not exactly a meaningful or worthwhile experience.

---

## Awkward Repetition

Effective repetition of words can make for emphasis; awkward repetition is merely wordy: It makes for dullness.

**Awkward**   The *driver drove* steadily; his *driving* made us feel safe.
**Revised**   The driver was steady; his skill made us feel safe.

**Awkward**   My *membership* application was accepted by the club and I was made a *member*.
**Revised**   The club accepted my membership application.

**Awkward**   If *one examines* the case, *one can* see that it is *one* of the *cases* that *cannot* stand close *examination.*
**Revised**   The case cannot stand close examination.

**Effective Repetition**   The average politician has a *sinister* past, a *sinister* attitude, and a *sinister plan* for the future.
**Effective Repetition**   *New* mouthwash, *new* deodorant, *new* toothpaste, *new* teeth—television sells them all with equal enthusiasm.

## Wordy Formulas

Eliminate from your writing phrases such as *to be, there is, it is, the type of, of the fact that, the use of.* These can just as well be left out of most sentences.

**Wordy**   She seems *to be* sad this morning. (Read the sentence without the italicized portion and notice that nothing is lost.)
**Wordy**   Higher mathematics appears *to be* difficult.
**Wordy**   The cowboy was considered *to be* a hero.

**Wordy**   *There is* something I have to say.
**Revised**   I have something to say.

**Wordy**   *It is* the truth that is important.
**Revised**   The truth is important.

**Wordy**   I got *the type* of job I wanted.
**Revised**   I got the job I wanted.

**Wordy**   Because *of the fact that* it was raining, we couldn't play the game.
**Revised**   Because it was raining, we couldn't play the game.

**Wordy**   His *use of* English is bad.
**Revised**   His English is bad.

## Passive Voice

By using the active instead of the passive voice, you can eliminate words and create a more vigorous style.

**Passive**   Anxiety about examinations *is felt* by some students.
**Active**   Some students *feel* anxious about examinations.

**Passive**   The holiday *was enjoyed* by everybody.
**Active**   Everybody *enjoyed* the holiday.

## Complicated Diction

Eliminate complicated diction from your writing. Invariably, the fancy way to say something requires more words than the plain way and is not more effective.

**Fancy**   It is my intention to make a careful scrutiny of the record.
**Plain**   I plan to look closely at the record.

**Fancy**   I observed that his behavior was somewhat less than intelligent.
**Plain**   I saw that he was acting foolish.

---

### *Test Yourself on*
### Eliminating Wordiness

Each of the following sentences contains awkward repetitions, wordy formulas, wordy passive voice constructions, or complicated diction. Correct each by using straightforward, active language.

 1. The important subject of my speech will be a subject important to students, educators, and others to whom the subject is of professional interest.
 2. It should be made clear to everyone that utmost silence is necessary while working in the library.
 3. Whenever he's in trouble, he makes use of rationalization.
 4. There is a special beach I'd like to take you to.
 5. It is a terrible thing to be chronically sick.
 6. That point was made by Darwin.
 7. He is the type of person unaware of the fact that people in this modern day and age are unhappy.
 8. Because of the fact that we used logic, we solved the problem and came up with the solution.
 9. George is known to be moody.
10. Some of the best times we had were when we were on vacation.

# The
# Research
# Paper

# The Nature of the Research Paper

If you were assigned to write a biographical sketch of your life and your family situation, you would have no trouble. You would simply reach into your memory for the necessary information. If the assignment asked you to write on your vocational plans, again you would have no trouble—you would speculate, gathering together thoughts and plans you have had on the subject. In both cases, you would be asked to come to some conclusion about the knowledge you would be presenting in the paper. Facts without a conclusion—that is, papers uncontrolled by a central idea or thesis statement—are dull stuff.

The research paper differs from these assignments in that you are asked to gather the knowledge not from your own mind but from the library.* The research paper is similar to the others in that you are also asked to come to a conclusion, that is, to control your material with a thesis statement or central idea, a conclusion about the facts.

You needn't be afraid at this point. By the time you finish your research you *will know* enough about your subject to come to a conclusion about it. In fact, you may even know *more* about it than your instructor.

# Finding and Narrowing a Topic

Three limitations govern the selection of a topic for your paper.

**1.** Certain subjective topics are eliminated. For example, it is futile to undertake to find out whether the Beatles were better musicians than the Rolling Stones or Walt Whitman a better poet than T. S. Eliot because such judgments depend on personal taste and no amount of library research can possibly decide the question.

---

*Of course, there are other kinds of research papers, based on laboratory experiments or other kinds of original investigation.

**2.** Topics that can rely on a single book or other kind of source are also eliminated. Photosynthesis or steel manufacturing, for example, can be explained with the use of a single source. One goal of the paper is to offer you practice in using many sources: eight to ten, depending on your instructor's ideas.

**3.** The length of college research papers—1,500 to 2,000 words—will limit your topic. You cannot, for example, fit a biography of Ronald Reagan into such a length. Nor can you do an adequate job with that length on the conflicts in the Middle East.

In light of these limitations, how should you go about finding a topic?

There are two ways, both based on your own interests. (1) If you have a question about something, say, *why are they fighting in Northern Ireland* or *why did Truman drop the atomic bomb instead of first demonstrating its power,* you are very far along toward a topic *and* a thesis statement (the *answers* to those questions will be thesis statements for the paper); simply research the answers. (2) If you have an interest in a large subject area such as communications or China or education, you must begin to narrow the subject down. The way to do this is by *qualifying* the word that describes your interest and to keep on qualifying it until you have a string of words that add up to a manageable research paper topic.

*China*—education in China—grammar school education in China—the kindergarten curriculum in China—kindergarten reading texts in China—the content of kindergarten reading texts in China—*the political content of kindergarten reading texts in China*

*John F. Kennedy*—the presidency of John F. Kennedy—foreign policy during the presidency of John F. Kennedy—foreign policy toward Communist countries during the presidency of John F. Kennedy—*President Kennedy's decision in the Cuban missile crisis of 1962*

The last strings of words in both examples are suitable topics, quite narrow enough for the size of the paper expected of you. But you cannot do this kind of narrowing in your head. You will probably have to worry over the main subject, first doing some preliminary reading (see below under that heading). This kind of narrowing can be done with *any* large subject matter.

The question the China paper would answer might be something like *how do the Chinese begin to indoctrinate their citizens into their political system?* The Kennedy paper might answer the question *what major considerations went into Kennedy's decision to institute the Cuban missile blockade?*

Another way to think of the "questions" that a paper can answer is to regard them as constituting a statement of purpose. That is, you might preface your paper with a statement of purpose in which you pose the question you propose to answer. In fact, if you can formulate this question (or questions) early enough, it will help to guide you more accurately in your research.

If you simply cannot "find" a topic, you must work harder at the search. You need to be continually *active* in your search for a topic by undertaking such inquiries as these:

**1.** Go over notes for other courses. What issues, people, or events puzzle you or excite your interest? Are there problems in anthropology, history, sociology that stick in your memory?

**2.** Look at your neighborhood or community: what aspects of these places are you curious about? Is there a problem on the streets or on the farm or in the town that you notice and care about?

**3.** Read a newspaper from cover to cover every day for as long as it takes you to uncover some group, person, or event that excites or interests you. Begin to work with one of those.

**4.** Ask for an appointment with one of your instructors. Explain your problem and see if the instructor can suggest a broad area of interest.

Finally, let us repeat, only your *active* search can land you a topic—and the sooner the better.

---

## *Test Yourself on* Identifying or Narrowing a Suitable Topic

Listed below are a number of possible topics for the research paper. If you think the topic is suitable, place a checkmark next to it and be prepared to explain why you think so. If it is not suitable, explain why. If it can be successfully narrowed down to make a good topic, do some preliminary reading, after consulting both the list of texts given in this chapter and your instructor, and make it into a useful topic.

1. How to manufacture steel
2. The energy crisis in the United States
3. Abraham Lincoln's military service
4. Norman Lear's situation comedies: what they have in common
5. Mohammed and Jesus
6. The Mormon Settlement of Salt Lake City
7. Symbolism in dreams
8. Gas rationing during World War II
9. The significance of agribusiness to American farming
10. The job market in America for 1979 college graduates

---

## Preliminary Reading

At this stage, you would do well to begin your work slowly by reading very general material about your topic in one or more of the general reference works listed in this section. The purposes of this preliminary reading, other than to help you narrow down your topic, are to make you broadly acquainted with the field you have chosen to explore and to suggest possible sources for further reading (most, if not all, the works listed here refer the reader to more specific and detailed reading matter).

# A List of Reference Works for Preliminary Reading

Below are listed a number of works in one or more of which you may begin your preliminary reading. The great majority of the works listed are encyclopedias and dictionaries with short general articles. Some, however, are bibliographies—books listing sources for further reading. Yet even these bibliographies are valuable for preliminary reading.

If the book you need is not here, do not despair. Ask either your instructor or your librarian to point you to the proper reference work, or consult the standard work on references, Constance M. Winchell, *Guide to Reference Books,* 8th ed.*

### Agriculture
*Cyclopedia of American Agriculture.* 4 vols. A popular survey of agriculture in the United States and Canada, covering such topics as crops, livestock, machinery, statistics on productivity.

### Arts (Architecture, Dance, Drama, Film, and Music)
*Art Dictionary.* A compendium of terms used in painting, sculpture, architecture, heraldry, and so on. Many of the definitions are accompanied by illustrations.

*Dance Encyclopedia.* Revised and enlarged edition. Numerous articles on all phases of the dance, from the so-called primitive to the most sophisticated modern and ballet.

*Dictionary of Architecture and Building: Biographical, Historical and Descriptive.* 3 vols. Many specialists write on all aspects of these subjects; covers the United States and foreign countries; profusely illustrated.

*Dictionary of Films.* Lists casts, plots, production information, and critical status of more than 1,300 important American and foreign films.

*Dictionary of Filmmakers.* Biographical sketches and filmographies of important film artists (actors, directors, producers, cameramen) from the beginnings of the art to 1971.

*Many of the annotations of these reference works are based on details given in Winchell.

*Encyclopedia of Folk, Country and Western Music.* Covers the development and aesthetics of these branches of popular music.
*Encyclopedia of Jazz.* Biographies of over 2,000 jazz performers from the beginnings through 1959; history of jazz on records; discography and bibliography.
*Encyclopedia of Painting: Painters and Painting of the World from Prehistoric Times to the Present Day.* Illustrated one-volume encyclopedia of art, artists, styles, and so forth.
*Grove's Dictionary of Music and Musicians.* 5th ed. 10 vols. Articles on music, forms, styles, instruments—and musicians of all periods.
*Harvard Dictionary of Music.* 2nd ed. rev. and enl. Omits biographies of musicians, but in its historical emphasis covers virtually all other aspects of music.
*New York Times Film Reviews.* Collects all this newspaper's film reviews from 1913 to 1970; contains index of titles, names of people associated with films, and awards.
*Oxford Companion to the Theatre.* Complete coverage of all aspects of theater in all countries of the world—plays, theaters, actors, scenery, etc.

## Biography

*Chambers's Biographical Dictionary.* Gives brief biographies of the more famous people who have ever lived in the world—includes kings, queens, princes.
*Current Biography.* 37 vols. and supplements. Valuable source of biographical data on people who have recently made some achievement.
*Dictionary of American Biography.* 20 vols. and supplements. Biographies of noted Americans no longer living.
*Dictionary of National Biography.* 22 vols. and supplements. The British equivalent of the preceding work.
*Notable American Women: 1607-1950.* 3 vols. Biographies of women, prominent or important members of American society.
*Who's Who in America.* Appears biennially. The companion is *Who Was Who in America.*

## Current Events

*Britannica Book of the Year.* Alphabetically arranged review of the past year. Contains detailed articles on a cross-section of topics, written by specialists; many charts, tables, photographs.
*Facts on File.* A weekly digest of world news, with annual index; useful compendium of events in politics, science, sports, education, and so on.
*Statesman's Yearbook.* Gives current information—including

statistics and some historical data—about all the countries of the world.

*Statistical Abstract of the United States.* Statistics of every imaginable kind on the status and activities of United States citizens.

*World Almanac and Book of Facts.* A one-volume work that reports international statistical information. Also contains short essays on various topics and biographical sketches of important people. Arranged by subject.

## Ecology

*Advances in Ecological Research.* A periodical first published in 1962. Articles on all aspects of the field.

*An Ecological Glossary.* Terms defined; bibliographies.

*The Ecology Action Guide.* Discusses man's influence on nature and the accretion of pollutants and suggests courses of action.

*The Environment Index.* An annual published since 1971; gives references to the literature.

*Environmental Conservation.* 3rd ed. Discussions of natural resources and the principles involved in their conservation.

*A Guide to the Study of Terrestrial Ecology.* Articles on the environment and experimental work in ecosystems.

*Man's Impact on Terrestrial and Oceanic Ecosystems.* Articles on various aspects of these subjects; includes bibliographies.

*Wildlife in Danger.* Contains short, detailed articles about endangered species and some on the verge of extinction. Discusses natural habitats, physical characteristics, ecological status of the animals; includes many photographs and illustrations.

## Education

*Dictionary of Education.* Gives definitions of technical and professional terms. It defines common foreign terms; cross-referenced.

*Encyclopedia of Education.* 10 vols. More than 1,000 signed articles dealing with various aspects of education: history, institutions, theory, philosophy, and so on.

*Encyclopedia of Educational Research.* Contains articles by educators on the latest developments in the field of education.

*World Survey of Education.* 4 vols. A publication of UNESCO; covers all levels of education, arranged by countries of the world.

## Ethnic Studies

*Black Studies: A Bibliography.* A guide to the literature.

*Directory of Afro-American Resources.* Gives a list of primary sources—documents, diaries, papers, narratives—available through organizations and institutions in the United States.

*Ethnic Studies in Higher Education: State of the Art and Bibliography.* Gives general information, sources, research issues on blacks, Chicanos, Asian-Americans, Native Americans, Puerto Rican and other Spanish-speaking peoples, and various white ethnic groups.

*Mexican Americans: A Research Bibliography.* 2 vols. A computer-assisted bibliography that covers the whole subject by theme and topic.

*Minority Studies: A Selective Annotated Bibliography.* Gives select materials available through 1974 on a rich selection of American minorities, including Hawaiians, Filipinos, Japanese, Chinese, blacks, Spanish-Americans, and Native Americans.

*The Puerto Ricans: An Annotated Bibliography.* Arranged by topic, covers history, geography, current status.

*Reference Encyclopedia of the American Indian.* 2nd ed. 2 vols. A guide to sources of information about Native Americans. Includes a who's who and bibliographies.

## History

*Cambridge Ancient History.* 12 vols. Immensely detailed history of the Western world from the beginnings through the middle of the 4th century A.D.

*Cambridge Medieval History.* 8 vols. The same for the Medieval period, to the beginning of the Renaissance.

*Chronology of the Modern World, 1763 to the Present Time.* This and a companion volume, *Chronology of the Expanding World, 1492–1762,* cover the history of all areas from Columbus onward.

*Dictionary of American History.* 7 vols. plus supplement. Consists of short articles on all aspects of American history.

*An Encyclopedia of World History.* 5th ed., rev. and enl. A one-volume treatment of world events.

*Harvard Guide to American History.* rev. ed. 2 vols. A guide to research; methods and resources; contains valuable bibliographies arranged by periods.

*New Cambridge Modern History.* 14 vols. A detailed history from the Renaissance onward.

## Literature and Mythology

*Cambridge History of American Literature.* 4 vols. From the Colonial through the modern periods, ending in the 1930s.

*Cambridge History of English Literature.* 15 vols. From the Anglo-Saxon beginnings through the modern period, ending in the 1930s.

*Cassell's Encyclopaedia of World Literature.* 2nd ed., 3 vols. rev. Articles on world authors, with biographies and bibliographies.

*Columbia Dictionary of Modern European Literature.* Begins at the end of the nineteenth century and gives critical commentary on many works of the modern period.

*Everyman's Dictionary of Non-Classical Mythology.* Emphasizes non-Western mythology.

*Funk & Wagnall's Standard Dictionary of Folklore, Mythology and Legend.* 2 vols. Covers the mythologies of the world. (1972 ed. is 1 vol.; it is a reissue of the 1949–50 ed. with minor corrections.)

*The Golden Bough.* 12 vols. (Also available in one-volume edition.) An exhaustive study of mythology.

*Mythology of all Races.* 13 vols. Mythologies in very great detail.

*New Larousse Encyclopedia of Mythology.* Essays on world mythologies.

*Oxford Classical Dictionary.* 2nd ed. Good brief articles on classical subjects.

*Oxford Companion to American Literature.* 4th ed., rev. and enl. Excellent source for brief articles on all aspects of American literature.

## Philosophy

*Encyclopedia of Philosophy.* 8 vols. Contains entries on both Western and Eastern philosophers and philosophies.

*History of Western Philosophy.* An excellent overview by a noted philosopher, Bertrand Russell.

*How to Find Out in Philosophy and Psychology.* A guide, for undergraduates, to research methods in these fields.

## Political Science

*Cyclopedia of American Government.* 3 vols. Brief articles on all aspects of government in the United States from the founding to the early twentieth century.

*Dictionary of American Politics.* A one-volume compendium of aspects and figures of American politics.

*International Encyclopedia of the Social Sciences.* 17 vols. Longer articles on political movements and ideas—as well as on comprehensive subjects in the social sciences.

*Palgrave's Dictionary of Political Economy.* 3 vols. Reprints of classic articles on economics as it relates to politics.

## Religion

*Book of Saints.* 5th ed. A dictionary of canonized saints, together with a calendar of their days and brief biographies.

*A Dictionary of Angels, Including the Fallen Angels.* Information about all the angels and angelology.

*Dictionary of the Bible.* Entries on people and places mentioned in the Bible.

*Encyclopedia of the Jewish Religion.* A compendium of information on theology and history of Jewish religion.

*Encyclopaedia of Religion and Ethics.* 13 vols. Very detailed articles on all aspects.

*History of Religions.* 2 vols. Detailed accounts of the rise of religions in Europe, Asia, and the Near East.

*New Catholic Encyclopedia.* 15 vols. Treats every aspect of Catholicism in great detail.

*Sacred Books of the East.* 50 vols. Contains translations of the major works of the seven non-Christian religions that have influenced Asian culture. The *Concise Dictionary of Eastern Religion* is an index to these volumes.

## Science

*Britannica Yearbook of Science and the Future.* Annual; gives the latest scientific developments—with illustrations.

*The Dictionary of the Biological Sciences* and *Encyclopedia of the Biological Sciences.* 2nd ed. Together, these cover all aspects of the field.

*Famous First Facts.* 3rd ed. A record of discoveries and inventions in the United States, with dates and descriptions.

*History of Magic and Experimental Science.* 8 vols. Details the history and development of the experimental sciences and ideas of magic which at one time or another served a scientific function.

*McGraw-Hill Encyclopedia of Science and Technology: An International Reference Work.* 15 vols. Supplemented by the *McGraw-Hill Yearbook of Comprehensive Science and Technology.* Contains general and specific essays dealing with every branch of science and technology. Biographical and historical material is not included. Psychology and medicine are treated only in their preprofessional aspects.

*Van Nostrand's Scientific Encyclopedia.* 5th ed. A one-volume compendium of inclusive scientific knowledge.

## Social Sciences

*Anthropology Today: An Encyclopedic Inventory.* Extensive bibliographies of work in this field up to 1952; gives the range and extent of the whole field.

*Dictionary of Psychology.* rev. ed. Defines terms and gives foreign equivalents.

*Handbook for Social Research in Urban Areas.* A guide to research on urban sociological themes; bibliographies.

*History of Psychiatry: An Evaluation of Psychiatric Thought and*

*Practice from Prehistoric Times to the Present.* A comprehensive review of ideas and developments in the field.

*International Encyclopedia of the Social Sciences.* 17 vols. A comprehensive set of articles on all aspects of the social sciences.

## Women's Studies

*American Women: The Official Who's Who Among the Women of the Nation.* 3 vols. Published from 1935–1940. A valuable source of biographies of accomplished women of the period.

*The Book of Women's Achievements.* A list of these achievements and notes on the achievers, arranged by area of work.

*Female Studies.* 6 vols. College syllabi for study; reading lists; a review of women's studies.

*Index to Women of the World from Ancient to Modern Times.* A list; brief biographies, bibliographies.

*Library on the History of Women in America.* 3 vols. Manuscript inventories and the catalogs of manuscripts, books, and pictures in the library of Radcliffe College. A useful sourcebook.

*Research Guide in Women's Studies.* A valuable guide to writing research papers in this field.

*Women and Society: A Critical Review of the Literature with a Selected Annotated Bibliography.* The title is accurate.

*Women and Sport.* Bibliography of research involving female subjects.

*Women's Rights Almanac.* State-by-state lists giving information sources and other resources of interest to women; discussions of legal issues important to women.

*The World Who's Who of Women.* Published from time to time; gives brief biographies of prominent women of the world.

# Other General Reference Works

Two other types of general reference works should be mentioned here.

## *General encyclopedias*

For preliminary reading as well as for bibliographic references, the most useful general encyclopedias are the *Encyclopaedia Britannica* and the *Encyclopedia Americana.* Good one-volume works are the *Columbia Encyclopedia* and the *Random House Encyclopedia.*

## Dictionaries

These rarely contain bibliographies, but the student working in the field of language should know about these useful sources:

### General

*A Dictionary of American English on Historical Principles.* 4 vols.
*The Oxford English Dictionary.* 12 vols. and supplement. Also issued in a two-volume *Compact Edition,* complete but photographically reduced.
*Webster's Third New International Dictionary*

### Special

*Dictionary of Afro-American Slang*
*Dictionary of Word and Phrase Origins*
*Oxford Dictionary of English Etymology*
*Dictionary of Slang and Unconventional English.* 7th ed.
*Dictionary of American Slang.* 2nd ed.

---

## *Test Yourself on* Using Reference Works

In order to gain practice in using general reference works in the library, find at least five general reference works in which you can find information on

1. your research paper topic,
2. a sample topic assigned by your instructor, or
3. one of the following topics: (a) the development of computers; (b) Napoleon Bonaparte (1769–1821); (c) the Iroquois Indians; (d) gas rationing in the United States; (e) the drug *laetrile;* (f) the origins of the Democratic party in the United States; (g) dolphins.

---

## Preparing a Bibliography

The *working bibliography* is a list of books, articles, pamphlets, and other reference materials—*the* list from which your paper will be written; it is kept on a series of index cards, one card for each publication (see below for a discussion of how to set up a working bibliography on index cards). The *final bibliography* is a typed list of those publications actually used in the preparation of your paper; it is appended to the final draft. Thus it is possible to end up with a final bibliography that is not identical with the working bibliography; along the way, you may drop some items from the working bibliography and, of course, add others. The following are the principal sources for your working bibliography.

## *The card catalog*

Probably your most important source will be the library's card catalog, which lists alphabetically on $3'' \times 5''$ index cards every piece of printed or filmed material the library owns. For each book, there are usually three cards: an author card, a title card, and a subject card (see page 348 for samples of all three kinds). Some books have additional subject cards and/or additional author cards if there are two or more authors. The author card is always the basic card; all other cards are duplicates of this card, with the title or subject heading typed at the top.

The different kinds of cards are there to help you in your research. You may, for example, remember that a particular author writes well on a subject that interests you. Finding that author's name in the catalog will lead you to the books you want. Or you may remember a title but not the author; the title card will be most useful to you in that case. Finally, if you know neither author nor title but have only a subject in mind, the card catalog lists books under numerous subject headings.

It is useful to read the explanatory key printed with the sample cards on page 348, because knowing what the card symbols mean can help you to select books on your topic that are especially valuable rather than just general. For example, a card may offer information on the book's contents, whether or not it contains a bibliography (and if so, how long), illustrations, maps, graphs, and so on. When you can quickly assimilate this information, you can make a much shrewder choice of books to add to your working bibliography than a researcher who cannot.

1. Author's name; following name, author's dates often are given.
2. Title of book, place of publication, name of publisher, edition, date of publication or copyright (brackets around year indicate that date is not printed on title page).
3. Call number in the library.
4. Number of pages (roman numerals indicate 7 pages of introductory matter); illustrations, if present; height of book in centimeters. (As this book is a little under 9″ high, it would normally be found in its regular shelf place; large books often are shelved on a separate large-size shelf.)
5. Explanatory notes; description of special features, if present.
6. Other places in the card catalog where cards for this book are filed. These other cards are shown here.
7. Call number under the Library of Congress System.
8. Call number under the Dewey Decimal System.
9. International Standard Book Number.
10. Title.
11. Subject.

Take another example: paying attention to dates of publication and information on the edition of the book (how many times it has been revised and reissued) can also be useful. As a researcher, you may be making a good choice by consulting a recently published work on your topic, but you should also consult a book whose first edition was published, say, ten years ago but whose latest edition is marked "4th ed." This information would suggest that the book may be on its way to achieving status close to that of a standard in its field—by virtue of its having been reissued so often over so short a period of time.

## Lists of periodicals

Researchers who want to locate a periodical should consult one of the following:

*Ayer Directory of Publications.* A standard source of information about newspapers and magazines published in the United States, Canada, Bermuda, Panama, and the Philippines.
*Ulrich's International Periodicals Directory.* Periodicals of the whole world, arranged by subject.
*Union List of Serials in Libraries of the United States and Canada*

## Indexes to periodical literature

Articles in newspapers and magazines are an important source for research material, but they are not listed in the library's card catalog and must be sought in the various indexes to periodical literature. The major index for articles on a wide variety of subjects published in nonspecialized magazines is the *Readers' Guide to Periodical Literature.* This is published twice a month and then cumulated in annual volumes. Articles are indexed by subject and author and by titles of certain creative works (including films). Here is a sample of entries from the *Readers' Guide.**

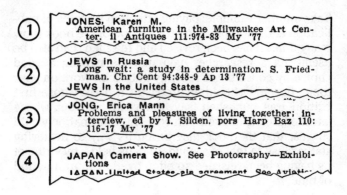

1. Author entry for illustrated article, "American Furniture in the Milwaukee Art Center," in *Antiques,* volume 111, pages 974–983, May 1977 issue.
2. Subject entry for article by S. Friedman in *Christian Century,* volume 94, pages 348–349, issue of April 13, 1977.
3. Another subject entry, but this subject is a person: the writer Erica Jong. The entry refers to an interview with her, illustrated with several portraits, in *Harper's Bazaar,* volume 110, pages 116–117, May 1977 issue.
4. Cross-reference entry that refers to the Photography section of the *Guide.*

Very useful for topics of current interest as well as for topics that require day-by-day information dating back to 1851 is *The New York Times Index.* The *Index* refers you to articles in the *Times,* giving date of issue and page number. Here is a set of sample entries:*

**BEARS. See** Hunting F 21, 2d Ag 8 par
  Wounded black bear sighted, Letchworth, NY; Rockland County areas alerted, Ja 26, 39:1
  R Murphy article on polar bears, threat of extinction and US move to preserve them; illus, Mr 28, VI,p38; depletion in Arctic area linked to high prices of skins at Vancouver fur auction, Je 6, 117:4; scientists from US, USSR, Canada, Norway and Denmark to conf, Anchorage, Alaska; more polar bears reptd being killed in Alaska by airborne hunters; illus, Jl 11,52:3
  Bears claw 2, Gt Smoky Mts Natl Pk, Je 1,31:3
  Drs F C and J J Craighead rev 7-yr experiment in which they drugged grizzlies in Yellowstone Natl Pk and attached devices to study their behavior; details; Natl Geographic Soc and Natl Science Foundation sponsors, D 19,58:1

(1)
(2)
(3)
(4)
(5)

BEARSTED, Lord (Marcus Richard Samuel). See
Hill, Samuel & Co
BEASLEY, (Asst Sec) D Otis. To retire, D 11,31:5
BEATLES, The (George Harrison, John Lennon,
Paul McCartney, Ringo Starr). See Motion Pic-
tures—Revs, Hard Day's Night; Help!.Music—Gen
F 13,19, My 19, Ag 11 par. Music—Tours, Foreign.
Recordings Je 10, Ag 9, N 9, D 14,17. TV—Pro-
grams, Beatles
    R Starr weds M Cox, London, F 12,19:1
    Queen Elizabeth names Beatles members of Brit
Empire Order, Je 12,1:8; Brit reaction, Je 13,3:2;
MP H Dupuis (Canada) to return his medal in pro-
test, Je 15,15:1
    2 Brit war heroes protest award of Brit Empire
Order, Je 16,13:1; Lt Col Wagg returns all 12 of his
medals to Queen in protest, Je 17,3:3; comment on
dispute; group of Labor MPs signs motion welcom-
ing award, Je 20,IV,5:3
        Investiture ceremony, Buckingham Palace; illus,
O 27,49:8
BEATON, Cecil. Diaries, 1939-44, revd, N 7,VII,
p90

Notes on the "BEATLES" entry:

1. Paragraph 1 compresses much information in a group of cross-references to full entries elsewhere: (1) Reviews and other news items about the Beatles' movies *A Hard Day's Night* and *Help!* can be located by looking up the titles under the index heading Motion Pictures—Reviews. (2) News items relating to the Beatles' music printed on February 13 and 19, May 19, and August 11 (paragraph) are described and further identified under the index heading Music—General, where the entries are arranged in order of dates of news items. (3) News items about the Beatles' tours can be found under Music—Tours, Foreign, alphabetically under "Beatles." (4) Items about the Beatles' recordings printed on June 10, August 9, November 9, December 14 and 17 are described and further identified under the index heading Recordings, where the entries are in order of dates. (5) Items about the Beatles' TV programs can be found under Television—Programs, alphabetically under "Beatles."

Following are a number of actual entries describing and locating general news items:

2. Paragraph 2 refers to a news story about Ringo's marriage to M. Cox in London; the article appears in the February 12 *Times* on page 19, column 1.

3, 4, 5. These paragraphs concern the award of the Order of the British Empire to the Beatles and the uproar this caused among certain British citizens. At the end of paragraph 4, the roman number "IV" refers to section 4 of the paper. At the end of paragraph 5, the abbreviation "illus" means that the article is accompanied by one or more photographs.

## Specialized indexes

In addition to the periodical indexes, you can consult a large number of specialized indexes, by subject area. The following is only a partial list:

*Agricultural Index*
*Applied Science and Technology Index*
*Bibliographic Index*
*Book Review Index*
*Business Periodicals Index*
*Engineering Index*
*Essay and General Literature Index*
*Index of Economic Journals*
*Index to Legal Periodicals*
*Music Index*
*Public Affairs Information Service Bulletin*
*Social Sciences and Humanities Index*

In addition to these, numerous other, even more specialized, indexes are available and listed in the card catalog. Look for the cards that follow a subject or author entry that have printed across the top in red the word *BIBLIOGRAPHY* or *INDEX*.

*Note:* All indexes, including the *Readers' Guide* and *The New York Times Index,* supply the reader with keys to their abbreviations. These "key" pages usually appear at the front of the volume. Looking over these pages before you begin to search the volume can usually save you a great deal of time and confusion.

## Government documents

The federal government publishes an enormous amount of material on numerous subjects. Guides to this literature are the *Monthly Catalog of United States Government Publications* and the *Monthly Checklist of State Publications.*

## *Test Yourself on*
## Sources of Information

Using your research paper topic or a sample topic assigned to the whole class, make a list of subject headings under which you might find sources of information. Take the list to the library and look up each subject heading in the following three sources:

1. *Readers' Guide.*
2. *The New York Times Index.*
3. The card catalog.

Add to your list of subject headings as you discover new ones. Which source was best for your particular topic? Why?

### *Setting up the working bibliography*

The mechanics of setting up your working bibliography are simple and may appear to you to be excessively tedious. But if you establish good work habits at this stage, your life (while working on this paper) will be free of stress. Skipping past the meticulousness required here will surely cause you grief later—the experience of millions of researchers attests to that fact.

For this work, you should acquire 3″ × 5″ lined index cards. Use one card for each book or article or pamphlet—*never* put more than one entry on a single card. Following are sample cards for a book and a magazine article. Note carefully the reasons behind including each bit of information.

Sample bibliographical entries for various kinds of published materials begin on page 355. You may use these entries as models in setting up your working bibliography. These are later transferred to a typed list and used as your final bibliography (see below for instructions on setting up the final bibliography). Note carefully the order in which information is presented and the exact punctuation used to separate the items.

1. The call number of the book or magazine volume; once you've noted it here, you need not return to the card catalog every time you want the book or article.
2. Your own item number. In your rough first draft of the paper, you can use this number in your rough footnotes. You also use this number on your note cards.
3. Name of author, exact title, facts of publication. Being exact here can save you trouble: you can use this card for your final bibliography.
4. An important note reminding yourself of an especially useful feature of the source.
5. Exact page numbers of the article.
6. Note reminding yourself that this article is one of a series and that it contains data of special interest to you.

## A Book

Waldhorn, Arthur. <u>A</u> <u>Reader's</u> <u>Guide</u> <u>to</u> <u>Ernest</u>
    <u>Hemingway</u>. New York: Farrar, Straus and
    Giroux, 1972.

## A Work in Several Volumes

Jaeger, Werner. <u>Paideia:</u> <u>The</u> <u>Ideals</u> <u>of</u> <u>Greek</u>
    <u>Culture</u>. Trans. Gilbert Highet. 3 vols.
    New York: Oxford University Press, 1943.

## A Later or Revised Edition

French, Robert Dudley. <u>A</u> <u>Chaucer</u> <u>Handbook</u>. 2nd ed.
    New York: Appleton-Century-Crofts, Inc.,
    1955.

## The Work of Several Authors

Lynn, Naomi B., Ann B. Matasar, and Marie Barovic
    Rosenberg. <u>Research</u> <u>Guide</u> <u>in</u> <u>Women's</u> <u>Studies</u>.
    Morristown, N.J.: General Learning Press,
    1974.

*Note:* Where there is more than one author, only the first author's name is inverted.

## A General Reference Work

"Fleming, Sir Alexander," <u>Chambers's</u> <u>Biographical</u>
    <u>Dictionary</u>. New Edition. P. 476a.

## An Article from An Edited Collection

Rovit, Earl H. "Ralph Ellison and the American
    Comic Tradition." In <u>Ralph</u> <u>Ellison:</u> <u>A</u>
    <u>Collection</u> <u>of</u> <u>Critical</u> <u>Essays</u>, ed. John
    Hersey. Englewood Cliffs, N.J.: Prentice-
    Hall, Inc., 1974.

## Articles from Weekly Magazines

Otten, Jane. "Living in Syntax." <u>Newsweek</u>,
    December 30, 1974, p. 9.
"Coming Across." <u>The</u> <u>New</u> <u>Yorker</u>, June 27, 1977,
    pp. 26-27.

## An Article from a Monthly Magazine

Mattingly, Ignatius C. "Some Cultural Aspects of
    Serial Cartoons, or Get A Load of Those
    Funnies." <u>Harper's</u>, December 1955, pp. 34-39.

### An Article in a Learned Journal

Erikson, Erik H. "The Problem of Ego Identity."
      Journal of the American Psychoanalytic
      Association, 4 (January 1956): 56–121.

### Newspaper Articles

Maitland, Leslie. "Story of an East Side Policeman
      Who Turned in Fellow Officers." The New York
      Times, July 3, 1977, sec. 1, pp. 1, 33.
"Eight Firemen Injured as Tenement Burns." The New
      York Times, July 3, 1977, sec. 1, p. 25.

### A Public Document

U.S. Congress. Senate. Committee on the Judiciary.
      Hearings before the Subcommittee to
      Investigate Juvenile Delinquency. Washington,
      D.C.: Government Printing Office, 1954.

## Setting up the final bibliography

To do this job, take your working bibliography cards, the ones you have actually used in writing your paper, and alphabetize them according to the authors' last names. For unsigned articles, alphabetize by the first letter of the first word, excluding the initial words *the* or *a.* Then simply type the cards into a list that looks like the final bibliography shown at the end of the sample research paper (p. 411). Be sure to use a heading and to follow the spacing and indentation of the sample—indenting five spaces for the second and subsequent lines of the bibliographical citation and double-spacing between entries. Notice that items in a final bibliography are not numbered.

---

## *Test Yourself on*
## Bibliography Form

Using the forms just discussed, set up working bibliography cards for each of the following items.

1. A book by Claude Lévi-Strauss called Structural Anthropology, translated by Claire Jacobson and Brooke

G. Scoepf and published in New York City in 1963 by Basic Books, Inc.

2. An article by Donald Kaplan called On Preaching Old Virtues while Practicing Old Vices: A Psychoanalytic Perspective on Morality. It was published in the Bulletin of the Menninger Clinic, volume 39, number 2, in March 1975, on pages 113–130.

3. A book in two volumes by Vernon L. Parrington called Main Currents in American Thought, published in New York by Harcourt, Brace & World, Inc., in 1954.

4. A newspaper article by Christopher S. Wren called Soviet Sharpens Criticism of U.S. Plans for Missile, published on page 1 of the New York Times for July 4, 1977, and continued on page 2.

5. A book edited by Mary Jane Moffat and Charlotte Painter called Revelations: Diaries of Women. It was published in 1974 by Random House in New York.

# Reading and Taking Notes

You are now ready to begin a period of intensive reading of the works you have compiled for your working bibliography.

How do you go about it and how do you take notes on what you've read?

First, avoid crashing; that is, avoid all emergency schedules—such as all-night sessions or forty-eight-hour squeezes. Instead, *plan* a reading period of, say, two work weeks, ten days, in which you read either in the library or in your room for two to three hours a session.

Second, what should you read? Obviously, you should read the whole of every article you select for your working bibliography, but should you read the whole of every book you have chosen? Not necessarily. How to decide? Look at the table of contents carefully; look at the index of the book carefully. For example, suppose you are writing on John F. Kennedy's handling of the Cuban missile crisis. You might have a book on your list that would take you through Kennedy's entire political career.

The shrewd move would be to examine the index carefully and read where the subject headings refer you to such topics as "Cuban missile crisis," "attitude toward Russians," and "pressure from Republicans regarding Cuba." You might want to read more of such a book—but you should understand that it is not entirely necessary to read from cover to cover every book on your list. The effective researcher learns to pick through the jungle of data to find what is *needed*.

---

*Totemism*                                              ⑨

   p. 30

   Maoris of New Zealand consider animals, vegetables, and minerals true ancestors. Therefore, "they cannot play the part of totems."

---

Notes on the "Totemism" card:

1. There is only one note on the card; that is, the note refers to one page of the source and sticks to a single subject; this makes for ease of handling: The card can be shuffled into any number of different positions in your final ordering.

2. The subject heading, "Totemism," is written at the top left and underlined; this also makes for ease of handling when sorting cards later.

3. The note itself *begins* with the page number at the left, above. It is written first so that you will have no trouble in identifying the page reference when you write your footnote.

4. The number in the upper-right-hand corner is the item number in your working bibliography that identifies the source, in this case *Totemism* by Claude Lévi-Strauss.

5. Part of this note is a direct quotation from the source. When you quote directly, be sure to include the quotation marks—*both* sets.

What kind of notes should you take and how should you record this material?

First, the easy part: Notes should be recorded on index cards. Researchers who do not use index cards are in for trouble—if not for downright misery; there is simply no way to keep and organize notes on ordinary note paper or in a notebook used for other purposes as well. *No way.* The good size for this job is the 5″ × 8″ *lined* card.* A lined card encourages neat writing (very important when it comes time to decipher what you've written!), and the extra size will enable you to get a good deal of information on the cards while still not sacrificing ease of handling. A rubber band to hold them together is essential.

If you've compiled an efficient set of working bibliography cards, all you need do when you record data on a note card is to use the number of the bibliography card and the page number where you got the data. Two examples are shown on pages 358 and 360.

What kind of notes should you take? What kinds of information should you record?

The best instrument for determining this is the rough outline of your paper. (See below for more about outlines.) Although you may not have a fully developed outline at this point, you may have either a topic outline or a rough idea of the main divisions of your paper. For example:

1. Advantages of nuclear power
2. Disadvantages of nuclear power
3. Advantages of solar power
4. Disadvantages of solar power

If you have something like this (and you may want to work in such a way or find yourself working in such a way that you will have), then your notes should of course fill out what you need for these main divisions.

*If you don't like the idea of carrying around 3 × 5 cards for your working bibliography and 5 × 8 cards for your notes, switch to 5 × 8 for both.

④

*Grief and depression*
*p. 155*
*Comparing real grief and the
state of depression :*

*real grief = loss by death of real
person*
*= world becomes poor
and empty*
*depression = unconscious loss of
image of person*
*= self becomes poor
and empty*

Notes on the "Grief and depression" card:
1. Note that this card is written in a kind of shorthand. This system is perfectly acceptable as long as you can interpret the shorthand you decide to use. Actually, this is good note-taking because it summarizes concisely a densely informative page from a difficult source, Freud's essay "Mourning and Melancholia." It is also possible to summarize *several* pages of a source on a single card.
2. As in the previous card, the subject heading that identifies the card is written at the upper left.
3. Also as in the previous card, the page number is placed above the note itself, and the item number that identifies the source is written at the upper right.

The other instrument you have for determining what kinds of information to record is your instinct; by this time you *know* something about your topic and you will be working to increase that knowledge. Thus the best advice is that you record whatever you think important, reserving for later the job of sifting through the cards and disregarding what is not useful.

But the biggest question you will face is whether to paraphrase information you gather from a particular page or pages or to quote it exactly onto your cards.

In nearly all cases, your decision should be to paraphrase. There are a number of good reasons for this, beginning with the fact that your paper will (because it *should*) use relatively little direct quotation. Papers that quote extensively appear to be nothing more than strings of undigested pieces of quotation; the reader tires of reading so much quoted material and is not prepared to take in the full significance of a réally important quote, because the writer has not been selective in the use of such material.

Direct quotation in your paper should only be used when (1) you need directly to prove something and only the actual words you have read will do that job; (2) you intend to be critical of the actual words an author has used; or (3) the words are so appropriate, dramatic, emphatic, or witty that no paraphrase can do them justice. For example, suppose you are reading about an event that took place in the 1950s, a hearing on the use of air power by the United States Air Force. The then commander of our Strategic Air Forces, General Curtis LeMay, Jr., you read, suggested to a congressional committee that we "bomb them into the Stone Age." You want to record General LeMay's attitude. Do you paraphrase and note that "LeMay favored total destruction of the enemy by air power" or do you quote him directly? No difficulty there.

Naturally, there are harder problems than this example. But as you read and take notes, you will become more expert at making these decisions and you can always go back—after gaining some experience—and check to see what you can do to improve your notes.

After each reading session, you are likely to have a pile of cards—perhaps ten or more. Whatever the number, you must now perform an important task. Read each card carefully and see what its essence is; that is, see if you can summarize each card in one or two words. Take a large felt-tip marker and write this word or words across the top. After your two-week reading period, you will have a large number of cards, ready to organize by the subject headings you've written across the top of each. These words, or subject headings, should correspond—or with slight revision can correspond—to the rough divisions you had already had in mind before you started the period of intensive reading. In any case, they are needed for the next step: preparing an outline.

# Preparing an Outline

An outline is an instrument for controlling the writing of a paper. It details the order in which you present your material. A *topic outline* is useful for the preliminary stages of a research paper, because it assists you to order your reading and your notes. Here is a typical—and simple—topic outline for a paper on the energy crisis in America:

I. The energy situation in the U.S. before 1973
II. Action by oil-exporting countries in 1973
III. Situation in U.S. between 1974 and 1977

This is an efficient way to order a chronological set of materials. But notice that while this kind of outline orders the material, it *says* nothing about that which it orders; it expresses no point of view, so that we have no idea of the writer's viewpoint on the material.

I. The energy situation in the U.S. before 1973 was already critical but little noticed.
II. The action by the oil-exporting countries in 1973 made the situation much worse.
III. The situation in the U.S. between 1974 and 1977 has been one of frantically and inefficiently scrambling after "a solution."

What makes this outline more useful than the topic outline is the fact that each of the roman numerals precedes a sentence—a statement that *says* something, that articulates a point of view, and that gives direction to the writer who must use it in writing the paper.

So important is it to develop the sentence outline that many instructors will not permit a student writer to begin composing a paper until this job is done. And at this stage, ready or not, the writer must take the plunge and begin to do the job.

What is most essential for the sentence outline is a

thesis—a controlling, central point of view, the conclusion you have come to after all your reading and thinking about your topic. And the thesis can emerge in one of two ways. (1) You have been, as you were engaged in intensive reading and note-taking, an avid reader of your own note cards; each day, after you finished, you thought about the notes you had taken, the subject headings you had written across them, and the implications of all this. Now you read your notes one last time and suddenly your thesis appears full-blown in your mind. (2) You work on your cards in an organized way until your thesis emerges from your subject headings.

## Working with your note cards: toward a thesis and an outline

Let us suppose that you have been researching an aspect of the energy crisis that developed in the United States after 1973. You have narrowed your topic to "The Relative Merits of Nuclear and Solar Power: Making a Rational Choice." You intend in your paper to answer two questions: (1) Which form of power is the more advantageous to fulfill our needs? (2) What are the prospects for America's adopting the one that seems more advantageous? You have done your reading and now have a batch of note cards under each of the following subject headings:

A. development of nuclear reactors for power needs
B. ancient devices for using the sun
C. nuclear accidents
D. nuclear waste disposal
E. advantages of solar power
F. advantages of nuclear power
G. absence of solar power technology
H. no portable systems for solar power
I. high nuclear costs
J. high solar startup costs
K. solar storage: a problem
L. costs of dismantling nuclear plants
M. industry's attitudes toward solar power
N. industry's attitudes toward nuclear power
O. government's sponsorship of nuclear power
P. government's failure to sponsor solar power

It seems easy enough to impose a preliminary order on these batches of cards. For example, A and B obviously go together in an introduction. M, N, O, and P belong at the end, where you would discuss the prospects for adopting the better choice (either nuclear or solar power). The remaining batches of cards belong in the central part of your paper, but they need to be put together under new subject headings. Logically, batches C through K fall into four separate categories under these headings:

1. advantages of nuclear power
2. disadvantages of nuclear power
3. advantages of solar power
4. disadvantages of solar power

To join these four, we should combine M, N, O, and P into two:

5. government and industry's attitude toward nuclear power
6. government and industry's attitude toward solar power

When you have done this, you are ready for an important task. You must *turn these six subject headings into sentences* that accurately express what *you* think is said by the totality of the cards you've arranged under these new subject headings. To do this, you must read each pack of cards carefully and, from the mass of details they contain, extract a generalization (a sentence) that accurately covers what the cards contain. Your sentence for any one pack need not contain *everything* on the cards—at this stage you may ignore some cards, deciding that some of the information is irrelevant to your sentence. But you do need a sentence for each subject heading.

Let us suppose now that you've done the job and the sentences come out like this:

1. The advantages of nuclear power are few.
2. The disadvantages of nuclear power are considerable.
3. The advantages of solar power are considerable.
4. The disadvantages of solar power are the same as those for any other newly developing technology.
5. The government has sponsored nuclear research, and industry is inclined to follow the path of nuclear development.

6. The government has given little aid to solar power research, and industry is reluctant to pay the costs of solar power development.

The reader who examines these sentences carefully will see that it is possible to find embedded in them a plausible thesis. What is required now are the *words* to express that thesis. As an exercise, before you read any further, try writing a rather longish sentence, using the materials in 1 through 6 above, that you think would do for a thesis.

Compare what you have written with the following:

The advantages that solar power has over nuclear power make it seem more suitable for America's energy needs, but government and industry are not inclined to press for its wide-scale adoption.

Now that you have a thesis, you are ready to "divide" it into an outline.

I. Introduction: Solar energy has been used successfully for thousands of years; nuclear energy is a recent development dating from 1945, when it was first used in the atomic bomb.

II. The advantages of nuclear energy are far outweighed by its disadvantages.
   A. The advantages of nuclear energy are few.
      1. There is a relatively stable supply of fuel.
      2. There is an available and developing technology.
      3. There is a body of engineers and workers trained in nuclear technology.
   B. The disadvantages of nuclear energy are considerable.
      1. It is thermodynamically inefficient.
      2. It needs extraordinary handling because of its deadly character, and its waste products remain deadly for centuries.
      3. It can give rise to catastrophic accidents.
      4. Its recycled products can be made into dangerous weapons.

III. The advantages of solar power far outweigh its disadvantages.
   A. The advantages of solar power are considerable.
      1. Its fuel, the sun, is in endless supply at no cost.
      2. It is thermodynamically efficient.
      3. It results in no deadly waste products.
      4. It cannot give rise to catastrophic accidents.

B. The disadvantages of solar power are virtually the same as those of any other newly developing technology.
   1. It will be fairly expensive to integrate solar power with current systems.
   2. It is not yet efficient to store solar power.
   3. It is not yet efficient to use solar power for transportation.

IV. Since government and industry are not enthusiastic about making the effort solar power will require and since both have heavy investments in nuclear technology, it seems unlikely that solar power will be adopted on a large scale in America in the near future.

## Notes on the outline

1. Note that the introduction rephrases into a sentence the materials on the original note cards, batches A and B (see p. 363).

2. Note that roman numerals II, III, and IV literally divide up the thesis statement on page 365. Note too that as we go from the A's and B's to arabic numerals, the dividing and specifying process continues.

3. Note that sentences II and III are parallel in form. Note too that the parallelism extends to the A's and B's, and that the numerical entries under these are also parallel.

4. The materials, the specific points made, in the statements marked by arabic numerals come, of course, from the note cards.

Of course, a different set of note cards for a different paper will present different problems, but the process is essentially the same: Consider your material until it yields more and more inclusive generalizations, from subject headings to sentences and from these sentences to a thesis. From the thesis to the outline is a matter of proper division and adding details from the cards.

The following few rules may be useful if you want to check your outline against some standard before submitting it to the instructor.

**1.** No outline should be written unless you are sure

the thesis is a satisfactory one. (For more on Thesis Statements, see the entry in Part 2.) Here is an example of an unsatisfactory thesis for the nuclear-solar power outline we have just discussed:

There are many advantages and disadvantages to using nuclear power and solar power.

This is unsatisfactory because it is too vague—and would remain so even if it named some of the advantages and disadvantages it speaks of. It is also a failure in not saying specifically what the writer thinks *after* doing the research; a statement like this one could have been made *before* reading about the subject. Compare it to the thesis statement on page 365.

**2.** The outline should always divide its material logically. For example, consider this piece of outline:

II. By hard work, Woodward and Bernstein tracked down their important sources.
   A. They tracked down a secretary at CREEP.
   B. They found an important source in the F.B.I.
III. They located a "leak" in the White House itself.

Notice that roman numeral III should be capital C. It clearly refers back to roman numeral II and is in parallel form with A and B.

**3.** The outline should present its material in logical order. Consider this preliminary outline:

I. Modern methods of early diagnosis cut down on heart disease fatalities.
II. Treatment of heart disease was hampered before 1950 by inadequate diagnostic understanding.
III. Treatment of heart disease cases used to consist of rest and only rest.
IV. Modern treatment of heart attack is based on the theory of prevention by physical and psychological conditioning.

Can you rearrange these into a more logical order? If you changed I to III, kept IV, and changed II and III to I and II, respectively, you have a good eye for logical order.

# Writing the Paper

If you have done your work efficiently to this point, you now have an outline in hand and batches of note cards in the same order as the divisions in that outline—and you are ready to write.

## *The mechanics*

You should be prepared to write at least two drafts. It is not inappropriate to suggest, in fact, that you write as many drafts as you need to write; it is hard to imagine extra attention spoiling your work. Depending on your preference in work habits, you may either write your drafts in longhand or type them; either way, be sure to keep careful track of your footnotes from draft to draft. (See below, Footnotes, for detailed information about them.)

When you are ready for a final draft, it should be typed on good white bond, $8\frac{1}{2}$ " $\times$ 11", on one side of the page only, with footnotes at the foot of the page or all together at the end, as your instructor requests. You should supply a title page (see Sample Paper) and a final bibliography. All of these should be proofread carefully.

Finally, you should know that there are a variety of words and phrases available to use in introducing quoted material. It is useful rhetorical strategy, for example, to introduce a quote with an expression like "as the noted astronomer and cosmologist Carl Sagan has observed. . . ." In this way, you let the reader know that an authority's words are about to be spoken, and the reader might be properly impressed. In any case, there are many ways to introduce quotes and you should think about the values inherent in each. For your convenience, here is a small list (there are many others):

As Prof. X *declared*                  In Kennedy's *analysis*
Dr. Falk *notes*                       By Freud's *definition*
Winston Churchill *observed*           Edward Heath *asserted that*
As Pablo Picasso *put it*              Nixon *summarized it as*
Nietzsche *has written that*

## *The rhetoric*

Everything you know about writing should, of course, be applied to the writing of the research paper. But this paper presents a special problem that you have not encountered before: the necessity to weave into your paper materials taken from a number of sources. The way to deal with this problem is to take the approach that these materials are *not* in and of themselves the heart of your paper; the heart of your paper is *your* purpose in writing, the thesis that you have set out to present. Once you have made the decision to take this approach, the materials you have been collecting will fall into their proper place. That is, you will see that they are to be used for your purposes, *woven* into the texture of your paper to support and illustrate your thesis and *not* strung together like strange beads because these pieces are all you have to present.

# Documentation

## The Mechanics

Documentation is substantiation, providing proof or evidence. In a research paper, documentation is in the form of footnotes that specify the source of something you have used in your paper. The things in your paper that require a footnote for documentation are the following:

1. A direct quote from a source.
2. Statistics, including graphs, tables, charts, or diagrams taken from a source.
3. A discussion in your own words based on someone else's words.
4. Your paraphrase of someone else's opinion.

You need *not* footnote specific details that you did not know before you began work on the paper *provided they are such that in the field of your topic they are common knowledge.* For example, you need not document the fact that Robert Kennedy was Attorney General of the United States during his brother's presidency; this fact is considered common knowledge in the history of the United States from 1960 to 1963.

You should consult your instructor if you have questions about documentation, because one of the goals of writing a research paper is to learn the accurate documentation of research materials, and the instructor's guidance in the matter can help you improve your skills.

## Ethics

In working with other people's material—an invariable part of writing a research paper—you may be faced with two ethical considerations. The first is the necessity to acknowledge the debt you owe to a source for words, ideas, or facts. The failure to make such acknowledgments is a serious breach of ethics known as plagiarism. For plagiarism, published writers are subject to court action and student writers to disciplinary action by the schools they attend. The second is the duty you have to present with absolute fairness the essential meaning of what you are quoting. Failure to make such a presentation has no name but deception.

To ensure that you are not guilty of plagiarism, you should be scrupulous in acknowledging the source of whatever you quote—whether you paraphrase it or quote it directly. Moreover, you should transcribe quoted material exactly as you find it in your source, being sure to include every punctuation mark, because even a misplaced comma can alter the meaning of a passage.

To avoid deceiving a reader, you should quote a passage without distorting its essential meaning. For example, suppose you had on one of your note cards a quoted passage such as this one:

The American parent seems solidly behind his teenage child, though numerous research studies and cultural articles like novels and television shows indicate that he is greatly troubled

by his child's participation in the drug culture or his early
involvement with sex. He is proud of his teenager's accomplishments and is likely to support teenage pursuits in sports,
hobbies, or socializing, but he admits to little awareness of how
to provide discipline or vocational guidance.

Since you have at your disposal ellipsis points, three
spaced periods (. . .), to indicate an omission, you might
quote in your paper a version of the above that goes like
this:

The American parent seems solidly behind his teenage child. . . .
He is proud of his accomplishments and is likely to support
teenage pursuits. . . .

But this would be a deceptive distortion, since the original passage clearly shows the parent to be much more
uncertain than the abbreviated quotation would suggest.

To be sure that your work follows the highest ethical
standard, the best guidelines are these: quote with ac-
curacy, convey the essential meaning of what you are
quoting, and acknowledge the source of the quotation.
To acknowledge the source, use a footnote.

## Footnotes

The physical form of footnotes follows one or another
convention. No single convention is universally adhered
to, so the form suggested here is based on one widely
adhered to: the *MLA Handbook for Writers of Research
Papers, Theses, and Dissertations* (New York: Modern
Language Association, 1977).

A footnote consists of two parts: (1) the superscript
number you use in the body of your text to mark the
passage to be documented and (2) the note itself, which
normally goes at the *foot* of the page (hence *footnote*),
but which may also go on a separate sheet of paper at
the end of your text before the final bibliography. Of
course, the note proper is numbered to correspond with
the superscript number in the text.

If you place your notes at the foot of the page, separate
the note or notes from the text with a triple space (set off

by a line typed across the page). Wherever you place the notes, separate them from each other with a double space. Footnotes should also be indented, as in the following examples, and the numbers should run consecutively throughout the paper; do not start a fresh set of numbers on each page.

It is important to note that a footnote reference is similar in form to that used on your bibliography cards—*but it is not identical.* Compare the sample footnotes given below with the bibliography samples given on pages 355–356 and with the final bibliography of the sample research paper on page 411.

The following sample footnotes give you the form of the first citation of a reference and the short form of each subsequent reference to the same source. You may use these as models for your own footnotes. In doing so, notice the order in which the information is presented and the exact punctuation that separates the bits of information.

### Reference to a Book

   1 Arthur Waldhorn, A Reader's Guide to Ernest Hemingway (New York: Farrar, Straus and Giroux, 1972), p. 98.

### Subsequent Reference

   14Waldhorn, p. 123.

### Reference to a Work in Several Volumes

   2Werner Jaeger, Paideia: The Ideals of Greek Culture, trans. Gilbert Highet (New York: Oxford University Press, 1943), II, 13.

### Subsequent Reference

   15Jaeger, III, 215.

*Note:* Note that in the Waldhorn references, the abbreviation "p." is used for the page number whereas in the Jaeger it is not. This is because the roman numeral for the volume number is used in the Jaeger. Wherever a volume number is used, the page number is cited *without* the "p." See below, under note 11.

### Reference to a Book in Which the Edition Is Cited

[3]Robert Dudley French, A Chaucer Handbook, 2nd ed. (New York: Appleton–Century–Crofts, Inc., 1955), p. 327.

### Subsequent Reference

[16]French, p. 299.

### Reference to a Book with Two or More Authors

[4]Naomi B. Lynn, Ann B. Matasar, and Marie Barovic Rosenberg, Research Guide in Women's Studies (Morristown, N.J.: General Learning Press, 1974), p. 32.

### Subsequent Reference

[17]Lynn, et al., p. 90.

*Note:* For more than three authors, use this form: "Naomi B. Lynn, et al...." omitting the names of the other authors; the abbreviation *et al.* means "and others." Note, too, that this is done in subsequent references to the work of three authors—as a convenient short form.

### Reference to a General Reference Work

[5]"Fleming, Sir Alexander," Chambers's Biographical Dictionary, New Edition, p. 476a.

### Subsequent Reference

[18]Chambers's, p. 476a.

*Note:* You need not supply publication facts in the case of a well-established general reference work, but only specify the edition and the page number.

### Reference to a Classic Play, Giving Act, Scene, and Line Numbers

[6]Hamlet, II.i.36

**Subsequent Reference: Follow Same Form**

## Reference to an Essay Included in an Edited Collection

[7]Earl H. Rovit, "Ralph Ellison and the American Comic Tradition," in <u>Ralph Ellison: A Collection of Critical Essays</u>, ed. John Hersey (Englewood Cliffs, N.J.: Prentice-Hall, Inc., 1974), p. 152.

## Subsequent Reference

[19]Rovit, p. 153.

## Reference to a Signed Article in a Weekly Magazine

[8]Jane Otten, "Living in Syntax," <u>Newsweek</u>, December 30, 1974, p. 103.

## Subsequent Reference

[20]Otten, p. 103.

## Reference to an Unsigned Article in a Weekly Magazine

[9]"Coming Across," <u>The New Yorker</u>, June 27, 1977, p. 26.

## Subsequent Reference

[21]"Coming Across," p. 27.

## Reference to an Article in a Monthly Magazine

[10]Ignatius C. Mattingly, "Some Cultural Aspects of Serial Cartoons, or Get a Load of Those Funnies," <u>Harper's</u>, December 1955, p. 35.

## Subsequent Reference

[22]Mattingly, p. 38.

## Reference to an Article in a Learned Journal ·

[11]Erik H. Erikson, "The Problem of Ego Identity," <u>Journal of the American Psychoanalytic Association</u>, 4 (January 1956): 57.

## Subsequent Reference

[23]Erikson, p. 60.

### Reference to a Signed Newspaper Article

¹²Leslie Maitland, "Story of an East Side Policeman Who Turned in Fellow Officers," The New York Times, July 3, 1977, sec. 1, p. 1.

### Subsequent Reference

²⁴Maitland, p. 33.

### Reference to an Unsigned Newspaper Article

¹³"Eight Firemen Injured as a Tenement Burns," The New York Times, July 3, 1977, sec. 1, p. 25.

### Subsequent Reference

²⁵"Eight Firemen," p. 25.

### Reference to a Public Document

¹⁴U.S. Congress, Senate, Committee on the Judiciary, Hearings before the Subcommittee to Investigate Juvenile Delinquency (Washington, D.C.: Government Printing Office, 1954), p. 112.

### Subsequent Reference

²⁶Senate Hearings, p. 200.

## *Subsequent references and Latin abbreviations*

For many years it was customary to use a number of Latin abbreviations in footnote citations. For example, in those years a set of footnotes might have looked like this:

⁶Jones, op. cit., p. 26.

Op. cit. is an abbreviation of *opere citato,* "in the work cited," and so the footnote would mean "in the work of Jones that was previously cited, on p. 26."

⁷Ibid., p. 76.

Ibid. is short for *ibidem,* "in the same place," and so this footnote would mean "in the same book [Jones] note 6 cites, only this time on p. 76."

⁸Smith, op. cit., p. 23.

⁹Loc. cit.

Loc. cit. is an abbreviation of *loco citato,* "in the place cited," and so this footnote would mean "in the same book [Smith] cited in the previous footnote and on the same page [23]."

However, the more recent trend is to eliminate Latin abbreviations like *ibid., op. cit.,* and *loc. cit.* and treat the same set of footnotes as follows:

6Jones, p. 26.

7Jones, p. 76.

8Smith, p. 23.

9Smith, p. 23.

The less complicated system of footnote citation has many advantages, not the least of which are an uncluttered set of footnotes and a style of reference that produces clarity.

If you refer in your footnotes to works by two authors with the same name, say Thomas Jones and Richard Jones, then in order to avoid confusion you would use the full name of each when you give their names in short, subsequent references (after the first, full citation).

6Thomas Jones, p. 75.

7Richard Jones, p. 112.

If your sources include two different works by the same author, then the form of your subsequent references to each cannot consist merely of this author's name. Let us suppose that your two books are Peter Clapps, *How Workers Triumph Over Unions,* and Peter Clapps, *Finding the Way Through Union Pension Funds.* Subsequent references to these would require the author's last name and an abbreviated title:

7Clapps, <u>Workers</u> <u>Triumph</u>, p. 179.

8Clapps, <u>Pension</u> <u>Funds</u>, p. 105.

### *Abbreviations used in footnotes*

The following list of abbreviations for terms used in footnotes may be useful. Note that abbreviations are followed by a period and that the abbreviations for Latin words are not italicized.

| | |
|---|---|
| anon. | anonymous |
| c., ca. (*circa*) | about (c. 1485) |
| cf. (*confer*) | compare |
| ch., chs., chap., chaps. | chapter(s) |
| diss. | dissertation |
| ed., eds. | edited by, edition, editor(s) |
| e.g. (*exempli gratia*) | for example |
| et al. (*et alii*) | and others |
| f., ff. | and the following page(s) |
| ibid. (*ibidem*) | in the same place |
| i.e. (*id est*) | that is |
| intro. | introduction |
| l., ll. | line(s) |
| loc. cit. (*loco citato*) | in the place cited |
| MS., ms., MSS., mss. | manuscript(s) |
| n. | note |
| n.d. | no date (of publication) |
| n.p. | no place (of publication) |
| numb. | numbered |
| op. cit. (*opere citato*) | in the work cited |
| p., pp. | page(s) |
| passim | here and there; throughout |
| rev. | revised |
| tr., trans. | translated by, translator |
| v. (*vide*) | see, consult |
| vol., vols. | volume(s) |

# Sample Research Paper

The sample research paper that follows is shown in final typed form. Commentary on the text, keyed to the numbered paragraphs, appears facing the appropriate paragraphs.

PHOBIAS:

WHAT WE KNOW ABOUT

THEIR HISTORY, CAUSES, AND CURES

Bryna Kaplon

English 110D

January 13, 1981

Statement of Purpose

    The purpose of this paper is to describe what
a phobia is, to survey the history of phobias in
human beings, to present what is known about the
causes and cures of phobias, including both the
theories and treatments in the fields of
psychoanalysis and behaviorism, and to comment on
what is known about phobias.

   I. Phobias are persistent, intense, irrational
      fears which continue to exist and affect
      people today just as they have done to people
      who lived many centuries before us.
      A. Recent accounts show that people who have
         phobias experience anxiety manifested by
         physiological symptoms.
      B. Historical accounts of people who have had
         extreme fears show that they have
         manifested physiological symptoms similar
         to those of people who we would now say
         have phobias.

  II. Classification of phobias can serve to
      describe them further and to indicate the
      numerous ones which exist.
      A. Phobias can be classified into four broad
         groups, with each group assigned similar
         objects or situations feared, as well as
         similar symptoms which accompany those
         fears.
      B. Phobias can be classified, as Freud
         classified them, into two groups according
         to the characteristics of the object
         feared.

 III. Freud felt phobias were produced as a result
      of defense mechanisms in the personality.
      A. Conflicts which ensue after repressed
         oedipal wishes surface into consciousness
         force the ego to defend itself, which, in
         turn, produces phobias.
      B. Two of Freud's case histories illustrate
         how phobias are produced.

  IV. How the two schools of psychology,
      psychoanalysis and behaviorism, view phobias
      determines their methods of treatment.

    A. Psychoanalysts view phobias as symbols of other unconscious conflicts within the individual.
   1. Psychoanalysts treat phobias through the process of psychoanalytic therapy.
   2. The process of psychoanalysis consists largely of free association.

    B. Behaviorists view phobias as behavior which is learned either by conditioning or imitation.
   1. Behaviorists treat phobias mainly by systematic desensitization.
   2. Other methods of treatment include flooding, modeling, and exposing phobic patients to pairs of scenes consisting of feared stimuli followed by pleasant stimuli.

V. Behavioral treatments for phobias are currently the most popular, but experiments in this field remain inadequate.

    A. Behavioral methods have proved effective for treating some of the simpler phobias but are not effective for treating agoraphobia.

    B. Behavioral treatments for simpler phobias are relatively fast and inexpensive.

    C. Experiments on phobias in this field lack long-term follow-up data on the small number of volunteers who participate in them.

**Pars. 1, 2, and 3:** Bryna chooses to begin on a dramatic and suspenseful note by describing three cases of phobic fears.

After consultation with her instructor, Bryna has chosen to place all her footnote citations at the foot of the page. (See p. 371 under Footnotes.) Of course, she might have placed them all together at the end of her paper. The advantage of her choice is that readers do not have to flip to the back every time a footnote number appears. The disadvantage is that sometimes notes at the bottom of a page interrupt a reader's concentration; besides, it's difficult to plan one's pages so that notes fit neatly at the bottom. The method you choose will depend on how you evaluate these conflicting claims and one other thing: If your notes are filled with supplementary information, you might wish to have them at the bottom so that they are easily accessible to the reader.

A 37-year-old married woman, with two children of her own, became terrified and panicked every time she saw a cat. She was so afraid of cats that when she walked outdoors she had to walk on the edge of the sidewalk to protect herself from being attacked by them. She couldn't go out at night alone for fear she would be attacked by cats. She also could not wear fur gloves or bear to be around those who wore fur coats. She even became upset when stumbling upon her daughter's stuffed koala bear.[1]

Men wounded in combat during World War II are known to have experienced extreme fear and anxiety when they were about to receive a hypodermic injection for treatment of their wounds.[2]

Another woman, 20 years old, was unable to

[1]H. L. Freeman, D. C. Kendrick, "A Case of Cat Phobia. Treatment by a Method Derived from Experimental Psychology," in Experiments in Behavior Therapy, ed. H. J. Eysenck (New York: The Macmillan Co., 1964), p. 56.

[2]Personal conversation between writer and Dr. Max Rast. July 1979.

walk the streets without the companionship of her mother and father.[3]

What these people have, or have had, in com- **4** mon is a phobia. Phobias are fears which are so intense that when people who have them come in contact with the particular object or situation which they fear they experience acute anxiety accompanied by such physiological symptoms as sweating, paleness, tachycardia, rapid breathing, nausea, excessive urination, vomiting, diarrhea, dizziness, and tightening of the chest.[4] Perhaps the best way to define a phobia would be to say that it is an intense, irrational, persistent fear of an object or objects, place, or situation which is out of proportion to the danger actually presented by the object or situation, is inexplicable and unresponsive to reasoning, is out of the realm of voluntary control, and which brings about an avoidance of the feared object, situation, or place.[5]

[3]Helene Deutsch, "The Genesis of Agoraphobia," <u>International Journal of Psycho-analysis</u>, 10 (1929): 57-58.

[4]Isaac M. Marks, <u>Fears and Phobias</u> (New York and London: Academic Press, 1969), p. 4.

[5]Marks, p. 3.

**Par. 5:**  After a series of important preliminary definitions and explanations, Bryna here introduces her thesis. After reading this paragraph, the reader knows where the paper is headed.

The two major approaches to psychological     **5**
health, namely, psychoanalysis and behaviorism,
maintain their own distinct theories concerning
the causes of phobias, with only some overlap
and agreement between the two approaches to
this disturbance. Though we can look back to
the beginning of Western civilization and find
phobic behavior manifesting itself, we still
know very little about what causes phobias,
about how such behavior starts and how it continues to nurture itself. Phobias have been
treated, however; case histories and clinical
and experimental studies exist on the treatment
of phobias, with the most recent research being
done in the field of behaviorism. At this point
there are, if not answers, then at least some
plausible, possible theories and treatments
which are capable of producing some cures of
some phobias.

Literature affords us the knowledge of the     **6**
long life which phobias have had in mankind.
Phobias existed in man long before the word
itself did. The word phobia is derived from the
Greek word <u>phobos</u>, which means fear, horror,

**Par. 6:** Bryna has been careful, as you will see, to use long quotes sparingly. There are just three in the whole paper. Can you see the value in this sparse use of the long, indented quotation?

The handling of the indented quote should be noticed: It is given *without* quotation marks, it is single-spaced, and it is indented for ease of identification as a direct quotation.

aversion.[6] And it was Hippocrates, the Greek
physician known as the father of medicine, who
wrote one of the first descriptions of a person
displaying phobic behavior:

> . . . the morbid condition of Nicanor. When
> he used to begin drinking, the girl flute-
> player would frighten him; as soon as he
> heard the first note of the flute at a ban-
> quet, he would be beset by terror. He used
> to say he could scarcely contain himself
> when night fell; but during the day he would
> hear this instrument without feeling any
> emotion. . . .[7]

Other writers, including both Shakespeare and
Descartes, can be noted as having written
descriptions of people with phobias. In 1621,
Robert Burton published the first comprehensive
study of phobias in his <u>Anatomy of Melancholy</u>.[8]
In this work Burton distinguished between the
emotions of depression, normal fears, and abnormal fears. Quite correctly, he asserted that
those people who had abnormal fears, such people as we would now say have phobias, could not
be held responsible for their seemingly bizarre
responses to the objects or situations which

[6]<u>The Compact Edition of the Oxford English
Dictionary</u>, Vol. II (1971), p. 786.

[7]Hippocrates: <u>On Epidemics</u>, V, Section
LXXXII, quoted by Marks, pp. 7-8.

[8]Marks, p. 8.

**Par. 7:**  Notice how Bryna has used the parentheses to define *agora*, thus avoiding interrupting the flow of her discussion.

they feared. He argued against the notion that
these people lacked willpower and stressed that
trust and confidence between doctor and patient
were most important in attempting a cure. In
1769, a French surgeon by the name of Le Camus
made a study of phobias, labeling them aver-
sions.[9] Various other references appeared concerning phobias up through the nineteenth century, but it was not until Westphal's article
"Die Agoraphobie," published in 1871, that
modern interest in and investigation of phobias
began.[10]

Westphal invented the term agoraphobia **7**
(agora—a Greek word meaning an assembly, the
place of assembly and marketplace[11]) to describe three of his patients who had fears
about going outdoors. He wrote that one of his
patients would start to tremble, have sensa-
tions in his head, and experience palpitations
every time he tried to cross a wide-open square
in Berlin. Westphal's patient feared wide-open
spaces, for he could manage places with people

[9]Marks, p. 9.

[10]Marks, p. 11.

[11]OED, Vol. I, p. 188.

**Par. 8:**   Bryna uses the name of the author of her source because she
does not intend to footnote that source until she has written several
more paragraphs.

At the beginning of this same paragraph, Bryna uses the words
*monosymptomatic* and *diffuse*. Should she have paused (say, in a
parenthesis) to define these terms? Or are they clear enough?

It is useful to examine three of Bryna's note cards shown on this page
and page 394. See if you can understand how and why she either
worked this material into her text or did *not* work it in.

Marks, "Perspe. on Flooding," pp 311-313

Flooding

Rapid presentation of either actual or imagined
anxiety producing stimuli. Essentially rapid
desensitization treatment. Can be given by
taped material or therapist. Actual stimuli
presented by therapist most effective.

and houses much better  Westphal noted that the thought of the feared situation was as upsetting to his patients as actually encountering the situation, and that anxiety when experiencing the phobic place could be alleviated by either bringing along a person, drinking alcohol or using a cane.[12]

The classification of phobias can be done **8** any number of ways. The simplest way to classify them might be to call them either monosymptomatic or diffuse. But to get a better idea of the various types of phobias perhaps a more specific classification, such as the one behaviorist I. M. Marks has made, would be useful. First of all, phobias can be fears of objects external to the phobic sufferer or fears of things internal to the phobic sufferer. Internal phobias involve fears of illness as well as fears of harming other individuals. External phobias, however, can be divided into four different groups: animal phobias, agoraphobia, social phobias, miscellaneous phobias.

Animal phobias are those which involve fears **9** of specific animals; they are generally mono-

[12]Marks, p. 11.

Marks, Years, pp. 6-7

<u>Counterphobic behavior</u>

Occurs when the phobic patient/person constantly seeks out the phobic object/situation. When phobia is relatively mild, phobic uses this method to quell phobia. Example: woman who was afraid of heights-- so afraid she would not ride in elevators--became an airline hostess and overcame her phobia (cite Frazier & Coxn 1967).

Slade, Psych. Today, p. 101

<u>Current Flight Phobia Treatment</u>

Can be and has been presented by audio-visual film. Phobics exposed to paired scenes: 1st anxiety-provoking, 2nd pleasurable. One study done of 40 women plus 11 men. 27 pairs of scenes presented. All but all, after treatment, felt they could fly.
Follow up of 32 after 3 1/2 yrs. 26 had flown; 24 still flying.

symptomatic. According to Marks, animal phobias are the rarest phobias found in psychiatric practice.

Agoraphobia is the most diffuse and compli-   10
cated of the phobias. It consists of a cluster of phobias centered around fears of going out into public places. The more diffuse the case, the greater the chances of agoraphobia being one of a number of neurotic disorders within the individual.

Social phobias revolve around fears of being  11
observed by other people while out in public. People with social phobias are afraid they will faint or behave inappropriately in some way in front of others. For instance, a person with a social phobia might fear that his hands will shake while drinking, eating, or writing in the presence of others.

Miscellaneous phobias are fears of such       12
things as heights, thunderstorms, closed-in places, darkness, and so on. These phobias, like animal phobias, are generally monosymptomatic.[13]

[13]This footnote refers to all the descriptions included in the classification of phobias. Marks, pp. 105-116.

**Pars. 15–19:** In these paragraphs, Bryna uses terms like *id, ego, superego, identification, displacement,* and *trauma,* terms that are common knowledge in the field of psychoanalysis. She does not define them on the grounds that readers of her paper might be expected to have this common knowledge. Are the terms clear to you? Do you agree or disagree with her decision?

It is obvious from this classification that **13** different phobias are not mutually exclusive. An agoraphobic's fears might include fears from each group, and a socially phobic person might eventually find his fears so debilitating that he has trouble leaving his house at all, thus acquiring the fears of the agoraphobic.

Freud, on the other hand, distinguished dif- **14** ferent kinds of phobias by dividing them into two different groups according to the characteristics of the object feared: (1) common phobias, normal fears, such as fear of getting sick, fear of death or darkness, blown out of proportion; and (2) specific phobias, fears of particular situations which normally do not inspire fear in the individual.[14]

Freud saw phobias as manifestations of **15** neurotic anxiety. Anxiety can arise from either internal or external stimulations, but the uncomfortable feelings produced by anxiety are governed by the autonomic nervous system. According to Freud's theory of personality, anxiety serves to warn the ego of danger. Freud

[14]Marks, p. 94.

believed, and psychoanalytic theory still maintains Freud's beliefs, that anxiety which pre-
disposes phobic behavior is internally induced.
Phobias are the product of the ego defending
itself against conflicts between the id and the
superego.[15] When wishes which have been repressed threaten to erupt, the ego defends itself by using such defense mechanisms as displacement—which is the primary defense mecha-
nism—reversal, regression, and identification.[16] A brief look at a couple of Freud's
case histories of phobic patients will help to
illustrate his psychoanalytic theory.

One well-known case is that of "Little          **16**
Hans," a study of a five-year-old boy with a
phobia of horses. Freud explained Hans's phobia
as originating in oedipal wishes. Hans was in
love with his mother and jealous of his father
toward whom he harbored hostile feelings.
These hostile feelings toward his father came

[15]Calvin S. Hall, _A Primer of Freudian Psychology_ (New York: The New American Library, Inc., 1954), pp. 61-66.

[16]Bertram D. Lewin, "Phobias," _International Encyclopedia of the Social Sciences_, Vol. 12, 1968, pp. 82-83.

into conflict with his love for his father. His aggression led him to fear he would be castrated. Hans then repressed his love for his mother and displaced his hostile feelings he had toward his father onto horses, which he thought would bite off his penis. So after repressing his original impulses, Hans produced his phobia by first displacing his fear to horses, then by reversing the aim of his aggression from his father to himself, and finally by regressing from the genital fear of castration to the oral fear of being bitten.[17]

In another one of Freud's case histories,    **17** known as the "Wolf Man," Freud attributed his patient's phobia of wolves to an inverted oedipal wish. This boy's phobia of wolves, though Freud did not treat this person until fifteen years after the wolf phobia no longer manifested itself and other neurotic symptoms had set in,[18] occurred some time after he had seen

[17]Lewin, pp. 82-83

[18]Sigmund Freud, <u>Three Case Histories</u>, ed. Philip Rieff (New York: The Macmillan Co., 1973), p. 189.

his parents engage in sexual intercourse. Freud explained that after this boy had seen his parents have sexual intercourse he identified himself with what appeared to him to be his castrated mother. He then feared that he would be castrated if he permitted himself sexual desires for his father. He then displaced his fear to a picture of a wolf in a book. When he saw the picture of the wolf he was afraid the wolf would devour him. His fear of being eaten by the wolf was the same desire, expressed orally, that he had for passive genital gratification.[19]

How one treats a phobia depends on how the **18** symptom, which is what a psychoanalyst would call it, or how the disorder, which is what a behaviorist would call it, is viewed. Both schools would agree that trauma can play a part in the development of a phobia, that once a phobia is developed the secondary gains which one might acquire from it can assist in maintaining the phobia, and that one must encounter the phobic object or situation in some way in

[19]Lewin, p. 83.

order to cure the phobia. Where the psychoanalyst and the behaviorist differ is not only
in how they view phobias but also in how they
view the behavior of human beings.

Psychoanalysts believe that our behavior is **19**
influenced by the thoughts which take place in
our unconscious. It is for this reason that
they view our unconscious thoughts as our
necessary thoughts. They feel, as Freud did,
that it is in the unconscious thought process,
rather than in the conscious thought process,
that the majority of our mental functioning
takes place.[20] Psychoanalysts view phobias as
Freud did: as arising out of a conflict brought
on by the resurgence of repressed wishes. Any
trauma involved would be that which triggers
off repressed wishes. Conflicts revolve around
temptation and punishment. Phobias are seen as
symbols for other fears unknown to the phobic
person, as concrete representations of other
unconscious conflicts existing within the
person.

[20]Charles Brenner, <u>An Elementary Textbook of
Psychoanalysis</u> (Garden City, N.Y.: Anchor Press/
Doubleday, 1973), pp. 9–14.

**Par. 20:** Notice the long quotation. Is it too long? Too complex? How would you have paraphrased it?

Behaviorists, on the other hand, look at      20
human behavior in a very mechanized way; the
thought process is not included to a very
significant extent. They believe that behavior
is produced by responses to reward and punishment. People learn things as a result of
conditioning. They would look at a trauma producing a phobia as a very strong conditioner.
More recent work has led behaviorists to
believe that learning can also take place
vicariously; this is where imitation of models
comes in. Though they would not claim that the
Learning Theory paradigm completely answers how
phobias are acquired, much of their treatment
for phobias is based on the principles of this
theory, so it is worth including:

> . . . phobias are acquired by classical
> conditioning in which the (future) phobic
> stimulus (the CS) is paired together with or
> shortly before a noxious stimulus (the UCS).
> Conditioning occurs through this temporal
> contiguity, and the phobia increases with
> the frequency of the pairing, with the
> strength of the noxious stimulus and when
> nothing can be done to stop the noxious
> stimulation. Once there is sufficient fear
> to cause avoidance of the phobic situation,
> the phobia is maintained in part by drive
> reduction and is hard to extinguish—this is
> a form of instrumental conditioning.[21]

[21]Marks, p. 91.

So the differences in how phobias will be treated lies in a fundamental difference between the two schools of psychology; the difference lies in how practitioners in the two fields look at human beings.

Psychoanalysts treat phobias according to the terms of psychoanalysis. That is, they believe that if the analyst and the patient can uncover what the phobia symbolizes, some other conflict going on in the unconscious thought process, then the phobia may be cured, resolved. Psychoanalysis places great confidence in the human intellect. Such treatment maintains that if a person can understand why he behaves in a particular way, he can then change his behavior. The process of psychoanalysis takes time, patience, and a strong desire on the patient's part to be cured. Psychoanalysis largely consists of the patient coming into his analyst's office and telling his analyst all the thoughts that come into his mind. The patient must refrain from consciously directing his thoughts, because the objective of psychoanalysis is to determine what is going on in the patient's unconscious thought process.

21

Dreams will most likely be analyzed during the course of this treatment and transference might take place; the analyst might employ word association with his patient, or even put him under hypnosis, but the majority of the work toward cure occurs by free association, that is, by the patient allowing his thoughts to surface and telling them to the analyst. Though psychoanalysts have written about their theories on the causes of phobias, little material exists that relates cases which have been cured by psychoanalysis.

In the field of behaviorism the most widely **22** used treatment, as well as one of the most successful forms of treatment for phobias, is Wolpe's Systematic Desensitization treatment. Wolpe's treatment for curing phobias is based on the phenomenon of reciprocal inhibition originally described by Sherrington.[22] This form of treatment, based on observations made during experiments on animals, suggests the following proposition:

[22]Joseph Wolpe, "The Systematic Desensitization Treatment of Neuroses," <u>Journal of Nervous and Mental Disease</u>, 132 (1961): 189.

> . . . if a response inhibitory to anxiety
> can be made to occur in the presence of
> anxiety—evoking stimuli so that it is ac-
> companied by a complete or partial suppres-
> sion of the anxiety response, the bond
> between these stimuli and the anxiety
> response will be weakened.[23]

Systematic desensitization treatment consists

of constructing a hierarchy of objects or

situations which provoke anxiety in the

patient. Then, after the patient has been

taught various relaxation exercises by the

therapist (though more recent studies have

shown that relaxation is not necessary for ef-

fective desensitization),[24] he is asked to

imagine an object or situation listed in the

hierarchy, starting with the item which

provokes the least anxiety in him, gradually

working up through the hierarchy to the object

which provokes his greatest anxiety. The

patient is not asked to imagine an object which

he fears more than another until he is free

from any anxiety which accompanies the less—

feared object. This method of treatment has

---

[23]Wolpe, p. 189. Information in the rest of
this paragraph is from Wolpe, pp. 189–203.

[24]I. M. Marks, "Perspectives on Flooding,"
in <u>Psychotherapy & Behavior Change</u>, eds. Marks
et al. (Chicago, Ill.: Aldine Publishing Co.,
1973), p. 313.

shown that when fear of an object is removed
when imagining the feared object, the fear will
also cease to exist when one encounters the
object in reality. Systematic desensitization
can be done, if necessary for relaxation purposes, when the patient is put under hypnosis.
The treatment can also be carried out by using
actual objects rather than asking the patient
to imagine the objects he fears. Desensitization treatment using actual stimuli was successful in effecting a cure of the woman's cat
phobia which was mentioned earlier in this
paper.[25]

Numerous other treatments for phobias exist **23**
in the field of behaviorism, most of which are
variations of densensitization treatment. Many
different names are given the same treatment,
but essentially they fall into the following
three categories:

The first of these treatments is called **24**
flooding. The name is a good indication of the
treatment. Here the patient is flooded, presented rapidly, rather than gradually as is the
case with desensitization, with the objects he

[25]Freeman and Kendrick, pp. 51-61.

fears. Flooding can be carried out in fantasy or in practice. It can be given by means of a tape recorder or by a therapist. Most cases treated by this method show that practical flooding administered by a therapist is more effective than imaginary flooding. [26]

Modeling is another form of treatment for **25** phobias in which the phobic patient observes a model, either live or on film, of a person encountering a phobic object and overcoming his fear. The films contain sound. This form of treatment suggests that phobic behavior can be learned vicariously. [27]

The last method for treating phobias is one **26** that has recently proved itself effective in curing people who have phobias about flying. This method of treatment can be presented in the form of an audiovisual film, so that a therapist is not even necessary to administer the treatment. The treatment involves present—

[26]Marks, "Perspectives on Flooding," pp. 311–315.

[27]S. Rachman, "Clinical Applications of Observational Learning, Imitation, and Modeling," in Psychotherapy & Behavior Change, eds. Marks et al. (Chicago, Ill.: Aldine Publishing Co., 1973), pp. 353–356.

ing phobic individuals with a series of paired scenes. First people are shown a scene which produces anxiety in them; this scene is then followed by a scene which evokes pleasure in the observer. After amateur therapists took 40 women and 11 men through 27 pairs of scenes, all but 11 said they felt they would be able to fly. Three and a half years after this treatment, the 40 people who said they thought they would be able to fly were interviewed. Twenty-six of them had flown since treatment; 24 of them continue to fly. Myron Denholtz, one of the people who has done research into this audiovisual approach to curing flight phobias, now has nonprofessionals administering this treatment at Elizabeth General Hospital in New Jersey. Denholtz is working on an audiovisual program for treating those who have phobias about heights as well.[28]

To sum up then, there is still little known **27** about the genesis of phobias. That they exist, we can be certain; but what causes them and how to cure them is still a matter for speculation

[28]Margot Slade, "Automated Phobia Foiling," Psychology Today, March 1979, p. 101.

and research. The behavioral approach to
curing phobias currently takes favor over that
of the psychoanalytical. Some of the behavioral
treatments for the simpler phobias have been
found to be effective. Because of the nature of
such approaches they are less time consuming
and less expensive than psychoanalysis. Behavioral treatments, however, have not been effective in treating the more complicated agoraphobia. In addition, though experiments are
numerous in this field, most of them involve
volunteers, not people debilitated by phobias.
Furthermore, most experiments test such a small
number of people and lack any long-term follow-
up data that it is hard to assess their
findings.

As can be seen, phobias have lived a long     28
life in mankind. We still do not know much more
about them than Hippocrates did. But must not
this always be the case when we deal with the
relationship between mind and body, body and
mind? Will not any answers found in a field
which seeks to know the how's and why's of
human behavior always lead to more questions?
Phobias . . . their causes and cures. . . .

BIBLIOGRAPHY OF WORKS CITED

Brenner, Charles. _An Elementary Textbook of Psychoanalysis_. Garden City, N.Y.: Anchor Press/Doubleday, 1973.

_The Compact Edition of the Oxford English Dictionary_. Vol. I. p. 188. Vol. II. p. 786.

Deutsch, Helene. "The Genesis of Agoraphobia." _International Journal of Psycho-analysis_, 10 (1929): 51-69.

Freeman, H. L., D. C. Kendrick. "A Case of Cat Phobia. Treatment by a Method Derived from Experimental Psychology." _Experiments in Behavior Therapy_, ed. H. J. Eysenck. New York: The Macmillan Co., 1964.

Freud, Sigmund. _Three Case Histories_, ed. Philip Rieff. New York: The Macmillan Co., 1973.

Hall, Calvin S. _A Primer of Freudian Psychology_. New York: The New American Library, Inc., 1954.

Lewin, Bertram D. "Phobias." _International Encyclopedia of the Social Sciences_. Vol. 12 (1968), pp. 81-84.

Marks, I. M. _Fears and Phobias_. New York and London: Academic Press, 1969. "Perspectives on Flooding." _Psychotherapy & Behavior Change_, eds. Marks et al. Chicago, Ill.: Aldine Publishing Co., 1973.

Rachman, S. "Clinical Applications of Observational Learning, Imitation, and Modeling." _Psychotherapy & Behavior Change_, eds. Marks et al. Chicago, Ill.: Aldine Publishing Co., 1973.

Slade, Margot. "Automated Phobia Foiling." _Psychology Today_, March 1979, p. 101.

Wolpe, Joseph. "The Systematic Desensitization Treatment of Neuroses." _Journal of Nervous and Mental Disease_, 132 (1961): 189-203.

# Glossary
# of Usage

Each of the entries in this section discusses words or phrases that are frequently usage problems for student writers—as well as for more experienced ones. Suggestions for correct usage given in the entries describe current usage among educated writers and are based on the best dictionaries and recent studies in usage. Naturally, not every problem is treated here. Elsewhere in the book, you will find a brief list of troublesome idiomatic combinations (pp. 131–133) and a list of homophones (pp. 252–256). However, if you are unable to find the word, expression, or rule you are interested in, you should consult either a good dictionary or your instructor.

The following labels are used in the glossary:

*Formal:* Words or expressions of standard educated usage; appropriate to a high level of serious writing. Students are expected to produce this kind of writing in most colleges and in most courses.

*Informal:* The language of the everyday world. Informal words and expressions occur widely, but are also widely avoided in formal writing.

*Colloquial:* The language used in conversation, mainly informal; used by writers and speakers both educated and uneducated; but should, in most cases, be avoided in all but the most informal writing.

*Standard:* The language used in most printed matter; includes formal and informal, but is understood to stand closer to formal.

*Nonstandard:* Applies to words or expressions that good dictionaries label as *illiterate, nonstandard, obsolete, slang, dialect,* or *substandard.* These are to be avoided in all kinds of writing.

*Illiterate:* A species of the nonstandard occurring only in the most uneducated writing and speaking; of course, items so labeled are to be avoided.

*Slang:* Also a species of nonstandard writing. Slang aims to be fresh, funny, and forceful. Often, slang develops into a kind of shorthand language and quickly becomes overused. Exercise care in using slang; it belongs only in informal writing and should be used there sparingly.

**A, an**  Use *a* before a word beginning with a consonant *sound*—even when the word begins with a letter classified as a vowel, as in *a university*. Use *an* before a word beginning with a vowel (*an egg, an orange*) or a word with a silent *h* (*an hour, an honor*).

**Absolutely**  Overworked when used as an intensifier: "It was *absolutely* the greatest experience of my life."

**Accept, except**  *Accept* is a verb, meaning "to receive" or "to agree to," and *except* is a preposition, meaning "other than" or "but."

I *accept* your invitation.
I have invited everyone *except* Charlie.

**Actually**  Overworked as an intensifier—like *absolutely* and *really*. Instead of "They were *actually* happy" use "They were very happy" or "They were happy."

**Ad**  An abbreviated form of *advertisement*, not appropriate to formal writing. Similarly shortened forms are *auto, exam, photo, math,* and *phone*.

**Adapt, adopt**  To *adapt* is to be able to adjust to a situation or set of circumstances; to *adopt* is to take in or to agree to a course of action.

Fred was not able to *adapt* to college life.
We would like to *adopt* a child.

**Advice, advise**  *Advice* is the noun, *advise* the verb.

I can give you good *advice*.
Let me *advise* you.

**Affect, effect**  Usually, *affect* is a verb, meaning "to influence." The verb *effect* means "to bring about or achieve"; the noun *effect* means "the result."

The music *affected* me deeply.
We can, through political action, *effect* a change in government.
The *effect* of a shave is to open little cuts on the face.

**Aggravate**  Means "to make worse" or "to intensify." Used colloquially to mean "annoy" or "provoke."

**Formal**  The argument *aggravated* my headache.
**Colloquial**  I was *aggravated* by his attitude.

**Agree to, agree with**  To *agree to* is to consent; to *agree with* is to concur.

I *agree to* the contract, but I do not *agree with* his estimate of how much money I will make under its terms.

**Ain't**  Contraction of *am not.* Extended frequently to *is not, are not, has not,* and *have not.* Not only nonstandard, but also strongly disapproved by most educated speakers and writers.

**All, all of**  Use *all of* before proper nouns or pronouns, as in *all of Africa, all of these.* The *of* may be omitted to make expression more concise in constructions like *all of his energy* (better: *all his energy*) or *all of her strength* (better: *all her strength*).

**All ready, already**  *Already:* "before" or "by a certain time"; *all ready:* "completely prepared."

When I arrived, she was *already* in the shower.
The Cosmos are *all ready* for the big game.

**All right, alright**  Most dictionaries say *alright* is nonstandard for *all right.*

**All that**  Colloquial when used in constructions like "I didn't like the course *all that* much." How much is *all that*?

**All together, altogether**  *All together* means "in a group." *Altogether* means "entirely" or "thoroughly."

We were *all together* in our decision.
Smoking is an *altogether* unhealthy vice.

**Allusion**  See **illusion, allusion.**
**Almost**  See **most, almost.**
**Alot**  Should be two words: *a lot.*
**Among, between**  *Among* is usually reserved for more than two persons or things. *Between* is commonly used only for two. However, it is possible to use *between* for three or more items when they are regarded as having a reciprocal relationship or to express the relationship of one to the others.

*Among* those at the meeting, there wasn't a single Democrat.
The choice *between* ice cream and pie is easy to make.
There's much competition *between* the three major car companies.
We sailed directly *between* the three big rocks.

**Amount, number**  *Amount* refers to quantities, like water and air, that cannot be counted individually; *number* refers to things, like trees, that can be counted individually.

The *amount of traffic* on the road is staggering.
The *number of cars* going through the tunnel is staggering.

**An, a**  See **a, an.**
**Analyzation**  Illiterate for *analysis.*

**And etc.**  A redundancy, since *etc.* means "and so forth"; together the words would mean "and and so forth."

**And/or**  A construction found in legal documents. Some find it objectionable in formal writing.

**And which, and who**  See part 2, **Parallel Construction.**

**Ante, anti**  *Ante* means "before" (as in *antedate*); *anti* means "against" (as in *anti-American*). Use the hyphen after *anti* when it precedes capital letters and when it precedes a word beginning with *i*—as in *anti-intellectual*.

**Anyone, any one**  Not interchangeable. *Anyone* means "any person at all"; *any one* refers to a specific individual or thing in a group.

*Anyone* can learn to drive a car.
*Any one* of those drivers can teach you to drive a car.

*Note:* This distinction also applies to *everyone* and *someone*.

**Anyways**  Nonstandard for *anyway*.

**Apt, likely, liable**  *Apt* refers to a habitual tendency or a natural talent; *likely* means "probable" or "to be expected"; and *liable* means "legally responsible" or "susceptible to."

**Correct**  She is *apt* at solving equations.
**Correct**  She is not *likely* to go to college this fall.
**Correct**  He is *liable* to prosecution for grand larceny.

Informal usage sometimes confuses these meanings.

**Informal**  She is *apt* to go to college this fall.
**Informal**  She is *liable* to go to college this fall.

**Around**  Colloquial for "about" or "near."

**Formal**  It was *about* four o'clock.

**As, as if, like**  See **like, as, as if.**

**At**  Nonstandard after *where,* as in the following:

Where is he *at*?
I know where he's *at*.

**Auto**  See **ad.**

**Awful**  See **real.**

**Awfully**  Commonly used in speech to mean "exceedingly," but not preferred in writing.

**Formal**  She was *very* late.
**Colloquial**  She was *awfully* late.
          The play was *awfully* good.

**Bad**  Sometimes confused with the adverb *badly*. But *bad* is an adjective.

She felt *bad* about breaking up with her boyfriend.
She was hurt *badly* in the accident.

**Beauty**  See **real.**
**Being that, being as how**  Illiterate. Use the correct subordinating conjunctions *as, since, because.*
**Beside, besides**  Writers should be careful to distinguish between *beside* meaning "at the side of" and *besides* meaning "in addition to" or "also."

He was *beside* me as we entered the room.
*Besides,* I'm tired.

**Be sure and, try and**  Colloquial for *be sure to, try to.*
**Between**  See **among, between.**
**Breakdown**  Standard when used to mean "collapse," but colloquial when used instead of "itemization" or "analysis."

**Standard**  She suffered a nervous *breakdown.*
**Colloquial**  He make a *breakdown* of our receipts from the dance.

**Bunch**  Colloquial when used to mean a *group* or a *gathering* of people, as in *a bunch of people,* but standard when appropriately applied to, for example, *grapes,* as in *a bunch of grapes.*
**Burst, bursted, bust, busted**  *Burst* is the standard past tense and past participle form of *burst. Bursted* is no longer standard. *Bust* and *busted* are slang.

**Standard**  The water main *burst* last night.
**Nonstandard**  The water main *bursted* last night.
**Slang**  The water main *busted* last night.

**But, hardly, scarcely**  Each alone is negative; thus they should not be used with other negatives. See Part 2, **Double Negative.**
**But that, but what**  Wordy substitutes for plain *that,* used as either relative pronoun or conjunction.

I wasn't sure *that* you were sick.

**Can, may**  In informal usage, *can* is used to signify both ability (I *can* play basketball) and permission (*Can* I get you a drink?). In formal writing, many reserve *may* for permission (*May* I get you a drink?). *May* also expresses possibility (I *may* not vote this year.).
**Case, in the case of**  Cases of wordiness. See that entry in Part 2.
**Center about, center around**  Some think it more logical to *center on.*

**Commence** Pretentious. Use *begin* or *start*.

**Compare with, compare to** Similar items are compared *with* one another; dissimilar ones are compared *to* each other.

*Compared with* Florence, New York is ugly.
*Compared to* an airplane, a bird is a model of flight efficiency.

**Compliment, complement** A *compliment* is an expression of praise; a *complement* is something that makes up or completes something else.

The remark was a *compliment*.
The remarks were a *complement* to the previous speaker's.

**Contact** There is some feeling against the use of *contact* as a verb meaning "to meet with" or "to talk to," but it is in wide use just the same. The trouble with the word is that it is too general, and it is better replaced in writing by more specific terms such as *meet, consult, talk to.*

**Continual, continuous** That which is *continuous* proceeds without interruption in time or space; the *continual* proceeds with some interruption.

The Alaska pipeline provides a *continuous* flow of oil.
We had a *continual* debate over the energy crisis.

**Could of** Nonstandard. Use *could have*.

**Couple** Should be followed by *of*, whether used to mean *a few* (in colloquial use) or *two* (in formal use).

**Cute, lovely** Very much overworked to indicate general approval.

**Data, phenomena** Plural forms of *datum*, "a fact used to draw a conclusion," and *phenomenon*, "a fact or event perceptible to the senses." Informally, *data* is used as a collective noun and agrees with a singular verb.

**Formal** These *data are* invaluable.
**Informal** This *data is* invaluable.

**Deal** Colloquial, but bordering on slang when used to mean "transaction" (a good deal on a car), "secret contract" (a deal with the D. A.), or "treatment" (bad deal from the teacher).

**Definite, definitely** Vague intensifiers, used colloquially, as in "He has a *definite* talent," or "I will *definitely* come tonight."

**Different from, different than** *Different from* is idiomatic.

*Different than* is becoming widely used, but should be restricted to introducing a clause.

Rugby is *different from* football.
Rome was *different than* I had expected.

See also Idioms under **Diction,** Part 2.

**Differ from, differ with** To differ *from* someone or something is to be unlike that person or thing; to differ *with* someone is to have a dispute with that person or hold an opposite opinion.

**Disinterested, uninterested** *Disinterested* means "without bias"; *uninterested* means "without interest." These words are often used interchangeably to mean "without interest," but the distinction is worth preserving.

**Don't** The contraction of *do not*—not of *does not.*

He *doesn't* (not he *don't*) have much money.

**Dose, does** A *dose* is a specified quantity of medication; *does* is the third person singular present tense form of the verb *to do.*

**Due to** Opinion is divided on this. Some authorities criticize the construction used in the sense of *owing to* or *because of.* The criticism objects to its use as a preposition at the head of an adverbial phrase, but this use is becoming widespread and can be used in all but the most formal circumstances.

**Formal** Our picnic was canceled *because of* rain.
**Informal** Our picnic was canceled *due to* rain.

**Each and every** Redundant for either *each* or *every.*
**Each other, one another** *Each other* refers to two people, *one another* to more than two people.

Tom and Jerry congratulated *each other.*
The Yankees congratulated *one another* after the victory.

**Effect** See **affect, effect.**
**Eminent, imminent, immanent** *Eminent* means "distinguished"; *imminent* means "about to happen"; *immanent* means "within a realm of reality or discourse."

Colin is an *eminent* sociologist.
Marvin's arrival is *imminent.*
David's book is on history as *immanent.*

**Enthuse, enthused** An informal construction. Recast the sentence and use *enthusiastic* instead.
**Equally as good** Omit the *as.*

**Etc.** Latin abbreviation for *and so forth*. Use it in formal writing only when its meaning is perfectly clear. Since etc. already includes *and,* never write *and etc.* See **Abbreviations** in Part 2.

**Everyone** See **anyone, any one.**

**Every so often** Colloquial for *frequently.*

**Every which way** Colloquial for *in every way, in every direction,* or *in great disorder.*

**Exam** See **ad.**

**Except** See **accept, except.**

**Expect** "I *expect* he'll be here soon" or "I *expect* I should be going now" are colloquial. Use *suppose* and *believe* instead.

**Fact, the fact that** A wordy way to say *that.* See **Wordiness,** Part 2.

**Wordy** Are you aware of *the fact that* she's leaving?
**Better** Are you aware *that* she's leaving?

**Fantastic, fabulous** Avoid these terms of exaggerated astonishment.

**Farther, further** *Farther* is the correct word to express physical distance; *further,* the correct term for all other distance.

His house is *farther* down the road than mine.
In politics, he is *further* to the left than I am.

In informal usage, *further* is widely used in both senses.

**Fewer, less** *Fewer* is used when countable units are discussed; *less* is proper when an uncountable amount is discussed.

There are *fewer* calories in diet soda than in regular.
If the pollution stories are true, we'll soon have *less* water to drink.

**Field** Much overworked, frequently unnecessary.

**Wordy** He was an expert in *the field* of computers.
**Better** He was an expert in computers.

See **Wordiness,** Part 2.

**Fine** Vague when used as a general term of approval (as in "We had a *fine* meal") and colloquial when substituted for *well* in a construction like "The car works *fine.*"

**Fix** Colloquial for *predicament.*

**Flunk** Colloquial for *fail.*

**Folks** Colloquial when used to refer to members of one's family or relatives as in the sentence "The *folks* all thought I looked well." Standard when it refers to people in general or a specific group: *young folks.*

**Foot, feet** As units of measurement, standard usage requires "a man six feet tall" or "a four-foot plank." "A man six foot tall" is nonstandard.

**Former, latter** *Former* is applied to the first of two items, *latter* to the second. Use *first* and *last* when there are more than two items.

**Funny** Colloquial for *odd, queer,* or *strange.*

**Gentleman** See **lady, gentleman.**

**Get** There are many colloquial and slang expressions of which the verb *get* is part. These are not appropriate in formal writing. Among them are the following: *get with it, get smart, get wise, get lost, get going.*

**Good** A good adjective that should not be used as an adverb.

**Good** The weather is *good* today.
**Not Good** She dances *good.* (Should be *well.*)

**Good and** Colloquial when used in phrases like "*good and* hungry."

**Great** See **real.**

**Guess** In a construction like "I *guess* you'll be happy with your motorbike," formal usage would prefer *think* or *suppose* to *guess.*

**Guy** Colloquial for *man, boy,* or *fellow.*

**had better, had best, better** Legitimate idioms for *ought to* and *should,* which are somewhat more formal; *better* without the auxiliary is colloquial.

You *had better* [or *had best*] go now.
You *ought to* [or *should*] go now.
You *better* go now.

**Had ought to** Illiterate for *ought to.*

**Illiterate** He *had ought to* change his oil.
**Standard** He *ought to* change his oil.

**Half a** *Half a* and *a half* are good usage; *a half a* should be avoided.

*Half a* loaf is better than none.
I have *a half* hour to spare.

**Hanged, hung** In formal writing, use *hanged* to refer to executed people, *hung* to refer to pictures or other objects.

**Hardly** See **but, hardly, scarcely.**

**He or she** This is a construction used to compensate for the allegedly sexist use of *he* to refer to both males and females. The construction is clumsy and logically leads to equally clumsy compromises such as *his or hers* and *him or her.*

**Clumsy**   When a student is well motivated, *he or she* earns good grades.
**Better**   When a student is well motivated, *he* earns good grades.

It is possible, of course, and often desirable to avoid the use of *he* to mean both sexes. This is done by rephrasing in some appropriate way:

**Rephrased**   When students are well motivated, they earn good grades.
**Rephrased**   A student who is well motivated earns good grades.

**Hisself**   Nonstandard for *himself*.
**Hopefully**   Used to mean "It is to be hoped" or "Let us hope," as in the sentence, "Hopefully, it won't rain while we're on vacation," *hopefully* is strongly disapproved by most educated speakers and writers. Nevertheless, it is widely used in those senses. Used as an adverb meaning "in a hopeful manner," it is correct.

The teacher entered the classroom *hopefully*.

**Idea**   Often an imprecise substitute for *intention, plan*, or *purpose*.

My *plan* [not *idea*] is to eat out tonight.
The *purpose* [not the *idea*] of the course is to acquaint you with the elements of geometry.

**If, whether**   Either *if* or *whether* may be used after such words as *say, ask, doubt, know, wonder*, or *understand*.

She asked if [whether] she could join us.
I wonder if [whether] you have a pencil to lend me.

In standard usage, choose *whether* when your sentence expresses alternatives.

I don't understand *whether* you're going or not.

**Ignorant, stupid**   An *ignorant* person has not been taught very much; a *stupid* one is not capable of learning.
**Illusion, allusion**   *Illusion* means a "false image or impression"; *allusion* means an "indirect reference to" something or someone.

It is an *illusion* to think you'll get a job this summer.
She made an *allusion* to the fact that she needed the money.

**Immanent, imminent**   See **eminent, imminent, immanent**.
**Impl**   See **infer, imply**.

**In, into, in to**   *In* denotes "within the confines of" or "inside." *Into* is the better word to mean "toward, to the inside of," but *in* is widely used in both senses. *In to* are separate words.

My shirt is *in* the closet.
Go back *into* the room and get it.
You may go *in to* see her now.

**In back of, in behind, in between**   Wordy formulas for *back of, behind, between.*

**Infer, imply**   *Infer* means "to draw conclusions from evidence"; *imply* means "to suggest obliquely without actually saying" something.

He *implied* he wouldn't go on the trip with us.
Therefore, we *inferred* that he didn't like the people who were going.

**Ingenious, ingenuous**   The former means "clever," the latter "naive."

**In regard to**   See **Regarding, in regard to, with regard to, relating to, relative to, with respect to, respecting.**

**In regards to**   Nonstandard when substituted for *as regards* or *in regard to.*

**Inside of, outside of**   Mainly, the word *of* in these constructions is unnecessary. *Outside of* is also informal for *except* or *besides.*

**Informal**   She'll be here *inside of* an hour.
**Formal**   She'll be here *inside* [or *within*] an hour.

**Informal**   *Outside of* me, nobody can operate the tractor.
**Formal**   *Except me,* nobody can operate the tractor.

**In terms of**   A vague and wordy expression; to be avoided.

**Wordy**   *In terms of* power, Aaron can hit home runs.
**Better**   Aaron has the power to hit home runs.

**In the case of**   A vague and wordy expression; to be avoided.

**Wordy**   *In the case of* my Shakespeare class, it's boring.
**Better**   My Shakespeare class is boring.

**Irregardless**   Nonstandard. Use plain old *regardless.*
**Is because**   See **reason is because.**
**Is when, is where**   Clumsy and illogical expressions when *where* and *when* are used to introduce noun clauses as the complement of *is.*

**Clumsy** Capitalism *is where* there is private ownership of capital.
**Better** Capitalism is a form of economic development with private ownership of capital.

**Clumsy** A neurosis *is when* there is a disturbance of ego function.
**Better** A neurosis is a disturbance of ego function.

**It is me, it is I** The latter is very (almost too) formal; the former is widely used informally. See **Case** in Part 2.

**It's, its** *It's* is the contraction of *it is*. *Its* is a possessive pronoun.

**-ize, -wise** The former suffix is frequently used to make a verb out of a noun or an adjective (*revolutionize, ionize*), the latter to make an adverb out of a noun or an adjective (*clockwise, otherwise, likewise*), but both are overworked, especially in bureaucratic jargon. Avoid their use except in established words.

Not "The agreement was *finalized*," but "The agreement was *made final.*"
Not, "*Moneywise*, it was a good decision," but "From a *financial* viewpoint, it was a good decision."

**Kind of a** Leave out the *a*.

**Know, no, now** *Know* is "understand"; *no* is the negative particle; *now* means "at present."

**Lack, need, want** As nouns, a *lack* is a shortage; a *need* is a condition brought on by a *lack;* and a *want* is a lack of things that are necessary combined with an awareness of that lack.

New York City has a *lack* of funds.
He had a *need* for friendship and affection.
The people feel a *want* of responsiveness to their problems.

**Lady, gentleman** *Man* and *woman* are plainer and therefore preferred to the pompous *lady* and *gentleman*—unless you are using the terms to make real distinctions in refinement. *Ladies and Gentlemen* is a conventional phrase used in addressing various gatherings.

**Latter** See **former, latter.**

**Lay, lie** This pair of verbs continues to give trouble. *To lie* is to "rest in or place oneself into a horizontal position." *To lay* something is "to set it or place it somewhere." The only way to correct the trouble is to memorize the forms of this pair.

| Infinitive | Past Tense | Past Participle | Present Participle |
|---|---|---|---|
| to lie | lay | lain | lying |
| to lay | laid | laid | laying |

Here are correct examples of the use of each form:

**Lie**
I want to *lie* down.
After I *lay* there awhile, I had an idea.
After I *had lain* there for an hour, I made my decision.
After *lying* down past lunch hour, I got up and made myself a snack.

**Lay**
Please *lay* the package on the table.
He *laid* the package on the table.
She *had laid* the package on the table.
I *was laying* the package on the table.

*Note:* **Lay**, unlike *lie*, has a passive voice:

The package *had been laid* neatly inside the drawer.
The body *has been laid* to rest.

**Leave, let** *Leave* means "to depart from"; let means "to permit." Nevertheless, "*leave* [or *let*] me alone" is a standard idiom. The trouble comes when you use *leave* for *let*.

**Nonstandard** I won't *leave* you go with me.
**Standard** I won't *let* you go with me.

**Less** See **fewer, less.**
**Let's us** Redundant, since *let's* already means *let us.*
**Liable, likely** See **apt, likely, liable.**
**Lie** See **lay, lie.**
**Like, as, as if** In formal use, *like* is a preposition; *as* and *as if* are conjunctions. *Like* is much used in conversation as a conjunction, but in writing this usage should be avoided.

**Correct** My daughter looks *like* me. (preposition)
**Avoid** My daughter speaks *like* I do. (conjunction)
**Correct** My daughter speaks *as* I do. (conjunction)

**Avoid** He spends money *like* he's rich. (conjunction)
**Correct** He spends money *as if* he were rich. (conjunction)

**Likely, liable** See **apt, likely, liable.**
**Lose, loose** *Lose* means "misplace; no longer having," or in betting terminology, the opposite of *win*. *Loose* is an adjective meaning "free or unattached."

If I don't make an A average, I'll *lose* my scholarship.
My notes are on some *loose* sheets of paper.

**Lovely** See **cute, lovely.**
**Mad** Colloquial for "angry."
**Marvelous** Avoid this overworked term of insincere approval.
**Math** See **ad.**
**may** See **can, may.**

**Maybe, may be**   *Maybe* means "perhaps"; *may be* is a two-part verb form.

It *may be* necessary to take Vitamin C in large amounts.
*Maybe* he hasn't got the money.

**Mighty**   Informal for "very" or "exceedingly." *Mighty* means "powerful."

**Informal**   This is *mighty* good coffee.
**Formal**   Hank Aaron was a *mighty* home run hitter.

**Moral, morale**   *Moral* as a noun is "a lesson" or "a conclusion to be drawn from a story"; the adjective *moral* means "pertaining to right or ethical conduct." *Morale,* a noun, refers to "the enthusiastic state of mind of an individual or a group."

Does this story have a *moral*?
His action was considered to be *moral* behavior.
The *morale* among the workers was high.

**Most, almost**   *Most* is an informal substitute for *almost.*

**Informal**   *Most* every time I see you, you're well dressed.
**Formal**   *Almost* every time I see you, you're well dressed.

**Mr.**   Never spell out *mister* except for special emphasis. In America, a period follows the abbreviation (unlike the custom in Britain, where it is omitted).

**Ms.**   A recently adopted abbreviation to identify women, married or unmarried. It answers the needs of those who believe it unfair that women—but not men—should have their marital status made public in the usual way (that is, *Mrs.* or *Miss*). Ms. is in widespread use. It can be used when you are uncertain of a woman's marital status. In other cases, the individual's preference should be respected.

**Must of**   Illiterate for *must have.*

**Myself (himself, etc.)**   Do not use *myself* where you would normally use *I* or *me. Myself* is used (1) reflexively, (2) for emphasis, (3) in absolute constructions, or (4) to indicate the normal, healthy state of the self. All other uses should be regarded as informal.

1. I'm going to buy *myself* a new car.
2. I *myself* will go to the station.
3. *Myself* a professor, I nevertheless avoided other professors.
4. I'm not *myself* today.

**Informal**   Joanna and *myself* went to visit her parents. (Formal: *I.*)
**Informal**   The property was left to my sister and *myself.* (Formal: *me.*)

**Need**  See **lack, need, want.**

**No, now**  See **know, no, now.**

**Nohow**  Nonstandard for *not at all.*

**Nothing like, nowhere near**  Colloquial for, respectively, *not like* and *not nearly.*

He was *not like* [not *nothing like*] my brother.
She was *not nearly* [not *nowhere near*] as tall as her mother.

**Nowheres**  Nonstandard for *nowhere.*

**Number**  See **amount, number.**

**Off of**  No need for the *of.*

**Okay**  This or abbreviations like O.K. or OK are all okay— standard—but use a more specific word in formal writing.

**One and the same**  Stale and wordy for *the same.*

**One another**  See **each other, one another.**

**Ought to of**  Illiterate for *ought to have.*

**Outside of**  See **inside of, outside of.**

**Over with**  Colloquial for *over* and *ended.*

**Colloquial**  I'm glad the game is *over with.*
**Formal**  I'm glad the game is *over.*

**Per**  Appropriate only in business or technical writing (*per diem, per capita, feet per second*) but stuffy in formal writing where *a* and *an* are preferable ($6 *an* hour, four miles *a* day).

**Percent, percentage**  Both mean "rate per hundred"; *percent* may be written as two words or as one, but *percentage* is always written as one. In formal writing, use *percent* to follow a numeral (*75 percent*). Do not use either word when you simply mean *part.*

**Formal**  A small *part* of my home is used as an office.
**Formal**  A small *percentage* of the team lacks spirit.
**Informal**  A small *percent* of government officials are corrupt.

**Phenomena**  See **data, phenomena.**

**Phone**  See **ad.**

**Photo**  See **ad.**

**Plan on**  In formal writing the correct idiom is *plan to. Plan on* is colloquial.

**Plenty**  Informal when used to mean "very."

**Plus**  As a preposition, means "increased by." It is informal when used in place of *and.*

**Informal**  Irv had a high fever *plus* he was breaking out in red spots.

**Pretty**  Overworked when used as an intensifier to mean "somewhat," e.g., *pretty* good, *pretty* happy.

**Principal, principle** *Principal*, a noun meaning "person in controlling authority" or an adjective meaning "main" or "chief," should be distinguished from *principle*, a noun meaning "fundamental law" or "concept."

The *principal* idea was to begin our vacation in January instead of June.
The *principal* of the high school came to dinner.
With him, it was a matter of *principle*.

**Prior to** Overblown usage for *before;* avoid it.
**Provided, provided that, providing** All three are now considered correct conjunctions.

I will go on the trip *provided that* you take your camera.
He will invite you to lunch *providing* you apologize.

**Quite a few, quite a bit, quite a little** Colloquial and wordy when used to substitute for *many, a substantial amount,* or *more than a little.*
**Raise, rise** Two different verbs. *Raise* (*raised, raised, raising*) is a transitive verb meaning "to cause or help to rise to a standing position." *Rise* (*rose, risen, rising*) is an intransitive verb meaning "to assume an upright position" or "to wake up from sleep."

He had *risen* at five and gone straight to work.
She *raises* chickens and sells eggs.

**Rap** Informal for "talk" or "chat," but slang when used to mean "punishment" or "blame."
**Real, swell, great, terrific, beauty, awful** However you may use these, they are becoming—or have become—vague and tired. Try for more specific words.
**Reason is because** *Because* in this construction should be replaced by *that.*

**Informal** The *reason* he can't see you tonight *is because* he has to make up a chem lab.
**Formal** The *reason* he can't see you tonight *is that* he has to make up a chem lab.
He can't see you tonight *because* he has to make up a chem lab.

**Reason why** The *why* is usually superfluous. The *reason* she lost him is obvious.
**Regarding, in regard to, with regard to, relating to, relative to, with respect to, respecting** High-blown substitutes for *on, about,* or *concerning.*

The Chancellor spoke on [not *with regard to*] the future mission of the university.

**Relating to** See **regarding, in regard to, with regard to, relating to, relative to, with respect to, respecting.**

**Relative to** See **regarding, in regard to, with regard to, relating to, relative to, with respect to, respecting.**

**Respecting** See **regarding, in regard to, with regard to, relating to, relative to, with respect to, respecting.**

**Rhetorical question** When you ask a real question (e.g., *What time is it?*), you expect an answer. When you pose a rhetorical question (*Is anyone more beautiful than my wife?*), you are simply making a point.

**Right** Dialect or colloquial form of *very* as in *right pleased* or *right new*. *Right away* is colloquial for *immediately*.

**Said** Adapted from legal language (*said* party, *said* action), it should be avoided in ordinary writing.

**Scarcely** See **but, hardly, scarcely.**

**Seeing as how, seeing that** Colloquial for *since* or *because*.

**Set, sit** Frequently confused pair. *Sit* (*sat, sat, sitting*) means "be seated." *Set* (*set, set, setting*) means "place" something somewhere.

The dog was *sitting* at my feet.
She *set* the dog down at my feet.
The package *was set* down beside me.

*Note:* Set has a passive voice; *sit* does not.

**Shall, will, should, would** *Will* is now generally accepted for all persons (*I will, you will, he will*) except for questions in the first person requesting an opinion or consent (*Shall* I order dinner? *Shall* we dance?) or in formal contexts (I *shall* hope to see you on Thursday in my chambers). Ordinary questions about the future still employ *will* (When *will* I see you again?). *Should* expresses obligation or condition for all three persons (*I should* go swimming; *you should* take a nap; *Manny should* write a letter). *Would* is used for all three persons for a wish or a hypothetical or a customary action (*Would* that he had taken the job! *You would* do it if you could. Every morning, *they would* take coffee on the verandah.).

**Shape up** Colloquial for 'proceeding or developing in a satisfactory manner."

My vacation plans are *shaping up.*

**Should** See **shall, will, should, would.**

**Show up** Colloquial when used to mean "appear" or "prove."

**Formal** John did not *appear* at the dance.
**Colloquial** John did not *show up* at the dance.

**Formal**   Charles *proved* superior to Frank.
**Colloquial**   Charles *showed up* better than Frank.

**Situation**   Unnecessary addition in such phrases as "a *crisis* situation" (a *crisis* will do) and "The *situation* is that we need money" (where the last three words will do).
**So**   In clauses describing purposes, *so* used in place of *so that* is colloquial.

**Formal**   We met in a hotel room *so that* we could discuss our plans in private.
**Colloquial**   We met in a hotel room *so* we could discuss our plans in private.

*So* used instead of *very* is colloquial and overworked.

**Formal**   She seems *very* sad.
**Colloquial**   She seems *so* sad.

**Some**   Colloquial when used as an adverb substituting for "somewhat" and as an adjective substituting for "remarkable, exciting, unusual." (We'll have to hurry *somewhat* [not *some*] to get there on time. This is *a remarkable* [not *some*] photograph.)
**Someone**   See **anyone, any one.**
**Sometime, some time**   The former is used when an occasion or time not specified is meant and the latter when a period of time (of unspecified duration) is meant.

*Sometime* I must visit the Empire State Building.
I must spend *some time* walking up Fifth Avenue.

**Sort**   See **these kind.**
**Stationary, stationery**   *Stationary* means "at rest" or "in a fixed posture or position." *Stationery* is "paper, envelopes," and other such materials.
**Stupid**   See **ignorant, stupid.**
**Such**   Colloquial when used as an intensifier.

**Formal**   He owned a *very* handsome dog.
**Colloquial**   He owned *such* a handsome dog.

**Supposed to, used to**   Don't forget the final *-d* in the words *supposed* and *used.*
**Sure**   Colloquial for *surely* or *certainly.*
**Swell**   Slang when used to mean "excellent" or "very good." See **real.**
**Take and**   Nonstandard usually. "He *drove* the car away," not "He *took and* drove the car away."
**Terrific**   See **real.**

**Than, then** Two different words. *Than* is a conjunction; *then* is an adverb or adverbial conjunction.

His grades are better *than* mine.
He had a long, cool drink; *then* he plunged into a cold shower.

**That** Colloquial when used as an adverb instead of *so* or *very* (as in "She was *that* poor, she was often hungry" and "I didn't like him *that* much").

**That, which** *That* always introduces restrictive clauses; *which* can introduce both restrictive and nonrestrictive clauses, but in formal speech and writing some prefer to limit *which* to introducing nonrestrictive clauses.

**Restrictive** The fruit *that I bought yesterday* is delicious.
**Nonrestrictive** The fruit, *which I bought yesterday,* is delicious.

**Their, there, they're** Frequently confused. *Their* is the possessive pronoun; *there* is an adverb or expletive; *they're* is a contraction of *they are.*

*Their* eyes stared straight at the flag.
*There* is no reason to be afraid.
*They're* going off on a holiday in July.

**Theirself, theirselves** Nonstandard. Use *themselves.*
**These kind** Should be *this kind* (or *that kind*) or *these kinds* (or *those kinds*). Same holds true for *sort.*
**Thing** Too often used for everything. Where possible, a more specific word should be used.
**This here, that there, these here, them there** Nonstandard all. Just use the first word of each pair.
**Through** Informal when used instead of *finished.*

**Formal** He is *finished* studying.
**Informal** He is *through* studying.

**To, too, two** Distinguish between the preposition *to,* the adverb *too,* and the number *two.*

If it isn't *too* much trouble, I'd like *two* pounds of candy to give *to* my mother.

**Transpire** Although the word means "to become known," it is widely used to mean "come to pass," "happen," or "occur," as in "It *transpired* that my scholarship check was late this month." Some authorities disapprove of this usage.
**Try and** See **be sure and, try and.**
**Type** Colloquial for *type of.*

**Formal** This *type of* air conditioner eats energy.
**Colloquial** This *type* air conditioner eats energy.

**Uninterested**   See **disinterested, uninterested.**
**Used to**   See **supposed to, used to.**
**Wait on**   Means to "serve" or "attend" and not, as in colloquial use, to "wait for."

**Correct:**   We *waited for* the counter girl to *wait on* us.

**Want**   See **lack, need, want.**
**Ways**   When referring to distance, *ways* is informal, *way* formal.

**Informal**   Davenport is a long *ways* from here.
**Formal**   Davenport is a long *way* from here.

**Where, were**   Pronounced differently, these are two different words. *Were* is the plural verb; *where* is an adverb, a conjunction, and a noun. Do not substitute *where* for *that.*

**Informal**   He could see *where* she was getting ready to leave.
**Formal**   He could see *that* she was getting ready to leave.

**Whether, if**   See **if, whether.**
**Which, who, that**   Use *who* or *that* to refer to persons, *which* or *that* to refer to all other things. See **that, which.**
**Who, whom**   See **case** in Glossary of Grammatical Terms or **Case** in Part 2.
**Will**   See **shall, will, should, would.**
**-wise**   Characteristic of governmental, business, or advertising jargon is the practice of converting a noun to an adverb by tacking on -*wise*. In formal writing, this is a vulgar practice.

**Jargon**   *Moneywise,* it's not a good deal.
**Better**   *Financially,* it's not a good deal.

**Jargon**   *Defensewise,* we need an early warning system.
**Better**   *For defense purposes,* we need an early warning system.

**With regard to**   See **regarding, in regard to, with regard to, relating to, relative to, with respect to, respecting.**
**With respect to**   See **regarding, in regard to, with regard to, relating to, relative to, with respect to, respecting.**
**Worst way**   Use *very much,* the formal way of saying *in the worst way.*

**Informal**   He wanted to go to the movies *in the worst way.*
**Formal**   He wanted *very much* to go to the movies.

**Would**   See **shall, will, should, would.**
**Would of**   Illiterate for *would have.* Based on sound perception by users who hear *of* instead of *have.*

# Index